"The political negotiations conducted by international human organisations to gain access to civil war victims has long taxed humanitarians and governing authorities. This illuminating account draws upon archives and other original sources to explore the clashes during civil wars between sovereign authorities in Sri Lanka, Russia, Ethiopia and Sudan and universalist organisations such as Médecins sans Frontières. Andrew Cunningham's approach demonstrates the complexity of negotiating structures and discordant discourses, in a book of many insights containing valuable lessons for humanitarians."

Michael Pugh, Professor Emeritus in Peace and Conflict, University of Bradford, UK

"Cunningham's book tackles a gaping fissure in today's humanitarian practice – the seemingly irreconcilable clash between the moral actions of the aid agency and the exercise of political power by the state. Given current trends in the establishment of state sovereignty, the mistaken humanitarian emphasis on 'state-avoiding' approaches will only further doom their access to people in crisis. Put simply, Cunningham's analysis of the state-INGO relationship makes not for interesting research; it should become required reading."

Marc DuBois, Independent Humanitarian Consultant, former Executive Director, MSF-UK

"Amidst increasing efforts by states to limit the actions of INGOs operating within their borders, Cunningham provides much-needed insight into the narratives, rules, norms and discourses that shape NGO-state relationships. He masterfully highlights the complex political realities faced by both humanitarian NGOs and the states in which they work, making this a must-read for policymakers, donors, NGO workers, and anyone interested in understanding when and why humanitarian interventions succeed or fail."

Jennifer N. Brass, School of Public & Environmental Affairs, Indiana University, USA

"How states and international humanitarian actors relate to each other matters because when the relationship breaks down people in need don't receive lifesaving assistance. This book is crucial reading for researchers and practitioners to understand how that happens and what could be done to build more constructive partnerships better able to assist and protect people in times of crisis."

Paul Harvey, Partner, Humanitarian Outcomes, UK

"Andrew Cunningham's carefully-researched book offers important insights, evidence and a framework that bridges academia and operational realities in the complex field of international humanitarian and development action, poverty reduction and social change in fragile states. His work offers a valuable contribution to the sector at a pivotal time in history."

Abby Maxman, CEO and President, Oxfam America, USA

"This is a thought provoking, empirically informed and very rich analysis of the complex and often fraught relationship between humanitarian NGOs and states in times of humanitarian crises. Written by someone with impeccable credentials for exploring that relationship in detail, it dissects the politics and political nature of humanitarian crises in eye-opening fashion."

Mats Berdal, Department of War Studies, King's College London, UK

"This book provides a long-awaited and most timely discussion of how humanitarian actors can better relate to the government in crisis areas. Theoretically well-informed and grounded in the author's vast experience, the book analyses aid-state relations in Sri Lanka, Ethiopia, Sudan and Russia. The book provides a solid escape from the usual idea of a battle between the high morals of humanitarians and the low politics of state. Rather than providing a simple tool-box for humanitarian diplomacy, the book seeks to support humanitarians (and states for that matter) with nuanced and context-specific understandings of how access can be negotiated."

Dorothea Hilhorst, Professor of Humanitarian Aid and Reconstruction, International Institute of Social Studies, Erasmus University, The Netherlands

"Are good intentions enough? More often than not, humanitarian imperatives clash with state prerogatives rendering the delivery of life-saving assistance more difficult. Cunningham convincingly argues the need for understanding contexts and for meaningful engagement between governmental and the non-governmental actors so that human life is saved and protected in times of crises. Essential reading for leaders, researchers, and aid workers."

Unni Karunakara, Yale School of Public Health, and US and International President, Médecins Sans Frontières (2010–2013)

INTERNATIONAL HUMANITARIAN NGOS AND STATE RELATIONS

International Humanitarian NGOs and State Relations: Politics, Principles and Identity examines the often discordant relationship between states and international non-governmental organisations working in the humanitarian sector. INGOs aiming to provide assistance to populations suffering from the consequences of conflicts and other human-made disasters work in the midst of very politically sensitive local dynamics. The involvement of these non-political international actors can be seen as a threat to states that see civil war as a state of exception where it is the government's prerogative to act outside 'normal' legal or moral boundaries. Drawing on first-hand experience of humanitarian operations in contexts of civil war, this book explores how the relationship works in practice and how often clashing priorities can be mediated.

Using case studies of civil conflicts in Sri Lanka, Darfur, Ethiopia and Chechnya, this practice-based book brings together key issues of politics, principles and identity to build a 'negotiation structure' for analysing and understanding the relationship. The book goes on to outline a research and policy development agenda for INGOS to better adapt politically to working with states.

International Humanitarian NGOs and State Relations will be a key resource for professionals and policy makers working within international humanitarian and development operations, as well as for academics and students within humanitarian and development studies who want to understand the relationship between states and humanitarian and multi-mandate organisations.

Andrew J. Cunningham is a humanitarian practitioner and consultant, with a PhD from the War Studies Department, King's College London, UK.

ROUTLEDGE HUMANITARIAN STUDIES

Series editors: Alex de Waal and Dorothea Hilhorst

Editorial Board: Mihir Bhatt, Dennis Dijkzeul, Wendy Fenton, Kirsten Johnson, Julia Streets, Peter Walker

The Routledge Humanitarian Studies series in collaboration with the International Humanitarian Studies Association (IHSA) takes a comprehensive approach to the growing field of expertise that is humanitarian studies. This field is concerned with humanitarian crises caused by natural disaster, conflict or political instability and deals with the study of how humanitarian crises evolve, how they affect people and their institutions and societies, and the responses they trigger.

We invite book proposals that address, amongst other topics, questions of aid delivery, institutional aspects of service provision, the dynamics of rebel wars, state building after war, the international architecture of peacekeeping, the ways in which ordinary people continue to make a living throughout crises, and the effect of crises on gender relations.

This interdisciplinary series draws on and is relevant to a range of disciplines, including development studies, international relations, international law, anthropology, peace and conflict studies, public health and migration studies.

People, Aid and Institutions in Socio-economic Recovery:
Facing Fragilities
Gemma van der Haar, Dorothea Hilhorst, and Bart Weijs

Anti-genocide Activists and the Responsibility to Protect
Edited by Annette Jansen

Disaster Management in Australia
Government Coordination in a Time of Crisis
George Carayannopoulos

Production of Disaster and Recovery in Post-Earthquake Haiti
Disaster Industrial Complex
Juliana Svistova and Loretta Pyles

International Humanitarian NGOs and State Relations
Principles, Politics, and Identity
Andrew J. Cunningham

INTERNATIONAL HUMANITARIAN NGOS AND STATE RELATIONS

Politics, Principles and Identity

Andrew J. Cunningham

Routledge
Taylor & Francis Group

LONDON AND NEW YORK

First published 2018
by Routledge
2 Park Square, Milton Park, Abingdon, Oxon OX14 4RN

and by Routledge
711 Third Avenue, New York, NY 10017

Routledge is an imprint of the Taylor & Francis Group, an informa business

British Library Cataloguing in Publication Data
A catalogue record for this book is available from the British Library

Library of Congress Cataloging in Publication Data
A catalog record has been requested for this book

ISBN: 978-1-138-04914-7 (hbk)
ISBN: 978-1-138-04915-4 (pbk)
ISBN: 978-1-315-16975-0 (ebk)

Typeset in Bembo
by Taylor & Francis Books
Printed and bound by CPI Group (UK) Ltd, Croydon, CR0 4YY

CONTENTS

List of illustrations	*viii*
Acknowledgments	*ix*
Abbreviations	*x*
Preface	*xii*
Introduction	1
1 The relationship of the external in the internal	14
2 The case of Médecins Sans Frontières and the Government of Sri Lanka, 2006/7	41
3 The case of Médecins Sans Frontières and the Government of Sri Lanka, 2008/9	71
4 Fear as discourse: The case of Chechnya	92
5 Law as discourse: The case of Ethiopia	109
6 Expulsion as discourse: The case of Sudan	128
7 Responses to securitisation	142
8 Politics, principles and identity	171
Conclusion: The future	194
Index	*201*

ILLUSTRATIONS

Figure

1.1 The negotiation structure: the relation of the external in the
internal   35

Table

7.1 Humanitarian INGO reaction options in a securitised context   143

ACKNOWLEDGMENTS

First, I wish to acknowledge all the input and support I received from colleagues at MSF-Holland and thank the organisation for allowing me complete and unhindered access to its Sri Lanka archives. Needless to say, my interpretation of MSF's work in Sri Lanka is my own. I would also like to thank all the other humanitarian colleagues who contributed to the case study research. Individuals and organisations requested to remain anonymous given the sensitivities involved with the subject matter, but you know who you are and I appreciate your input and support.

As much of the original research this book is derived from my PhD thesis, appreciation must also go to my thesis supervisor Mats Berdal and my secondary advisor Oisin Tansey, both at the War Studies Department at King's College London. I wish also to thank all those who provided assistance with organising my aborted field research trip to Sri Lanka, as well as those who facilitated other aspects of my other case study field research trips. Again, you requested to remain anonymous, but the gratitude is real.

In an age of budget cuts in the UK where the utility of public libraries is being questioned, a special mention should go to the Hackney (London) library system for providing such wonderful spaces in which to work.

Last, but certainly not least, a huge thank you to my wife, Clea Kahn, for her patience, understanding and support during the book-writing process.

ABBREVIATIONS

ACF	Action Contre la Faim
CFA	Ceasefire Agreement
CHA	Consortium of Humanitarian Agencies
CHF	Cooperative Housing Foundation
CID	Criminal Investigation Department
CNO	Centre for National Operations
CPA	Comprehensive Peace Agreement
CSP	Charities and Societies Proclamation
EC	European Commission
ECHO	European Union Humanitarian Aid and Civil Protection Department
EPRDF	Ethiopian People's Revolutionary Democratic Front
EU	European Union
GoE	Government of Ethiopia
GoS	Government of Sudan
GoSL	Government of Sri Lanka
GWoT	Global war on terror
HAC	Humanitarian Affairs Council
HAD	Humanitarian Affairs Department
HRW	Human Rights Watch
ICC	International Criminal Court
ICRC	International Committee of the Red Cross
IDP	Internally displaced person
IGO	Intergovernmental organisation
IHL	International Humanitarian Law
INGO	International non-governmental organisation
IPKF	Indian Peace Keeping Force

IRC	International Rescue Committee
JEM	Justice and Equality Movement
JHU	Jathika Hela Urumaya (National Heritage Party)
JVP	Janatha Vimukthi Peramuna (People's Liberation Front)
LLRC	Lessons Learnt and Reconciliation Commission
LTTE	Liberation Tigers of Tamil Eelam
MDM	Medicos Del Mundo [Spanish section of Médecins du Monde]
MENA	Middle East and North Africa
MoD	Ministry of Defence
MoH	Ministry of Health
MoU	Memorandum of Understanding
MSF	Médecins Sans Frontières
MSF-E	Médecins Sans Frontières (Spain)
MSF-F	Médecins Sans Frontières (France)
MSF-H	Médecins Sans Frontières (Holland)
NAM	Non-Aligned Movement
NGO	Non-governmental organisation
NPC	National Peace Council
NRC	Norwegian Refugee Council
NWPC	North Western Provincial Council
PADCO	Planning and Development Collaborative International
PSC	Parliamentary Select Committee on NGO Abuses
P-TOMS	Post-Tsunami Operational Management Structure
R2P	Responsibility to Protect
RPF	Rwandan Patriotic Front
SLA	Sri Lankan Army
SLFP	Sri Lanka Freedom Party
SLM	Sudan Liberation Movement
SUDO	Sudan Social Development Organisation
TRO	Tamil Relief Organisation
UN	United Nations
UNF	United National Front
UNHCR	United Nations High Commissioner for Refugees
UNICEF	United Nations Children's Fund
UNOCHA	United Nations Office for the Coordination of Humanitarian Affairs
UPFA	United People's Freedom Alliance
VOICE	Voluntary Organisations in Cooperation in Emergencies
WFP	United Nations World Food Program

PREFACE

My interest in the theme of this research – the relationship between states and humanitarian international non-governmental organisations (INGOs) against the backdrop of civil conflict – is derived from my 20-plus years of work with humanitarian organisations, including 14 years' full-time engagement with Médecins Sans Frontières (MSF), both in managing field operations and in headquarters. Humanitarian organisations are faced with many challenges working amid conflict, and the difficult relationship with states has become one of the dominant themes over the last decade or so. In my MSF work I dealt with many contexts where the relationship with states was tense and difficult, such as Sudan, Russia, Turkmenistan, Pakistan, Ethiopia, Eritrea, Zimbabwe and China, amongst others. These experiences led to the development of a research theme within the organisation that began a process of reflection on this evolving relationship. This project included the co-editing of an MSF-sponsored special edition of the journal *Disasters* on the topic of state sovereignty and humanitarian action.[1] However, I was aware that much more work needed to be done on the topic and I decided to dedicate my PhD thesis research to it, focusing on the humanitarian organisation I knew best, MSF. I was able to leverage my MSF connection to obtain complete and unhindered access to the MSF-Holland Sri Lanka archives, which greatly enhanced the empirical depth to my research. The decision was made to focus on the Sri Lankan context partly because I had had no prior engagement with MSF's work in that conflict (as I had with the other countries considered), and therefore could come to that humanitarian context with a relatively fresh and objective eye.

That study was but one component of a larger research project that aims to develop a more sophisticated and nuanced understanding of the relationship

---

1 Clea Kahn and Andrew Cunningham (eds), 'Special Edition: State Sovereignty and Humanitarian Action', *Disasters*, 37, Supplement 2 (2013).

between states and INGOs in times of civil conflict. Although the often tense relationship with states is seen by INGOs as one of the dominant challenges facing humanitarian action, this thematic has lacked in-depth empirical research, which has resulted in a lack of theoretical grounding for action, ill-informed policy formulation and often unproductive interactions. The original study initially aimed to research the state's perspective directly through conducting field research in Sri Lanka. The goal was to interview government and civil society actors to better understand the thinking behind the government's actions vis-à-vis INGOs, MSF in particular. Unfortunately, the necessary permissions to conduct the field research were not granted by the Government of Sri Lanka (GoSL). In addition, access to GoSL officials was not forthcoming, severely limiting the potential value of the field research even if it had been possible to conduct it. This was in and of itself an interesting finding which reinforced the importance of the central problematic, and in many ways the lack of direct access to GoSL authorities put me as a researcher into the shoes of humanitarian actors who often only have a government's discourse to go by in interpreting the rationale for government decision-making. Discourse, accessible from a distance, then became the lens through which the Sri Lankan government's side of the story was established. Rather than weakening the research project, in the end it was methodologically strengthened, as the discursive environment within which both actors worked is rich in explanatory potential and forms a firm basis for theory development.

The next step was to publish my PhD findings as a professional oriented book, kindly facilitated by the Humanitarian Studies group at Routledge. It was necessary to widen the research for the purposes of this book, as a broader interest was demanded for the mixed audience of practitioners, academics and students. The widening of scope entailed opening the research up to other organisations and locations. As a result, three new cases studies were researched, based on recommendations made in previous research. Implementing the research accomplished three essential goals. One was to start the process of including multi-mandate organisations into the theoretical framework. The second was to include new contexts, regions and types of context. And the third was to expand the definition of discourse to include thematic aspects.

Finally, this book has benefited from editing and rewriting that has oriented the book away from a purely academic audience and towards a professional audience. The research has, therefore, come full circle. The interest in the topic derived from my operational experiences, then became a topic of academic theorising, and has now (hopefully!) been put back into the realm of practitioners, or least put into a form useful to humanitarians. The research agenda presented in the concluding chapter should therefore be considered integral to the book, as the hope is that the findings will be carried forward to help us do a better job for the populations needing humanitarian assistance.

INTRODUCTION

> He who knows only his own side of the case, knows little of that. His reasons may be good, and no one may have been able to refute them. But if he is equally unable to refute the reasons on the opposite side; if he does not so much as know what they are, he has no ground for preferring either opinion. The rational position for him would be suspension of judgment, and unless he contents himself with that, he is either led by authority, or adopts, like the generality of the world, the side to which he feels most inclination.
>
> *John Stuart Mill,* On Liberty[1]

Humanitarian international non-governmental organisations and states

Following Mill's warning, there are two sides to a story and proponents of each should strive to understand the other's perspective. The story told in this book relates to the interaction between states and humanitarian international non-governmental organisations (INGOs) in times of civil conflict. The question to be addressed is how these two actors understand each other: What process do the two actors use to form and develop their relationship and within what type of negotiation structure? The response to this question demands both deep empirical study and the development of a theoretical framework, for as will be seen there is a gap in our understanding of how INGOs and states interact in times of humanitarian crises. The first step in this process of understanding is to appreciate the starting perspectives and backgrounds of the two actors involved.

Humanitarian INGOs provide assistance to populations living amid man-made crises, disasters arising from natural events, or armed conflicts.[2] The internal

---

1   Mill, 2002: 38.
2   Although all humanitarian organisations, whether national or international, operate on the same principles, this book concerns international humanitarian non-governmental

narrative of humanitarian actors is that they are moral agents performing good works for people in dire need. Their goal is to save lives, alleviate suffering and help restore dignity to people living in crisis. Humanitarian action is believed to inhabit a moral universe that should be sheltered from the harsh realities of the political sphere. This identity is the basis for action and provides a functional framework by which humanitarians desire their action to be understood. Humanitarian workers, however, do not implement their activities in isolation and operate within a complex global political environment.

Debates in the humanitarian sector have increasingly called into question the viability of the 'humanitarian project' itself.[3] The sanctity of the humanitarian principles – humanity, independence, neutrality and impartiality – has been questioned; the relationship with governmental and intergovernmental donors is often politically and ethically problematic; the Western identity of the majority of the large international agencies is commonly seen as a liability; and the contexts within which humanitarian actors work are perceived to be increasingly more dangerous than in years past. The relevancy of humanitarian action in relation to longer-term development aid projects is often questioned, and multi-mandate organisations – those that implement both humanitarian and development aid projects – are seen by some to be muddying the pure waters of humanitarianism.[4] And finally, serious concerns have been expressed over aid 'politicisation' – when states use aid and aid actors for political purposes – and aid 'criminalisation' – when aid provision is made a criminal act if assistance is thought to support proscribed organisations.

Another prevalent theme, and the theme of this book, concerns the relationship between humanitarian INGOs and states receiving humanitarian aid in times of civil conflict. On a practical level, the narrative as told by humanitarian actors is that states are 'reasserting their sovereignty' and 'pushing back' against INGOs. In the humanitarian sector, this is often referred to as the 'strong states' thematic (Kahn and Cunningham, 2013). Humanitarian agencies perceive a world in which states – both donor and aid recipient states – manipulate humanitarian actors for cynical political objectives, deliberately interfere with the 'right' and duty of humanitarian agencies to provide humanitarian assistance, and impose undue bureaucratic constraints on INGOs for economic gain, as a symptom of autocratic tendencies or simply out of spite.

organisations specifically. As such, 'humanitarian organisations' should be understood as international humanitarian organisations, with no prejudice intended towards national humanitarian actors.

3   The literature is vast. Starting points would be: Collingwood and Logister (2005), Lancet (2010), Leaning (2007), Macrae (2002), de Montclos (2006) and Pugh (2004).

4   Whereas humanitarian organisations work in contexts of crisis, development organisations work in more stable environments to meet longer-term development goals. Such organisations typically have a closer relationship with host governments than humanitarian organisations that attempt to distance themselves from the parties in a conflict. Some organisations, however, combine both mandates and are often criticised for the perceived incompatibility of the two mandates. See, for example, Hofman (undated).

States, naturally, have their own narratives. States inhabit a world of other states – an international political system – and thus have a formal and legal understanding of sovereignty upon which they base their rights, responsibilities and duties as political actors. Actors external to the state, its territory and population are viewed as potential threats. A countervailing narrative of interference by external actors pervades. If INGOs believe they inhabit a moral space, states inhabit a fundamentally political space, one where INGOs are viewed as political actors and humanitarian assistance is considered to be a fundamentally political act. A view has emerged that states, particularly in the developing world, have begun reinforcing the sanctity of the notion of sovereignty in relation to emerging external 'threats', such as the work of the International Criminal Court,[5] an increasing number of military humanitarian interventions,[6] and the growing recognition of the concept of the 'Responsibility to Protect' (R2P).[7] Over the last decades there have also been tensions between the perceived domination of Western ideology, particularly concerning human rights norms, in the global debate on the form and function of the international order, and a concomitant push-back by many non-Western states, found most notably in the 'Asian values' discourse.[8]

The context within which humanitarian INGOs and states interact and build their relationship is therefore complex and strained. The fact of the relationship cannot be disputed, but what form the relationship should take is contested, as international humanitarian actors and states differ fundamentally on the parameters of their engagement. Consequently, the relationship is ever evolving and difficult to conceptualise. The task at hand is to develop a theoretical framework that can describe and explain how the relationship functions in practice. Although contested, it is argued that there are still rules and norms which guide how the relationship is constructed over time. Following Mill, it is hoped that a better understanding may assist humanitarian INGOs in improving their relationships with states, not for their own sakes, but to better enable populations suffering amid humanitarian crises to access humanitarian assistance. The way to do this is through a careful examination of how humanitarian INGOs and states interact in practice through the analysis of a series of case studies, and to do so with reference to an empirically derived analytical framework.

The literature provides an inadequate explanation of the contested relationship between states and INGOs; however, a number of illuminating themes can be elaborated upon from a review of the predominately practitioner-oriented literature.[9] A common strand relates to complaints by INGOs about the interference of states

5   See Kimenyi (2013).
6   See, for example, Goodman (2006), Greenwood (1993), Lyons and Mastanduno (1995), Ryniker (2001), Slim (2001) and Watanabe (2003).
7   See, for example, Cunliffe (2007), Jackson (2000), Jones (2008), Schreur (1993) and Sorensen (2001).
8   See, for example, Acharya (2009), Boll (2001) and Langguth (2003).
9   The Feinstein Center at Tufts University and the UK's Overseas Development Institute tend to dominate the research on practice-oriented humanitarian issues.

in their work,[10] and also to critiques of the humanitarian system as a whole, including how states fit into the system.[11] Case studies of natural disaster responses by affected states focusing on bureaucratic and legal mechanisms,[12] and the desirability of building resilience with people, communities and states as a way to mitigate the effects of future disasters,[13] form another strand. The 'clash' between humanitarian action and sovereignty and its effects on the security of humanitarian actors,[14] how aid is politically contextualised in the global political order,[15] ethical dilemmas with working with 'less-than-democratic' states and in armed conflicts,[16] and the political implications of aid provision,[17] form yet another thread. Works investigating the necessity of taking a conflict-sensitive approach to working in emergencies (associated with the 'do no harm' approach)[18] as well as the role and importance of customary and informal institutions at the local level in fragile states suffering from conflict[19] can also be grouped together. Finally, the importance of establishing legitimacy by NGOs in peace-building settings has also been elaborated upon.[20]

More pertinently, a framework for understanding how states deny access to humanitarian organisations has been elaborated (Labonte and Edgerton, 2013). In this view, there are three types of denial: bureaucratic obstruction, the intensity of the hostilities itself (insecurity) and targeted violence against humanitarian personnel and theft (ibid.: 39). But the important question is *why* do states want to deny access in the first place, especially if state behaviour is not ad hoc and denial 'can constitute a valuable policy tool for national authorities and reflects prevailing perceptions of the norms associated with humanitarian access and civilian protection' (ibid.: 40). Normative perceptions of humanitarianism and how they align with political goals inform a state's policy response.

Each of these themes is relevant and adds nuance to a description of the relationship between humanitarian INGOs and states, and it is important to ground research in the context of the global aid system. However, a gap exists in the literature related to both how humanitarian INGOs and states negotiate the parameters of their relationship in practice and, more importantly, why they interact in those ways and not others.[21] With few exceptions the literature describes the

---

10 See Dempsey and Kyazze (2010).
11 See Collinson and Elhawary (2012).
12 See Cochrane (2008); Harvey (2009) and Humanitarian Policy Network (2009).
13 See European Commission (2014).
14 See Security Management Initiative (2009).
15 See Feinstein International Famine Center (2004).
16 See Bell and Carens (2004) and Slim and Bradley (2013).
17 See Keen (2008: 116–148), Duffield (2001: 75–107) and Mills (2005).
18 See Zicherman et al. (2011) and Okumu (2003).
19 See van der Haar (2013).
20 See Walton (2008).
21 MSF attempts in their book *Humanitarian Negotiations Revealed: The MSF Experience* (Magone, Neuman and Weissman (eds) (2011)), to give its side of the story concerning negotiating access, but this examination fails to adequately consider the respective governments' viewpoints. In addition, the crucial question of why states act the way they do is not adequately explored. This work is illustrative of the gap in the literature.

problem without examining it in a theoretically coherent way. This book attends to this gap by examining the evolving relationship between humanitarian INGOs and a series of states, specifically Sri Lanka (the 2006 and 2008/9 periods of the civil war), Ethiopia (the new NGO law instituted in 2009), Sudan (the INGO expulsions in 2009) and Russia (the 2006 NGO law and fear and insecurity during the second Chechen war). The background context of the case studies is civil conflict and political insecurity, a precarious setting for a state and a natural operating environment for a humanitarian agency.

A theoretical framework was used to conceptualise and analyse the evolving case study relationships. It is argued that the actors determine the form of their relationship through an ongoing process of negotiation, a negotiation between moral and political imperatives mediated through various forms of discourse – textual, or thematic, such as the law, fear and expulsion. This should not be understood as simply the representatives of two parties sitting across the table negotiating their terms of engagement. Rather, negotiations occur through a wide variety of methods, but always involving discursive interactions. The essential point is that these negotiations take place within a structure – a set of rules, norms and procedures that can be described and understood. Such a relationship is constructed and not predetermined or simply based on material factors.

The concepts of principles, politics and identity dominate the case study's findings. Principles should be viewed as the manifestation of the moral project in which humanitarian actors engage. The humanitarian imperative can be boiled down to the expression of the humanitarian principles of humanity, impartiality, independence and neutrality. Politics is obviously the milieu of the state, the reference point for its identity, and its primary concern. Identity is the nexus of the clash between the two worldviews. To a large extent the relationship between humanitarian INGOs and states can be characterised as an evolving interpretation of identity, involving each actor's own identity and the perceived identity of the other. This relationship is mediated, and negotiated, through discourse. More concretely, the structure of the relationship is built on two core elements – the striving of a humanitarian INGO to access populations in need amid crisis and the instinct of a state to treat such actors as threats. In this process, the state fulfils its duty as a sovereign actor with the prerogative to decide who is a friend and who is an enemy and to deal with each appropriately, whether within or outside the bounds of the normal legal order. Humanitarian INGOs, conversely, fulfil their duty as moral actors in attempting to help others in need. To label this clash of imperatives it is argued that a process of securitisation occurs, which INGOs have a number of options to respond to, namely desecuritisation, accommodation, withdrawal, counter-attacking or concealment.

There are, therefore, two normative frameworks in tension in the relationship between states and humanitarian INGOs – a domestic sovereignty and state responsibility set and an internationally applicable humanitarian set. The literature, however, is largely focused on the effects of the international *on* the domestic – how international norms, expressed by actors operating externally, have influenced domestic political developments within a state.[22] The current research has taken an alternative perspective by focusing on the international *in* the domestic – how INGOs as external actors developed a norms-based relationship with the states while operating on their territories. Although global organisations may have an impact on domestic policy development without operating within a state, humanitarian organisations attempt to work on a state's territory and alongside a state structure, intimately proximate to the ongoing political sensitivities resulting from civil crises. Sovereignty is challenged and securitisation is contemplated.

The concept of sovereignty can be understood in relation to the idea of prerogative: 'The sovereign is he who decides on the state of exception' (Schmitt, 2005: 5). This idea of deciding on a 'state of exception' – and the related prerogative to make decisions based on this state of exception – is at the core of the interaction between states and INGOs. In this book, a state of exception will be correlated to a context of civil war, or at least a politically precarious situation. An additional aspect of this view that is particularly relevant to this research is the 'friend and enemy' distinction: 'The specific political distinction to which political actions and motives can be reduced is that between friend and enemy' (Schmitt, 2007: 26). The friend and enemy distinction is independent of other judgments, such as 'good and evil' or 'beautiful and ugly', and does not 'draw upon all of those moral, aesthetic, economic or other distinctions' (ibid.: 26–27). The enemy is a 'stranger', and 'in an especially intense way, existentially something different and alien, and so in the extreme case conflicts with him are possible' (ibid.: 27). Such a distinction, particularly in times of conflict, will generate an emotional reaction whereby the enemy is *treated* as evil and ugly, even though such characterisations are not at the basis of the political distinction, and indeed those who are truly evil and ugly are not by definition the enemy and can be, politically speaking, a friend.

Securitisation is, precisely, this process of defining an issue, or in this study's case a type of international actor, as an existential threat (Buzan and Hansen, 2009: 214). An issue or an entity can be non-political, which does not elicit state involvement, politicised, which does entail a state's interest, or securitised, which, in effect, brings forth a state of exception and inspires sometimes extra-judicial, but most certainly quick and decisive, governmental involvement in the management of the threat. An issue is securitised 'only if and when the audience accepts it as such', and one argues one's case through the use of discourse (Buzan, Waever and de Wilde, 1998: 25). Friends and enemies can be designated by a political actor, but these designations must be described and justified and this process is implemented through discourse. This process of securitisation implemented through discourse plays a prominent analytical role in these case studies, as does the underlying nature of the political as defined above.

Humanitarian INGOs have a number of options in reacting to this securitisation process. At one extreme is ignoring the threat, lying low and trying to weather the storm. If this tactic does not work, an INGO is at high risk of being found

22 For an exemplary work, see Finnemore (1996).

unprepared and forced to react hastily. The other extreme is counter-attack. In this reaction, the INGO does not try to desecuritise itself – rather, it tries to securitise the state. This is a high-risk tactic with little chance of success because an INGO has much less credibility and room for manoeuvre than a state. Another choice is to withdraw from the game, ceding the field altogether. A further option is to submit to the demands of the state, thus remaining on the field but giving complete control to the state as final arbiter of the rules of play. The final alternative is to try to negotiate a positive space within which to work through a process of desecuritisation. Each context brings a different response. These options are examined in the case studies and reviewed in chapter 7.

The theoretical framework

As argued, the primary relationship under consideration in these case studies is one of negotiation, and each side has its own objectives and interests which must be met and considered. For a humanitarian INGO, a condition of being labelled an enemy and a threat is hopefully replaced by a condition of being seen as a legitimate actor with whom a state can negotiate. The objective of negotiation is thus to create this positive discursive space. For INGOs engaged in negotiation the primary objective is to create the 'space' – physically, legally and morally – for an identified population in crisis to safely and securely access humanitarian assistance. Humanitarian actors will commonly reference humanitarian principles in this negotiation. States are concerned with issues of national security, the social contract with their populations, their international standing and their sovereignty, amongst other issues.

This negotiation structure describes the relation of the external (a humanitarian INGO) *in* the internal (a state). Two norms sets are in tension, and their relationship is constructed through discourse. The actual interaction needing explication is the attempt of humanitarian INGOs to work and the resistance of states to their work, within the context of civil conflict. The outcome of the negotiation is informed by political considerations – that is, the designation of friends and enemies and the prerogative of sovereign actors to determine a threat profile and mitigate against threats through securitisation. Action must however be argued for, and this is done through discourse. Securitised agents have the option to try to desecuritise themselves, also through discourse.

Each of the four case studies was examined using this theoretical framework. The case studies were chosen to provide a variety of civil conflicts, types of states and geographical areas. The Sri Lanka case study examines the 2006 and 2008/9 periods of the civil war, comparing experiences of those two periods and why the relationship between humanitarian actors and the government changed over time. This first case study forms the reference point for comparing and contrasting other experiences. The next three chapters explore other forms of discourse. The Chechnya study looks at fear as discourse, the Ethiopia case examines the law as discourse and, finally, the Sudan example elaborates on expulsion as discourse.

Each context provides a different perspective on how the relationship between a state and a humanitarian INGO developed. A variety of INGOs are considered in the case studies.

The relationship between INGOs and states must be viewed from both sides – the discursive environments as created by states and the reactions to these environments by humanitarian organisations. As a starting point, and the basis for the discourse analysis conducted in the Sri Lanka case study, discourse was considered to be the public manifestations of the views of the actors – it was therefore any text or verbal communication that demonstrated these views, inclusive of internal documentation and public statements. From the states' side, outside of direct communications with individual organisations, the media are often the most efficient way to communicate its policies, warnings and the like. The media, where available, are therefore heavily used by states to create a discursive environment upon which actions are based and justified. For states, discourse then compromises the discursive environment as articulated in a wide variety of media, civil society, academic and governmental sources.

For the next three case studies, however, the concept of discourse was expanded to include thematic conceptions of discourse: fear, the law and expulsion. Rather than being strictly textual, discourse was considered to be inclusive of other channels of communications, sometimes textual, sometimes political, sometimes even emotional, but most often based on action. Each case study first makes the case for its thematic form of discourse, then analyses the relationship between a state and INGOs in that context. This expanded conceptualisation of discourse in the securitisation process is the major theoretical contribution of this book.

Summary of findings

The research findings can be distilled into a discussion of politics, principles and identity, the key themes that tie everything together. As way of introduction to the book's themes, a brief summary of the findings is provided below.

The first hurdle for most INGOs, whether solely humanitarian or multi-mandate, when considering how best to engage with states is to reflect on the question of the role of politics in humanitarian action. The findings from this book's case studies supports the view that the environment within which INGOs work is political. Apparent also is the fact that humanitarian crises are, fundamentally, political crises and are some of the most politically sensitive contexts conceivable. External actors attempting to intervene in such circumstances must engage with a highly politicised context and form relationships with all relevant political actors. The work of humanitarian INGOs – their actions and presence – will have political consequences and will be perceived as political action by the political actors cohabitating the zone of crisis. It is, therefore, vital for INGOs to understand the political motivations of states and the political context, and well as understand their own political roles. Whichever option an INGO uses to react to being securitised, the response depends not only on a political analysis but also on proactive political engagement.

As INGOs often believe that politics is for states and they are not themselves political agents, it is also sometimes believed that principles are reserved for humanitarian organisations. The case study findings, however, show that states also rely on principles. Political principles are, of course, those related to statehood and sovereignty, and their use will play a prominent role in the case studies. This book argues for a clash of the moral with the political – the humanitarian project grounded in the moral principle of humans helping humans and states representing hard political choices. Although this basic view survives the test of the four case studies, it is also true that the actually existing world is a messy place. It is certainly not the case that humanitarians have a lock on principles or moral action and that state action is, by definition, immoral. In the end there are going to be tensions between the two distinct identities – states and INGOs are fundamentally different. It is enough to recall that *non*-governmental organisations establish their identity in opposition to governments.

Politics, principles and identities are powerful forces that will inform how the negotiation process progresses and the relationship is constructed. The theoretical framework, backed by sound empirical research, allows for a nuanced view of how these three concepts inform the development of the relationship between states and humanitarian INGOs. Although found useful, no theory is perfect, and the last chapter ends with a discussion of a proposed research agenda.

Structure of the argument

The book follows a general–specific–general logic. First the theory is presented, followed by a test of the theory in four cases studies. The Sri Lanka case study should be considered the baseline and the next three are modifications of the overall theoretical framework. And while the Sri Lanka case study focuses on one humanitarian organisation, the other cases studies open up the discussion to a wider variety of actors, including multi-mandate organisations. The case studies are presented from the states' perspectives, whereas the response options available to INGOs are covered in a stand-alone chapter. The book's findings are summarised in the penultimate chapter and a research agenda for the future is presented in the conclusion. The content of the chapters is summarised below.

Chapter 1: The relationship of the external in the internal

This chapter lays out the theoretical basis for the rest of the book. In the first part, the sets of norms used and understood by both the external and the internal are presented, focusing on the normative concepts of 'statehood' and 'humanitarianism'. Following this is a brief review of the historical and contemporary interactions between these two norms sets. In the second part of the chapter, the theoretical framework is introduced and the concepts of the state of exception and securitisation are discussed. Finally, the methodology used in the book will be more fully presented.

Chapters 2 and 3: Humanitarian securitisation – Médecins Sans Frontières and the Government of Sri Lanka 2006–2009

These two chapters examine the relationship between the Government of Sri Lanka and the international humanitarian non-governmental organisation Médecins Sans Frontières (MSF) during the Sri Lankan civil war. The case study is presented in two parts covering the 2006 and the 2008/9 periods.

The first chapter describes the example of how MSF tried to re-engage with the Government of Sri Lanka in 2006 against the political backdrop of the time. MSF at this time had not been active in Sri Lanka since the tsunami and was re-engaging with the context due to the escalation of the war. MSF had many problems with the government and, as with the other case studies, the theoretical framework is used to analyse these tensions. The analysis focuses on how the Government of Sri Lanka securitised MSF and other international actors and why it chose to use this strategy. The concepts of principles and identity are brought in to the discussion as relevant.

Whereas MSF was successful in negotiating its presence and work by the end of the period described in chapter 2, in the 2008/9 period MSF, as was the case with almost all other organisations, was severely constrained in its activities. Chapter 3 examines an extreme form of securitisation, termed 'bare life' securitisation, based on the work by Giorgio Agamben. Chapter 3 ends with a discussion of the differences between the two periods – what changed, why and how.

Chapter 4: Chechnya – Fear as discourse

The Chechnya case study is full of vagueness, uncertainty and indistinction. This chapter elaborates on the use of fear as discourse. The securitisation framework is used to analyse the relationship between the Russian state and INGOs in the context of the second Chechen war. In addition, the case study examines the new NGO law introduced in 2006.

Fear comes in many forms, but for humanitarian organisations working in zones of conflict, fear most often relates to insecurity. Some contexts, such as Chechnya, witnessed an especially wide-scale and insidious environment of insecurity. The threat of kidnapping was the prevalent security threat for organisations working in Chechnya. Concerns about security lead to an overriding atmosphere of fear. The Chechnya case describes a situation of indistinction between violence and the law. Throughout the discussion the critical themes of agency and truth are in the background. The importance of developing a viable narrative is stressed.

Chapter 5: Ethiopia – Law as discourse

The Ethiopia case study further develops how states use the law in managing the external. In this chapter 'the law' is understood to be inclusive of allied administrative rules and regulations. The terms 'state', 'government' and 'regime' are given more nuance. The law is a form of discourse, one that combined control with fear.

The law needs to be properly interpreted by INGOs – there is meaning behind it and clear messages are communicated by the government. Organisations must be able to perform this interpretation if they are to be able to properly respond to the actions of the government. The law is a political issue and is often in tension with the principles upon which international organisations base their behaviour and thinking.

Chapter 6: Sudan – Expulsion as discourse

This chapter explores the use of expulsion in the securitisation process. Against the backdrop of the war in Darfur, this chapter examines the securitisation process in Sudan in 2009 when a number of INGOs were expelled from the country. Focus is placed on the international–domestic political nexus as one explanation for why INGOs were expelled. The concepts of corporate expulsion, deportation and exile are discussed.

Chapter 7: Responses to securitisation

International humanitarian NGOs have options regarding how to respond to a securitisation process. This chapter first presents the various response options INGOs have. A chart tabulates these options: desecuritisation, accommodation, withdrawal, counter-attack and concealment. Organisations have different views on the response process given their differing mandates and political orientations, and these variations are discussed. Practical examples from the case studies are examined. The chapter ends with the development of key findings concerning the response options.

Chapter 8: Politics, principles and identity

This chapter wraps up the findings and provides some answers to the research question – how do states and international humanitarian NGOs construct their relationship? First, the utility of the theoretical framework is reviewed. Following this is a discussion of the perspectives of both states and INGOs on their relationship. The discursive themes are given special attention in the discussion. To end the chapter, summary reflections focus on the concepts of indistinction and politics, principles and identity.

Conclusion: The future

Based on the research findings, the conclusion outlines a research agenda that aims to more fully elaborate on the relationship between states and international humanitarian NGOs. This research proposal suggests research priorities, as well as practical recommendations for INGOs to better adapt politically to working with states. The need for a more constructive relationship between academics and humanitarian practitioners is stressed.

References

Acharya, A. (2009). *Whose Ideas Matter? Agency and Power in Asian Regionalism*. Ithaca, NY: Cornell University Press.

Bell, D. A. and Carens, J. H. (2004). The ethical dilemmas of international human rights and humanitarian NGOs: Reflections on a dialogue between practitioners and theorists. *Human Rights Quarterly*, 26, 300–329.

Boll, A. M. (2001). The Asian values debate and its relevance to international humanitarian law. *International Review of the Red Cross*, 83(841), 45–58.

Buzan, B. and Hansen, L. (2009). *The Evolution of International Security Studies*. Cambridge: Cambridge University Press.

Buzan, B., Waever, O., and de Wilde, J. (1998). *Security: A New Framework for Analysis*. London: Lynne Rienner.

Cochrane, H. (2008). The role of the affected state in humanitarian action: A case study on Pakistan. Humanitarian Policy Group Working Paper. Overseas Development Institute, London.

Collingwood, V. and Logister, L. (2005). State of the art: Addressing the INGO 'legitimacy deficit'. *Political Studies Review*, 3, 175–192.

Collinson, S. and Elhawary, S. (2012). Humanitarian space: A review of trends and issues. Humanitarian Policy Group Report, 32. Overseas Development Institute, London.

Cunliffe, P. (2007). Sovereignty and the politics of responsibility. In C. Bickerton, P. Cunliffe and A. Gouvrevitch (eds). *Politics Without Sovereignty: A Critique of Contemporary International Relations*. London: University College London Press.

de Montclos, M.-A. P. (2006). Neutrality and humanitarian NGOs as political actors: A review. Annual Meeting of the International Studies Association, San Diego, CA.

Dempsey, B. and Kyazze, A. (2010). At a crossroads: Humanitarianism for the next decade. Save the Children, London.

Duffield, M. (2001). *Global Governance and the New Wars: The Merging of Development and Security*. London: Zed Books.

European Commission (2014). Building resilience: The EU's approach. EU Factsheet. Humanitarian Aid and Civil Protection, Development and Cooperation.

Feinstein International Famine Center (2004). Ambiguity and change: Humanitarian NGOs prepare for the future. Tufts University, Medford, MA.

Finnemore, M. (1996). *National Interests in International Society*. Ithaca, NY: Cornell University Press.

Goodman, R. (2006). Humanitarian intervention and pretexts for war. *American Journal of International Law*, 100(107), 107–141.

Greenwood, C. (1993). Is there a right of humanitarian intervention? *The World Today*, 49(2), 34–40.

Harvey, P. (2009). Towards good humanitarian government: The role of the affected state in disaster response. Humanitarian Policy Report, 29. Overseas Development Institute, London.

Hofman, M. (undated). Less is more: The case for a purely humanitarian response in emergencies. *Opinion and debate*. MSF-UK. https://goo.gl/v1Z5MK [accessed 4 October 2017].

Humanitarian Policy Network (2009). The role of affected states. *Humanitarian Exchange*, 43, June. Humanitarian Policy Group, London.

Jackson, R. H. (2000). *The Global Covenant: Human Conduct in a World of States*. Oxford: Oxford University Press.

Jones, A. (2008). NGOs and the retreat of the state? *E-International Relations*, 29 February. https://goo.gl/9scmJ1 [accessed 4 October 2017].

Kahn, C. and Cunningham, A. (2013). Introduction to the issue of state sovereignty and humanitarian action. *Disasters*, 37 (supplement 2), S139–S150.

Keen, D. (2008). *Complex Emergencies*. London: Polity.

Kimenyi, M. S. (2013). Can the international criminal court play fair in Africa? *Africa in Focus*, 17 October. Brookings Institution. At: https://goo.gl/UpC5jg [accessed 4 October 2017].

Labonte, M. T. and Edgerton, A. C. (2013). Towards a typology of humanitarian access denial. *Third World Quarterly*, 34(1), 39–57.

Lancet (2010). Growth of aid and the decline of humanitarianism. *The Lancet*, 375(9711), 253.

Langguth, G. (2003). Asian values revisited. *Asia Europe Journal*, 1(1), 25–42.

Leaning, J. (2007). The dilemma of neutrality. *Prehospital and Disaster Medicine*, 22(5), 418–421.

Lyons, G. M. and Mastanduno, M. (1995). *Beyond Westphalia? State Sovereignty and International Intervention*. Baltimore, MD: Johns Hopkins University Press.

Macrae, J. (ed.) (2002). The new humanitarians: A review of trends in global humanitarian action. HPG Report, 11. Overseas Development Institute, London.

Magone, C., Neuman, M. and Weissman, F. (eds) (2011). *Humanitarian Negotiations Revealed: The MSF Experience*. London: Hurst & Company.

Mill, J. S. (2002). *The Basic Writings of John Stuart Mill: On Liberty, the Subjection of Women and Utilitarianism*. New York: The Modern Library.

Mills, K. (2005). Neo-humanitarianism: The role of international humanitarian norms and organizations in contemporary conflict. *Global Governance: A Review of Multilateralism and International Organizations*, 11(2), 161–183.

Okumu, W. (2003). Humanitarian international NGOs and African conflicts. *International Peacekeeping*, 10(1), 120–137.

Pugh, M. (2004). Peacekeeping and critical theory. *International Peacekeeping*, 11(1), 39–58.

Ryniker, A. (2001). The ICRC's position on 'humanitarian intervention'. *International Review of the Red Cross*, 83(842), 527–532.

Schmitt, C. (2005). *Political Theology: Four Chapters on the Concept of Sovereignty* (2nd edition). Chicago: Chicago University Press.

Schmitt, C. (2007). *The Concept of the Political* (expanded edition). Chicago: Chicago University Press.

Schreur, C. (1993). The waning of the sovereign state: Towards a new paradigm for international law? *European Journal of International Law*, 4, 447–471.

Security Management Initiative (2009). Report of the 4th senior security management seminar: Sovereignty, security and humanitarian action. Geneva, 22–24 November.

Slim, H. (2001). Military intervention to protect human rights: The humanitarian agency perspective. International council on human rights meeting on humanitarian intervention: Responses and dilemmas for human rights organisations. Geneva.

Slim, H. and Bradley, M. (2013). Principled humanitarian action and ethical tensions in multi-mandate organizations in armed conflicts. World Vision.

Sorensen, G. (2001). *Changes in Statehood: The Transformation of International Relations*. Basingstoke, UK: Palgrave Macmillan.

van der Haar, G. (2013). States and non-state institutions in conflict-affected societies: Who do people turn to for human security? Occasional Paper, 6. Wageningen University.

Walton, O. (2008). Conflict, peacebuilding and NGO legitimacy: National NGOs in Sri Lanka. *Conflict, Security and Development*, 8(1), 133–167.

Watanabe, K. (2003). *Humanitarian Intervention: The Evolving Asian Debate*. Tokyo: Japan Center for International Exchange.

Zicherman, N. et al. (2011). Applying conflict sensitivity in emergency response: Current practice and ways forward. Humanitarian Practice Network Paper, 70. Overseas Development Institute, London.

1

THE RELATIONSHIP OF THE EXTERNAL IN THE INTERNAL

Introduction

The goal of this chapter is to lay out the theoretical basis for the rest of the book. In the first part, the sets of norms used and understood by both the external and the internal will be presented, focusing on the normative concepts of 'statehood' and 'humanitarianism'. This will be followed by a brief review of the historical and contemporary interactions between these two norm sets. In the second part, the theoretical framework will be introduced, with a discussion of the state of exception concept and securitisation theory and a presentation of the methodology used in the book.

Norms in tension

An introduction of the norm sets provides the necessary background to properly relate the external to the internal. As will be seen, the theoretical framework is based on this positioning. The state norm set will be discussed in relation to the political concepts of sovereignty, prerogative, the state of exception and securitisation. The contrasting humanitarianism norm set, grounded on moral concepts, will be discussed in terms of principles. This discussion will set up a tension that is the basis of the later analysis, a tension mediated through negotiations between the actors, negotiations that are conducted through discourse. First, however, the concept of norms must be introduced.

Norms

In this book 'norms' will be understood as 'shared expectations about appropriate behaviour held by a community of actors' (Finnemore, 1996: 22). Norms are socially constructed, rather than dictated, and in an idealised world are whole-heartedly shared by the relevant actors, although in the real world they are often highly contested and prone to mutual disagreement. Even within a set of norms there is often disagreement on what constitutes the proper understanding of the 'shared' norms. For example, individual humanitarian organisations may understand the norm of humanitarianism in a particular way. Difference are particularly marked between INGOs that only implement humanitarian programming and those that also implement development activities, as the role of humanitarian principles in negotiating access can sometimes vary.

What an actor understands to be appropriate behaviour – for itself and others, inside and outside their norm sets – creates a potential for action. How that understanding is actualised in behaviour, and how others react to these actions, is a critical question. The two 'shared' sets of norms under consideration in this study are those concerned with state behaviour and the behaviour of humanitarian actors. If even within norm sets there are differences of opinion, then between norm sets there can be considerable tensions. One specific way in which tensions can build is when there is a clash between international and local norms, as the global distribution of norms has not been straightforward. Newly introduced international norms do not encounter a normative vacuum at the local level. Local norms, even those borrowed from global sources before being adapted to local conditions, will often have a 'robust legitimacy' which moderates the reception of international norms (Acharya, 2009: 5). This point should be remembered when the case studies are reviewed.

Statehood

Defining the concept of the state is highly problematic. The term could more rightly be considered 'an idea or cluster of concepts, values and ideas about social existence' than an objective reality (Vincent, 1987: 4). A state is an abstract construct, a legal and political designation, a convenient fiction used to regulate political interactions. The term, and the designation, facilitates how different actors engage with each other – discrete universally accepted categories are easier to manage than vague ethnic or cultural constructs. But such a category is only superficial in nature. In practice, each state develops in a unique historical, geographical, cultural and religious context and will focus on different aspects of what it means to be a state. States have 'different structures, political institutions, cultures and values. We do not see "the state"' (ibid.: 7). The modern state system has been greatly influenced, and can be said to be derived from, Western political and philosophical developments. Although this model has greatly informed how non-Western states have formed and developed, there are regional and national differences that inform attitudes to the roles and responsibilities of states. The Asian values rhetoric and debate of the 1990s points to this[1] and will play a part in the Sri

1   See, for example, Boll (2001) and Langguth (2003).

Lanka case study; as will be seen, the non-Western view on statehood will feature importantly in the other case studies as well.

Regardless of the problematic nature of the concept, a working definition of statehood should be proposed. Rather than a highly theoretical definition, commonalities will be elaborated upon. In this book, a state will be considered as a political entity that is acknowledged internationally to represent a defined geographical area and population. The key point is that a state is a political entity which faces outward – in other words, it can decide on who is a friend and who is an enemy. Changing perspective 180 degrees, a state is only a state if considered as such by other states. The rules of the game are that states are autonomous, that other states should not interfere in their affairs, and that all states are equal – de jure, if (certainly) not de facto.

Domestically the situation is muddier. In Max Weber's oft-cited definition from his lecture 'Politics as a vocation' (1918), 'a state is a human community that (successfully) claims the monopoly of the legitimate use of physical force within a given territory' (Weber, 1946). Coercive authority is an essential element of a state and helps a government to tie together its subjects (Laski, 1935: 21). Coercion plays a major role in both the creation of a humanitarian crisis itself and the need for negotiations to define the space for humanitarian action within the crisis. Allied with coercion are the themes of fear and the law, themes that will form the basis of all the case studies.

Another key aspect is that the state is separate from society – the public and private spheres are different constructs (Dunleavy and O'Leary, 1987: 2). States claim their 'hegemony or predominance within a given territory over all other associations, organizations or groups within it' (Vincent, 1987: 19). A state will, therefore, consider itself above society and, it will be argued, take a fundamentally political and instrumentalist view in its relations with civil society. The external face of statehood will be much less important in this analysis than an understanding of the relationship between those who represent a state and society and how political actors use coercion, fear and the law domestically to meet their political objectives.

Even more than for the definition of a state, sovereignty is an evasive concept. Indeed, 'in spite of the agreement on some ... basic issues, sovereignty remains an ambiguous concept' (Biersteker and Weber, 1996: 2). In this book sovereignty will be very simply defined. Two core ideas should be understood: that there is 'no final and absolute authority exist[ing] elsewhere' – that is, outside the state – and that 'there is a final and absolute political authority in the political community' – that is, internally (Hinsley, 1986: 26). Therefore, a state is 'sovereign' in the sense that there is no higher *external* political authority that has the authority to make decisions[2] and that *internally* the state apparatus is the final political decision-making body.

---

2   Of course, there are a wide variety of inter-governmental organisations and treaty mechanisms which states may be a part of, and a system of international law binds states to certain norms of behaviour. The conceptualisation in this book is, however, based on a political view of sovereignty.

In this sense sovereignty is one aspect of statehood; it is not itself so much a legal as as an integral aspect of the political classification of being an internationally recognised 'state'. In the contemporary world sovereignty 'bestows supreme political authority upon the government. That sovereignty is an institution simply means it is a set of rules that states play by' (Sorensen, 2004: 103). Finally, as with statehood, the concern here is with the 'internal face' of sovereignty, for, 'even though states may be sovereign relative to one another, they possess clearly different authorities over their own societies' (Lake, 2008: 49). This book is concerned with this, the domestic understanding and use of sovereignty, which is the most important location of tension concerning the relationship between states and humanitarian INGOs.

Finally, it is important to be clear about the use of the terms 'state' and 'government'. In this book, a government is made up of individuals who perform the actual 'steering' of the ship at any given time (Vincent, 1987: 29). Governments, which represent states, are in practice

> composed of political actors who are simultaneously members of social sectors, classes and interest groups; they have their own ideological, ethical and religious beliefs; their own programmatic priorities; and their specific views on how best to fuse these complex personal traits with their roles as state officials.
> *(Pempel, 1992: 118)*

Therefore, a government is a collection of officials holding formal power at a given time and place. A government represents the sovereign state. It is the only actually existing political entity that can be directly interacted with, as it is made up of people, and decisions are made by them, rather than by abstract political constructs.

Humanitarianism

The concept of humanitarianism is defined and used in different ways by different actors. A state-led humanitarian intervention which uses military resources will not be discussed, debated, understood and reacted to in the same way as a non-violent intervention by a humanitarian INGO. Even within the humanitarian NGO sector the term will be used in somewhat nuanced ways depending on the mandate and perspective of the organisation. In this book, humanitarianism will be defined as a Dunantist humanitarian organisation would define it. Dunantist organisations, named after the founder of the International Committee of the Red Cross Jean Henri Dunant, aim to subscribe strictly to the humanitarian principles upon which the Red Cross was founded and limit their action exclusively to humanitarian crises.

The core humanitarian principles are humanity, independence, neutrality and impartiality. Independence refers to proactive disengagement from political and military actors by humanitarian actors to limit coercive control of their action; neutrality to not taking sides in a conflict or engaging in political controversies; and impartiality to offering assistance to those in greatest need without discrimination. But at the heart of humanitarianism is, obviously, humanity. Humanitarians are concerned with human suffering, human interaction and the human ability to feel empathy and compassion for, and then respond to, the suffering of other humans. Humanitarianism is, in essence, a moral project. As a moral concern, there are characteristics humanitarianism is meant *not* to exhibit. Humanitarian action must not be profitable and must not be overtly political. Humanitarianism can be 'conceived of as an unchallenged good characterised by impartial charity for a common humanity, and something which transgresses the confines of state sovereignty' (Campbell, 1998: 498).

Discussions of principles often dominate debates within humanitarian organisations. On the notion of neutrality and remaining apolitical, there have been long arguments within the sector about whether humanitarian organisations are, indeed, existentially and practically, political or not. As not being a political agent is often seen as an essential component of humanitarianism, this is a core identity question. In theory, humanitarianism should be limited to humans helping other humans without any underlying political agenda, and as such NGOs are to remain politically neutral and independent from the control of political actors. Thus, to be internally coherent and consistent with the notion of humanitarianism they must stay outside of politics in the sense of not being overtly political actors. One should be reminded, though, of Schmitt's warning that 'we have come to recognize that the political is the total, and as a result we know that any decision about whether something is *unpolitical* is always a *political* decision, irrespective of who decides and what reasons are advanced' [italics in the original] (Schmitt, 2005: 2). Humanitarian INGOs, almost by definition given the work that they do and the contexts within which they operate, are intimately involved with highly political issues. Humanitarian crises are some of the most politically complex and sensitive contexts imaginable, and politics is at the core of their cause, continuation and resolution. In this way, although not being political actors, humanitarian INGOs engage with political actors and work in contexts of intense political contestation. These political actors will, obviously, view any other actor – internal or external, self-proclaimed apolitical or not, as political actors in some regards. At the least, their activities will have political consequences that will be reacted to on the part of the main political participants in the crisis (Lockyear and Cunningham, 2017).

On another front, there is much confusion amongst states and aid organisations alike concerning the difference between actors that engage in 'humanitarian' activities as well as development operations (multi-mandate NGOs) and those that should be considered as purely humanitarian organisations. A Dunantist humanitarian actor, such as MSF, only implements activities in what are considered to be 'humanitarian crises'. Humanitarian crises are situations where a population's very existence is in jeopardy, either through structural violence, war, displacement, massive outbreaks of disease or natural or human-made disasters. Multi-mandate organisations, such as CARE or Oxfam, implement both development and humanitarian activities, and sometimes implement both kinds of activities in the same context. Purely humanitarian organisations ground their legitimacy in humanitarian principles exclusively, and differentiate themselves from development or multi-mandate organisations that are widely perceived to be more 'political', 'activist' and even sometimes 'collaborative' in nature. In making this distinction no negative judgement is usually implied, but the differences in perspective and scope of activities is germane to how an international NGO is perceived by the state.

From an operational perspective, humanitarian aid is understood to be assistance and action designed to save lives, alleviate suffering and maintain and protect human dignity amid crises. It is intended to be short-term in nature – once a crisis is over the need for humanitarian action stops. Humanitarian aid traditionally focuses primarily on material assistance – food, shelter, water, sanitation and medical aid. Development programming is, by definition, longer-term in perspective, and involves types of activities outside the remit of immediately saving lives, such as livelihood development, agricultural programming and education, as well as such activities as security-sector reform, governance capacity building and conflict resolution. This book will discuss the experiences of both types of actors in the following case studies and how their different perspectives impact on their relationship with the governments will be teased out where relevant.

States and INGOs

Given the above, how have, and how do, states and INGOs interact? This section will provide a brief overview of key themes in how states and the aid system have interacted from the Cold War onwards. The relationship between states and the aid system has changed and developed over time. Different issues have predominated and different types of actors have been at the centre of action and debate. A background knowledge of the changing relationship is necessary to situate the recent critiques of the aid system by states and states by aid actors. For the purposes of this historical review, aid is inclusive of all manner of aid mechanisms and is not limited to humanitarian aid.

The Cold War era

In much of the recent literature on the relationship between states and aid actors the issues are presented as newly emerging trends. But the discussion of foreign aid through the lens of politics is not new. Morgenthau, in 1962, discussed the fact that 'policies of foreign aid are frequently suspect, as serving in disguise the traditional ends of colonialism' and that 'foreign aid is no different from diplomatic or military policy or propaganda. They are all weapons in the political armoury of the nation' (Morgenthau, 1962: 306). From the beginning of the Cold War era aid was a tool in a state's foreign policy toolbox. The Cold War era can be conceptualised as a period of hegemonic states (donor states) relating to recipient states (mostly post-colonial states) in a period of geopolitical polarisation. Aid was not based on need but was a political tool, driven by strategic geopolitical necessity – aid programmes were heavily influenced by short-term foreign policy decisions guided by the foreign policy establishment (Fleck and Kilby, 2008: 1). The objective was political influence rather than aid effectiveness (Dunning, 2004: 409–423). Aid was then seen as a method of buying influence, and military and economic interests were the most important determinants of aid, especially in the later part of the Cold War period (Bermeo, 2008).

Viewing aid from the perspective of a recipient state, aid created a 'moral hazard' (Dunning, 2004: 409). They could put into place policies and set goals at variance with the aims of donor states as donor states needed the support of the recipient states in the geopolitical manoeuvrings of the Cold War. Aid was used freely by local elites in recipient states to repress or co-opt local populations. Donor states turned a blind eye to such practices, or even preferred these 'strong states' – authoritarian regimes – as they were considered more reliable and efficient.

The beginning of the 1970s saw the development of the *san frontieriste* ('without borders') perspective that interjected new concepts into the debate about the role of aid, most notably the role of advocacy in calling attention to the plight of the suffering populations during such crises.[3] As stated by MSF, the 'principles of impartiality and neutrality are not synonymous with silence'.[4] Key debates revolved around whether there was the right of humanitarian assistance on the part of victims of humanitarian crisis, the right of a humanitarian organisation to provide such needed assistance, and the right of such organisations to do so *unhindered*. It will be seen how these concepts made states increasingly uncomfortable.

The post-Cold War era

The expectation moving into the post-Cold War era was that aid would be re-focused on needs. Humanitarian and development goals would take over from military and political objectives. Non-development aid resources (mostly military aid) were to be freed up for other uses, and as such the percentage of development aid funding would rise. Donor state leverage increased in this period as the polarised geopolitical world was deconstructed. Threats of sanctions and conditionality became more plausible and effective. The era of the 'moral hazard' was over. In fact, democratisation became increasingly important and donors expressed more distrust of corrupt and authoritarian regimes.

Interestingly, in this period attitudes also started to change regarding sovereignty: 'Change in the normative and legal environment in the aftermath of the Cold War means that state sovereignty is no longer sacrosanct; rather, it is conditional on good state behaviour with a responsibility to protect its own citizens' (Kennedy, 2008: 27). This is a key point and informs all subsequent discussions on both the

3 For a detailed discussion of MSF's place in the political context of this period, see: Davey (2012).
4 All background information can be found at www.msf.org/msf-charter-and-principles/ [accessed 5 October 2017].

role of aid and how donor states view the duties and responsibilities of recipient states. It can be argued that what was increasingly debated was less the fundamental concept of state sovereignty than the expectations for how states were to fulfil their responsibilities to their own populations. Related to this was the important question of what role the international community was to take if states did not fulfil these expectations.

The 1990s and the rise of NGOs

The 1990s saw a major growth in the numbers and influence of NGOs and a growing focus on the importance of civil society in the aid project. The 2002 UNDP Human Development Report recounted that nearly 20 per cent of the then 37,000 INGOs were formed in the 1990s (United Nations Development Programme, 2002: 5). There are many explanations for the massive growth in the number of NGOs (summarised from: McGann and Johnstone, 2006: 65–77; and Reimann, 2006: 45–67):

- Increased recognition of the role of civil society in democratisation and increased number of aid programmes focused on democratisation.
- Increased demand for independent information and analysis by donor states and inter-governmental organisations (IGOs).
- Increased possibilities for inter-connectedness based on improved communications (the fax machine in the 1990s; later, the internet and social media).
- Increased availability of funding for NGOs. Donors became more mistrustful of working through certain types of states and specific governments, fearing corruption and the misuse of aid monies.
- In general, the poor performance of the public sector was given more attention. A 'public is bad, private is good' ideology formed (unattributed, 2007: 5).
- Increased political access for NGOs. As international and inter-governmental organisations expanded to tackle global issues, NGOs were increasingly promoted by donors to act as service providers, advocates and agents of democratisation.

This new structural environment was advantageous for NGO growth and a 'pro-NGO' norm developed. For the most part, states bought into, or were pressured into, this new normative structure. As states became members of international organisations they adopted standard practices, policies and features of governance and were socialised into new norms of behaviour through peer pressure. Donor states and IGOs such as the United Nations also attempted to 'teach' states the legal models of development of civil society which were imported from the West (Reimann, 2006: 58–61). This was, though, often perceived as a paternalistic approach by the recipient states.

In summary, NGOs became more useful as part of broader political developments in the role of aid and the relationship between Western-dominated IGOs such as the United Nations, financial institutions such as the World Bank, and developing states. The role and expectations of civil society also changed, especially related to the process of democratisation. The traditional concept of sovereignty was being challenged. States were pressured to accept these new norms as donor state leverage was strengthened and new international norms developed which were often hard to resist. But this was often an essentially contested process.

Post-9/11 and the global war on terror

In many ways, the 1990s can be viewed as an 'inter-war period', as the situation began to change yet again post-9/11 and the start of the Global War on Terror (GWoT). Aid in this period in some circumstances reverted to its role as an important geopolitical tool. For the 35 years before the beginning of the GWoT, the weight given to need in aid allocation rose; post-9/11 the weight lessened (Fleck and Kilby, 2008: 2). A new concept of 'strategic development' arose during this period, where donor states' development aid to recipient states focused on areas where returns from development *to the donor state* were the greatest (Bermeo, 2008: 3). Benefit could be judged from a political, cultural, economic or national security perspective. Concerns also increased that some NGOs were open to be used as platforms for terrorists (McGann and Johnstone, 2006). Therefore, there was a re-emergence of geopolitical considerations in aid allocation in certain circumstances, and in some situations civil society was actually seen as a threat from a national security standpoint if not properly controlled by states. This was a perspective shared by both donor and recipient states.

Contemporary issues and developments

For the most part, the contemporary era remains defined by the Global War on Terror. However, two additional evolving themes to mention are the development of the 'responsibility to protect' concept and integrated UN missions. The Responsibility to Protect (commonly known as 'R2P') idea was derived from UN Secretary-General Kofi Annan's report to the 2000 Millennium Assembly, where he asked the international community to arrive at a consensus on the question of 'humanitarian interventions' – that is, cases where one or more states intervene militarily in another state in the name of protecting that state's population. The International Commission on Intervention and State Sovereignty published its findings at the end of 2001 (International Commission on Intervention and State Sovereignty, 2001). These findings can be summarised as stating that a state has the primary responsibility to protect its own citizens, but if unable or unwilling to do so it is up to other states to intervene. It should be stressed that the primary responsibility to protect remains with the host state. The international community plays a monitoring and secondary role. But the fact that there is a developing consensus that there is a duty to respond in other states to protect the citizens of those states is a powerful one. The R2P concept relates to the debate on the *droit d'ingerence*, which has long been a particular feature of discussions in France on the role of the humanitarian imperative in foreign policy.

Another background development has been the concept of UN integrated missions, where all aspects of the UN's involvement in a crisis – political, humanitarian and military, are put under one coordination mechanism. This type of coherence has been widely debated, particularly concerning the inclusion of humanitarian operations in the grouping (Metcalfe, Giffen and Elhawary, 2011). The logic is clear – intervene in a comprehensive manner so that all actors are working on the same problem in a coherent way. The concern on the humanitarian side relates to the idea that humanitarian action should be apolitical, impartial and neutral, and thus should not be guided by and associated with political and military objectives.

The general point to be taken from this review is that humanitarian aid is provided within a political context. This has always been the case, although the political context itself has changed over time. That is, the political reference points have changed over time – from the Cold War bi-polar to the war on terrorism schema, but the fact of political reference points has remained constant. This does not imply that INGOs are political actors in the sense that states are political actors, only that humanitarian assistance itself is often considered to have political consequences, regardless of the moral foundations of the humanitarian norm.

The view of humanitarian international non-governmental organisations

Humanitarian action in one view is founded on the following logic: 1) the right to humanitarian assistance is universal, 2) victims are defined as those who are not receiving this assistance, and 3) agencies assert their right to have access to these victims (adapted from Hours, 2008). In practice, what this means is that aid agencies show up, declare an emergency based on their own definitions of crisis, and start to save lives. But often this is done on their own terms with little reference to the policies, concerns and capacities of the state involved. This self-proclaimed 'right to interfere' has in fact turned out to be 'more of a political problem for states than a victory for humanity' (ibid.: 2). These types of interventions also often lack legitimacy: they 'presuppose a global civil society which gives a mandate to aid groups to intervene and that these groups have no nationality or agenda of their own' (ibid.: 2–3).

Most humanitarian international agencies are Western in outlook and share a Western-based worldview concerning the role of humanitarian action. For such humanitarian INGOs neutrality, impartiality and independence are often taken as a shorthand for disengagement *from* state structures rather than necessitating principled engagement *with* them. Principles are often used to 'protect' INGOs from 'interference' from states. Humanitarian INGOs view states as becoming more 'assertive' in their dealing with international actors (Harvey, 2009). The principle of independence is especially difficult to maintain against state assertiveness. Increasingly, bureaucratic means are being used to restrict the activities of NGOs (Harvey et al.,

2010). A few examples will assist in presenting the INGO perspective. The focus here is on the perspectives of humanitarian INGOs and the discourse used, rather than a review of the 'facts' of the matter.

The Voluntary Organisations in Cooperation in Emergencies (VOICE) Newsletter number 13, May 2011, was dedicated to the question: 'Is independent humanitarian action a myth?' (VOICE, 2011). Instrumentalisation was a key theme. In an editorial, the view was expressed that instrumentalisation of aid can be defined as 'the illegitimate interference on the part of governments into the field activities of humanitarian agencies' (Wolf-Dieter Eberwein, President of VOICE, in VOICE, 2011: 33). Instrumentalisation on the part of donor governments is 'illegitimate', while NGOs 'influencing' donors to change their practices is 'legitimate'. The idea is clearly that states should not interfere with humanitarian INGOs, but INGOs can advocate with states. In an article from the same newsletter entitled 'No go for NGOs? Worrying trends presents new challenges for aid agencies', it was argued that

> A prerequisite to an effective response to human suffering is the right of NGOs to decide when, where and how they exercise their duty to assist vulnerable populations. Aid operations must be guided by the fundamental values of humanity, independence, impartiality and neutrality: every person in need should be granted assistance regardless of political, strategic, economic and other non-humanitarian interests.
>
> *(Chopin, 2011)*

This is the standard view of INGOs on the use of principles. The article went on to say that 'NGOs must live up to their acronym and remain *non-governmental*, maintaining a clear separation between their activities and state action. Only this clear separation will guarantee acceptance among the population we wish to help, and therefore ensure the efficient provision of aid'. But this was thought not to be the actual case, as 'recent developments, alarmingly, have highlighted **a tendency by states to forget these fundamental principles**' [bold in original]. States, then, are viewed as the culprits.

A Save the Children report from 2010 on the state of the humanitarian project made the following observation, also in line with the above view: 'Most worrying, however, is an increase in governments taking an actively obstructive or antagonistic stance towards humanitarian response' (Dempsey and Kyazze, 2010: 12). The language is illustrative of the INGO perspective: 'Obstructive' and 'antagonistic', rather than, say, careful and cautious, or even responsibly deliberative. The report goes on: 'in some cases, governments attempt to exercise greater control over humanitarian activity in their countries, and may have political incentives to restrict aid to certain troublesome regions, erect blockades or establish restrictions on people's movements' (ibid.: 12–13). On the one hand, the sentence fully admits that the countries are, indeed, under the responsibility of the governments, but on the other hand access to aid actors should not be constrained.

The above two quotes explain well the process of the securitisation of INGOs – making them into a threat which must be dealt with, a process which will be discussed more fully below. However, this process can be viewed from different perspectives. What is the objective behind a state's action? To the World Movement for Democracy, in a report on defending civil society from 2008, it is stated that

> Governments have tried to justify and legitimize such obstacles as necessary to enhance accountability and transparency of non-governmental organizations ('NGOs'); to harmonize or coordinate NGO activities; to meet national security interests by countering terrorism or extremism; and/or in defence of national sovereignty against foreign influence in domestic affairs. This report exposes such justifications as rationalizations for repression, and, furthermore as violations of international laws and conventions to which the states are signatories.
>
> *(International Center for Not-for-Profit Law (ICNPL) and the World Movement for Democracy (WMD) Secretariat at the National Endowment for Democracy (NED), 2008: 3).*

This is a very clearly stated perspective on the behaviour of states. The securitisation process is acknowledged, but any rational basis for it is discounted. Discourse is used by states as a way of justifying bad behaviour, rather than a justified reaction to valid security threats. Intriguing assumptions are made about how governments think, act and use discourse. This is of course not to say that governments do not use discourse in this cynical way, only to point out the underlying assumptions that are often made by INGOs when considering the behaviour of governments. In response to external actors – treated as political agents regardless of the motivation of the actor – governments are often seen to use concepts such as sovereignty to create a mystique of legitimate authority, and it can be argued that 'this mystique of the state simply shields the people behind it in government' (Vincent, 1987: 29). Sovereignty, in fact, in one view, serves to keep the international community out of the places and minds where decisions are really made (Uvin and Bayer, 2012: 17). The case studies provide interesting tests of these views.

The common feature of the above views is that INGOs stress the moral side of the equation – aid assistance is good, the political is bad, the moral should win over the political. Principles should be respected and aid should be allowed if based on these principles, regardless of the situation on the ground. Even when it is admitted that governments have the primary role in ensuring aid provision, the behaviour of governments in this process is often viewed as a cynical expression of political and security agendas which interfere with aid provision. But as has been discussed, humanitarian aid itself has political consequences – as much as INGOs attempt to remain apolitical states will of course respond to these consequences.

The view of recipient states

From the standpoint of a government there is 'a continuum between one extreme in which non-state authority sustains and reinforces the authority of the state, and, at the other extreme, a non-state authority which contests and challenges, or threatens to supplant that of the state' (Strange, 1996: 92). It is up to the state to decide if an INGO is a threat, a hindrance, a help or a friend. This fits in well with the Schmittian friend–enemy dichotomy, as will be discussed below. The relationship is thus often fraught, as 'humanitarian norms, more than most kinds of norms, challenge central notions about sovereignty and the organization of international politics in important ways' (Finnemore, 1996: 70). But no norm set is adhered to completely. Many decisions that are made by both parties are based on interest rather than adherence to a norm. This may often be the case for legal directives aimed at INGOs by states, for, 'like every other order, the legal order rests on a decision and not a norm' (Schmitt, 2005: 10). INGOs themselves can also act instrumentally. They may come from a moral norm set, yet make decisions to implement their objectives based on self-interest. Although requests to states for access may be justified in terms of need and moral good, there are other interests at play for organisations, such as the need to sustain funding flows, public relations and job security, amongst others. This fact has not gone unnoticed by states.

States are not passive and static entities. Developing states faced with evolving international norms concerning the rights, duties and responsibilities of sovereign states, especially in the domestic realm (norms that are often perceived as being Western-defined and dominated), will, and do, react. One reaction has been to sometimes view NGOs as replacing hegemonic states. Concerns over the infringement of sovereignty are valid no matter who is doing the 'interfering'. The pro-NGO norm developed through peer and donor pressure has increasingly been resisted. States often use discourse, and securitisation, in their reactions, attempting to counter these assumptions about the legitimacy and desirability of NGOs.

States therefore have legitimate concerns about how aid agencies work. But concurrently there are sometimes hidden agendas at work when governments consider how they will interact with aid actors. The following (non-exhaustive) list reviews some of these concerns and agendas:

- States may be unwilling to acknowledge that their capacity to cope with a crisis has been exceeded and that international assistance is required.
- Under some circumstances, state control of aid delivery goes beyond the legitimate interest states have in ensuring a well-coordinated and managed response.
- States often perceive the mere presence of humanitarian actors as a threat to their authority; this may be especially the case when dealing with authoritarian regimes.
- In certain contexts, states fear exposing their population to outside influences.
- States under intense international criticism will especially fear political manipulation and are prone to see all foreigners as spies.
- Aid organisations are often seen to be attempting to access the hidden.

But on the other hand, and regardless of the above 'hidden agendas', it is acknowledged by most aid actors that states retain the primary responsibility for the delivery of humanitarian assistance on their territories. The roles and responsibilities of states in relation to humanitarian aid are commonly conceived to be as follows (adapted from: Harvey, 2009: 6):

- States are responsible for calling a situation a 'crisis' and inviting foreign aid.
- States should provide assistance and protection (to the population) themselves.
- Sates should monitor and coordinate aid.
- States should set up regulatory and legal frameworks for aid delivery.

This dichotomy between hidden agendas and rights is, however, troubling to many aid actors. And if it is true that states have the primary responsibility to respond to crises, then the involvement of outside actors is problematic to states. 'State policies toward NGOs range from governments treating them as threats, to cooperating with them, with policies that ignore, seek to institutionalize (co-opt) them, or passively accept them falling in between' (Weir, 2003: 16). Each side faces a difficult situation.

But in the end the work of international aid actors does depend on the consent of states, whether legally, physically or politically. This is the case whether the state is weak, abusive or strong. There may be cases where the state exists in name only, such as Somalia, but in the vast majority of cases INGOs must seek consent (or at least the absence of a 'no') to operate from the state, especially in cases where the state is 'strong' (meaning internationally legitimate, fully formed and concerned with ensuring their sovereignty is respected). What is interesting is that, normally, strong states provide aid, weak states receive it. The situation INGOs are most perplexed with is when populations of strong states need aid. As an Overseas Development Institute report on 'affected states' put it: 'Humanitarian agencies operating within Pakistan have to be aware that they are working within the boundaries of a sovereign state' (Cochrane, 2008: 11), a state with a strong identity and bureaucracy. It is striking that it is felt that INGOs need to be reminded that states are sovereign and must be treated as such.

Case study: Médecins Sans Frontières and strong states – major issues[5]

MSF-Holland (MSF-H), being concerned with the issue of state control over humanitarian action, investigated the theme in 2010 which led, through a series of case studies, to a report entitled 'A line in the sand: States' restrictions on humanitarian space' (HAD, 2010). The case studies related to the experiences of MSF-H in the Ogaden region of Ethiopia, Sri Lanka and Turkmenistan.

5   The background context for this section is based on a close reading of a wide range of internal MSF-H documents on the theme, interviews with MSF-H officials, and personal knowledge and participation in MSF-H internal discussions.

When considering the organisation's experience in working under repressive regimes, it was thought that, 'although other motives may play a part in some instances (e.g. the resentment of having to rely on foreign charity), the main reason for restricting MSF's space is that governments perceive the organization as a threat'. Where an armed conflict existed, such regimes feared that agencies such as MSF would provide support to opposition forces, either with the provision of medical services or by extending credibility through interacting with them. But to MSF the most important reason the organisation was thought to be dangerous was because such governments had something to hide and feared that this 'something' would be exposed by international agencies, which were thus seen as threats to the regime's authority or its political objectives. What was it states wanted to go unrevealed? It could be violations of International Humanitarian Law or International Human Rights Law, or 'simply the lack of capacity to adequately respond to a disease outbreak'. The latter was of most concern to a medical agency, often associated with fears by governments of negative publicity concerning their inadequate response capacity. In MSF's view, a correlation could be made between the 'perceived importance of information control' and the level of authoritarianism exhibited by a government. The more authoritarian, the more important was the control of information to such governments, as well as the increased tendency to deny populations political and civil rights. To summarise, to MSF the logic was clear: the more authoritarian and repressive a regime, the more it had to hide, and thus the more threatening were organisations 'as free-minded and outspoken as MSF'.

The principle of neutrality also factored into the discussion of why humanitarian agencies were sometimes considered a threat. In the MSF perspective, 'when the control of information is a tool in the government's strategy to consolidate its power, any information not in support of the government quickly becomes anti-government, and therefore a potential threat'. Whether an actual threat – in the sense of being a challenge which was meant to cause harm – existed or not was thought to be irrelevant to the government concerned, as the very fact of the expression of a contrary view, however benignly stated, was itself considered to be a threat. And as such neutral space in such contexts was at a premium. This point should be emphasised in relation to MSF. Given MSF's dual mandate and the fact that it was 'a big and credible global player' that had the ear of Western diplomats, in at least MSF's mind authoritarian regimes would be fearful of its presence. It was thought that these facts played against the agency being given access.

Maintaining impartiality was also a major concern for MSF when operating in authoritarian states. It will be remembered that the humanitarian principle of impartiality refers to providing assistance to those most in need regardless of their ethnicity, race, creed, political persuasion or other such characterisations. It was thought that states were liable to manipulate humanitarian action that would disallow the provision of aid in an impartial manner by humanitarian organisations, as states would be fundamentally biased towards, or against, certain groups within society and would desire that agencies work with those positively viewed and not work with undesirable segments of the population. The latter would commonly be those whom humanitarian organisations would most want to assist. Disturbingly to MSF, such manipulation could create a situation where the agency's work could potentially cause harm to the very population that was meant to be served due to its association with an external agent. Avoiding these situations was a challenge when working with authoritarian regimes.

Many of the key findings concerning MSF's relationship to authoritarian regimes related to the role played by the organisation's 'public voice'. To an organisation that had a dual mandate of medical action and witnessing, the (in)ability of speaking out was an important factor in any decision-making concerning negotiating access. The organisation's public voice was also a mark of its identity. The use and restrictions on its public voice was commented upon in relation to the manipulation theme. It was thought that MSF may have underestimated the 'leverage' of its public voice in terms of negotiating access. The sense here is that the threat of speaking out could assist with negotiations. But on the other hand, gaining access at the cost of speaking out also risked MSF being manipulated by authoritarian regimes (as MSF's leverage would have been lost) and, even more seriously, being made complicit in the activities that the organisation witnessed but could not speak out about. The fear of complicity was strong. Self-censorship was also a risk, as in certain circumstances, dictated by the behaviour of the government, MSF refrained from exposing the 'something' which was meant to remain hidden, either by remaining silent or by avoiding the sensitive subjects in its public communications. Not speaking out often carried as strong a message as speaking out.

But given the above analysis, why was MSF tolerated at all? Why would an authoritarian state allow any humanitarian international agency to work on its territory and interact with its population, let alone one with a reputation of speaking out? There were a number of explanations according to the 'A Line in the Sand' case study research. For states that had slowly drifted into authoritarianism, the fact that MSF had been in the country for a substantial period of time could be a factor, especially if credit and leverage with certain authorities, such as technical ministries or local authorities, had been banked. In such situations, there would be costs incurred, in terms of international standing and image, by the expulsion of the agency. If these outweighed any negative consequences concerning its continued presence, especially if control was tightened, then it was more rational to allow the agency to continue to work. On the other hand, the presence of an international agency, if well managed, could actually be used by the regime to gain credibility and legitimacy. In such situations agencies could also provide useful services, filling gaps the government was unable, or unwilling, to fill. Or, as MSF conceded, it was possible that the regime, though authoritarian, was truly concerned about the welfare of its population and welcomed humanitarian assistance. But in most cases, it was certainly a combination of these reasons.

Intriguingly, the last overall finding of the MSF research related to MSF's internal weaknesses that limited its ability to respond to the above-outlined challenges. These involved the organisation's poor performance in understanding the contexts within which it worked and its inadequate networking with key local and international actors. These weaknesses had resulted in decreased access and increased manipulation (as described above), and were considered by some to be so serious as to preclude work in authoritarian regimes until rectified.

The MSF-Holland case is but one example of how humanitarian INGOs view working with states and relates to a limited number of case studies. Many of the themes, however, may also apply to other organisations and other contexts. The findings as presented above should, therefore, be kept in mind as the case studies are discussed and this book's overall findings are analysed.

The theoretical framework

Against this background this section goes into details of the political themes under consideration: The state of exception concept and securitisation theory. The role of these concepts as they pertain to the state–humanitarian INGO relationship will be elaborated upon and the theoretical framework will be introduced which will be used as the analytical tool in the case studies.

The nature of the political

As it is a foundational concept, it is important to first think about what exactly it is to be 'political'. A standard dictionary definition of politics is that it is the art and science of government. Many would expand this definition to include other aspects of social interaction, such as gender roles, economic systems or class relations. When considering how a government reacts to the presence of an external agent on its territory – the external in the internal, Schmitt's 'friends and enemies' dichotomy may be the most useful (Schmitt, 2007: 26–27). In Schmitt's sense, the 'friends and enemies' distinction does not define one actor as evil and one as good, but it does allow for one actor to, at least temporarily, define another actor as a stranger, an outsider, an 'other'. A third party, however neutral, cannot determine who is in which category, the designations must be determined by the political actors themselves. It is important to note that 'the friend and enemy concepts are to be understood in their concrete and existential sense, not as metaphors or symbols' (ibid.: 27).

Determining who is a friend and who is an enemy is based on a sense at any given time of who is a threat and who is being supportive (Schmitt, 2007: 27). By designating another as an enemy a conflictual relationship is established. Adding nuance to this general Schmittian approach, it is here argued that norms, though to Schmitt not a valid reference point for the final decision itself, must at least be factored in to an actor's justification. A norm does not dictate to an actor who is a friend and who is an enemy, but when making such a distinction an actor must refer to how this decision relates to established norms. This will become clearer when the securitisation approach is added to the theoretical framework and the important role of discourse is discussed. When considering this process, context matters. The case studies in this book are all associated with a context of civil conflict, although the Ethiopia case study opens the discussion up to the more general theme of political instability. Humanitarian agencies work in many types of crises, but for the purposes of exploring the tensions between states and humanitarian INGOs a context of civil war presents the most fertile ground, and is therefore the focus of this book.

The context of civil war is one of the most perilous times for a state. In such an environment, the involvement of external actors is particularly sensitive. But how then to define 'civil war' – what are the essential features? The simplest definition of civil war includes the following four elements: 1) 'Protracted internal violence aimed at securing control of the political and legal apparatus of a state', 2) a situation involving incumbents – i.e. the government – and insurgents – i.e. anti-government militant groups, 3) a context where members of society must define their attitudes in reference to the conflict, a potential polarisation of society, and 4) the potential of third party involvement, whether diplomatic, economic or military in nature (Evans and Newham, 1998: 64–66). This basic set of features will be taken as the working definition, but absent from point 4 in the list concerning third-party involvement is mention of the aid system. This is an often-missing aspect of civil war that must be included in the analysis of any context where aid actors are present. Whether aid actors consider themselves as politically involved or not, states may very well consider them as third-party actors, to be thus either pushed away or manipulated to decrease their negative influence.

In terms of examining the relationship between humanitarian INGOs and governments in times of civil war, the most intriguing ideas are those of prerogative and state of exception. The context of civil war is an especially sensitive time for a government. These are the periods when the prerogative of a government to proactively manage an emergency demands them to define the rules, informal and formal, concerning the engagement of external actors, and these feed into the negotiations between the actors. These negotiations therefore must be contextualised. By prerogative it will be understood as an exclusive power to command, decide, rule or judge. This concept of prerogative leads directly to the concept of the state of exception.

Securitisation

Exposing the parameters of prerogative is a first step, but how that decision-making power is used when confronted with an emergency such as a civil war is another question. What constitutes a 'state of emergency', or better, a 'state of exception', and what powers a sovereign actor has in relation to such contexts, needs further development. The concept of state of exception should be understood as a policy or decision that is not in conformity with a general rule, principle or law. In other words, the authority to make exceptions to the law – in this context either to increase or to decrease the space within which INGOs work. Law can mean both domestic and international law. Humanitarian INGOs enter into a context with an idea about what is legally correct and possible, though governments are often perceived to be capricious in how they manage the rules of the game. It is important for INGOs to understand the factors and thinking which underlie a government's change in behaviour and the changing legal rules.[6]

A legal code bases itself on a set of agreed upon norms, while a 'guardian of the constitution' may need to act outside those norms (McCormick, 1997: 214). In the 'personalistic decisionism' view, a sovereign decides on the best approach outside formal legal limits (ibid.: 213–216). Leaders, such as those confronted with a civil conflict, or indeed any type of humanitarian crisis, man-made or otherwise, may certainly agree with the weight placed on decision-making, and all the case studies test this view. Importantly, legal norms are also only effective if they are enforced. Without being enforced they cannot be realised. The Ethiopian case explores this aspect head on.

In practice, the concept of the state of exception should not be confused with an actual declaration of a state of emergency, as not all states of exception end with such an emergency declaration. In this book, a state of exception is viewed as any point in time when the normal legal and administrative system related to humanitarian INGOs is fundamentally changed in ways negatively affecting the work of humanitarian INGOs. Examples are new INGO registration systems, changed visa policies or adapted reporting systems, each in their own way restricting or even blocking the work of humanitarian INGOs and instituted in sometimes opaque and legally questionable ways. In most such cases, the government explains the changes on the basis of national security, a perceived threat to sovereignty and the like. In such a context, the questions INGOs ask are: what is the limit of a government's prerogative? What laws and legal codes apply, to the INGOs and in relation to the evolving context? How do these changes inform the status of the relationship with the government and the population? The important point is for it to be understood that the rules have changed and that the government has entered into a new way of conceptualising the boundaries of its action and the acceptability of external actors' actions.

This, then, is the type of context in which humanitarian INGOs attempt to negotiate access. Without an adequate understanding of the state of exception concept, as is the case with prerogative, INGOs will not understand the basis for negotiations. Schmitt's work, however, did not adequately elaborate on the actual process of defending a state of exception to the population and other actors. Therefore, the second part of the theoretical framework – securitisation – must now be introduced.

Thus far, a picture has been painted of a state as an autonomous political agent, at least domestically, which has the prerogative and capacity to make decisions based on current political and security needs in relation to external, and internal,

6   For a discussion about exceptionalism in the contemporary era, see Huysmans (2006): 11–29. Are changes in exceptionalism more about changes in how international politics and diplomacy are viewed than about debates about international law?

actors and factors. Distinctions are made between friends and enemies, whereby friends may be supported but enemies will be resisted and managed. A state of exception, such as a civil war, spurs a government to take decisive action, often outside the normal bounds of the law. The securitisation approach is an elegant way in which to frame this process of distinction, and it can be argued that the securitisation perspective is rooted in 'the politics of enmity, decision, and emergency' (Williams, 2003: 515).

A state, as represented by a governmental apparatus, must protect the interests of the population it purports to serve. Faced with an identified threat a government will attempt to stabilise the situation caused by this threat to achieve security. Security issues are sometimes serious enough to be framed as existential threats. In the standard securitisation structure, the thing that is existentially threatened is the referent object.[7] The actor that reacts to the threat on behalf of the referent object is the securitising agent. In addition, functional actors are those which 'affect the dynamics of a sector' and who 'significantly influences decisions in the field of security' (Buzan, Waever and de Wilde, 1998: 36). Given the fact of an existential threat a securitising actor will feel justified in instituting emergency measures beyond the rules that would otherwise be in place. It is important to understand that amity and enmity 'are generated by the actors and are not reflections of material conditions' (ibid.: 19). In this view security is essentially a matter of survival.[8] In the political sector sovereignty and ideology are the major issues under consideration, and in the societal sector collective identities such as religion are the most important themes. A threat is often another political or military actor, but even civil society actors can serve this role. Regardless, these threats endanger a referent object. This may be a community, a nation, an ecosystem or a state, among other examples. A securitising actor then acts on behalf of the referent object and responds to the threat by instituting actions outside the normally acceptable realm. Other actors may function in roles that affect the dynamics of the securitising act, such as pressure groups.

A basic grammar of security can exist, though each sector will have its own dialect, i.e. political, social, military or humanitarian. The key to emphasise here is how the concept 'security' is used and textual analysis is vital to determining this logic. Essentially, the securitisation act isn't about the threats that exist, but about how the issue is presented. And the way to study this process is to analyse the discourse used to communicate the nature and urgency of the perceived existential threat. The question is, when does an argument sufficiently resonate with an audience to convince that audience to tolerate violations of rules that would normally be in force? It should be understood, though, that a securitising act is not always successfully implemented. On occasion, a securitising act is attempted – referred to as a securitising move – but the intended audience is not receptive to the argument and will therefore not consider the 'threat' a security issue. As such the securitising

7   This study uses a generic version of the standard form of the securitisation approach. For
    a review of criticisms and responses of this approach see Williams (2003).
8   On state 'fears', see Knudsen (2001): 355–368.

process is a negotiation between the securitising agent and audience. As will be seen in the case studies, the definition of the audience is at times tricky. Once a securitised context has been established discussion ends and actions are taken on the newly established priorities.

Finally, in this view the concept of security should be considered in a negative light, as a failure to deal with issues in a normal manner. But this failure can be reversed by implementing a desecuritisation process that puts the situation back 'into the ordinary public sphere' (Buzan, Waever and de Wilde, 1998: 29). The desecuritisation process works by removing the existential threat in the minds of the audience, thus allowing for a reversion back to relying on normal policies, rules and ways of interacting with the security threats. The goal should be desecuritisation, and in many ways it is the more important, though challenging, process. In a desecuritised world there would be no need for behaviour outside normal modes of behaviour. Chapter 7 will discuss the various types of responses INGOs have at their disposal, including desecuritisation.

The negotiation structure

It is in this environment that humanitarian INGOs and governments negotiate the parameters – moral, legal and political – of their relationship. The question isn't about sovereignty per se, but about the state's prerogative, as fulfilled by a government – its executive power – to decide on a state of exception and, more importantly, to manage the state of exception. It is a process of securitising humanitarian INGOs using discourse. A period of civil conflict, framed as a humanitarian crisis, is the specific state of exception under consideration. The relevant government is understood to have the prerogative – the authority – to declare a state of exception, to securitise certain issues and actors, to make decisions about how to manage such a crisis point and to justify their actions through discourse. The four case studies will elaborate in detail on the nature of securitisation discourse.

Based on these findings a negotiation structure is proposed to conceptualise the evolving relationship between states and humanitarian INGOs. It is argued that the two actors construct their relationship through an ongoing process of negotiation, a negotiation between moral and political imperatives, mediated through the discourse of identity and informed by principles. This should not be understood to be simply the representatives of the two parties sitting across the table negotiating their terms of engagement. Rather, negotiations occur through a wide variety of methods, but always involving discursive interactions. The essential point is that these negotiations take place within a structure, a set of rules, norms, and procedures that can be described and understood. Such a relationship is constructed and not predetermined or simply based on material factors. The negotiation structure can be visualised in the diagram below.

Each of the four cases studies, as well as the chapter on INGO response to securitisation, utilise this basic analytical structure. The next section will go into more detail about the methodology used in the case studies themselves.

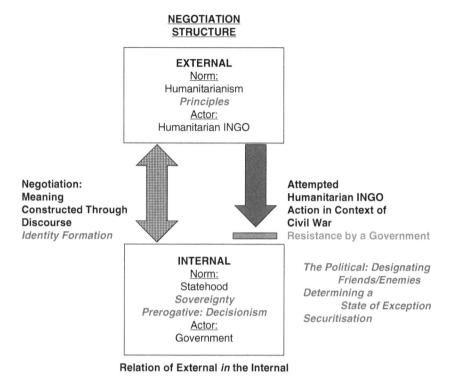

FIGURE 1.1 The negotiation structure: the relation of the external in the internal

The case study methodology

A case study methodology allows for an exploratory approach, in that variables and hypothesis will be inductively identified (George and Bennett, 2005: 75). In other words, it is important to establish and test the theoretical framework from the bottom up. The Sri Lanka case study provides the first test. For Sri Lanka, a methodology was used that allowed changes over time to be traced. The Sri Lankan context is a prototypical case – that of civil war, where humanitarianism and state responsibility are both most clearly tested, and the Sri Lanka case can be compared to other (like) examples of civil conflict. The themes that are the basis of the other three case studies (fear, the law and expulsion) were derived from the Sri Lanka case – appropriate contexts were found that matched. Once the usefulness of the theoretical framework was established, other themes could be isolated and studied.

A word about process tracing, an essential methodology to be used in this type of research. Process tracing is a method to examine the link between different contextual elements and how this link expresses itself in a given context. The aim is to examine not only what happened but also how it happened, including how actors explain their 'actions and behaviour' (della Porta and Keating, 2008: 232). At a fundamental level, 'uncovering the reasons that actors give for their actions is a key aspect of the empirical investigations' (ibid.: 233). Understanding the reasons governments gave for their policy decisions and the factors which went into their decisions was of prime interest in these case studies. The 'narrative explanation' of the causal path that led to a specific outcome was an important research interest (ibid.: 234). It should be noted, however, that process tracing findings do not determine an ironclad cause and effect relationship between events and policy decisions, as establishing a truly scientifically provable causal relationship is unrealistic. The findings can, however, point to significant associations between events, discourse and policy changes.

The actual process being traced in the case studies concerns how domestic and international events led the governments to construct the discursive and policy environment it did and how INGOs reacted to these developments. The end point was INGOs being securitised; the process was how this happened and why. The core questions are: what happened, who made it happen, who was it directed at, where, and when? And what events were important from the perspective of the themes – how were the relationships constructed in practice? The process tracing exercise is told in narrative form and first sets out the factual story before a presentation of the uncovered associations between events, discourse, and policies.

Discourse analysis and sources

As indicated above, tracing the use of discourse is a key element in constructing the case studies. As the book progresses, the definition of discourse will be expanded. However, it is important to first present the initial logic, as used in the Sri Lanka case study, before elaborating on the changing practice.

In the Sri Lanka case study, the analysis of the available discourse focused on what words were used and what meanings were ascribed to them and how these words, and meanings, were understood – or misunderstood – by each actor. What concepts, experiences and worldviews lay behind the semantic choices and the form and structure of the communications? And finally, how were these meanings negotiated through discourse? The analysis of the texts was informed by the approach of *verstehen* – understanding – which highlights the necessity of understanding the context, experiences and worldview of the actors and situating the study in a particular time and place, accomplished by the above-described process tracing exercise. Without this 'understanding', the texts could not be properly analysed. Indeed, the epistemology underlying *verstehen* states that knowledge must be understood historically and that there are no timeless bodies of truth (Hausheer, 1996: 48).

Discourse in the context of the Sri Lanka case study was considered to be the public manifestations of the views of the actors and was therefore any text or verbal communication that demonstrated these views. For INGOs this included internal documentation and public statements. For the government, it comprised the discursive environment as articulated in a wide variety of media, civil society, academic and governmental sources. From the government's side, outside direct communications with individual organisations, the media were the most efficient way to communicate its policies, warnings and the like. The media were therefore heavily used by the governments to create a discursive environment upon which actions were based and justified. As such this study considered the media as an essential channel of communication and meaning formation between the INGOs and the governments.

It must be asked, however, how far media reports can assist in establishing associations between events and policy decisions. It would of course be better to have access to internal governmental documentation and records of behind-closed-doors governmental deliberations. But as this was not possible, other sources had to be relied upon. Media sources, paired with the other primary and secondary sources – academic works, public statements and public documents – all coalesced to form a sense of the government's decision-making. In addition, if the theory is valid that the GoSL used discourse to securitise humanitarian INGOs, then the media would be a key channel of communication for the government. In the end, it is difficult to adequately answer this question, as without intimate knowledge of the government's views – their backroom discussions – it is impossible to know how far the discursive environment as presented in the press matched the actual views of government officials. But, it should be noted, INGOs such as MSF believed this was so and acted on this belief. It was this initial observation in fact which led this researcher to focus on the analysis of the discursive environment as the analytical starting point. Regardless, this is a limitation of the research and this methodological question needs further development.

For the remaining three case studies – Chechnya, Ethiopia and Sudan – the concept of discourse was expanded. The logic of each expansion will be dealt with in the relevant chapter, but in essence discourse was taken away from being text-based and made thematic. The central idea is that one can focus on a theme, and proxy indicators that speak to that theme, rather than on texts only. The theme itself becomes discourse. For Sudan, the discursive theme is expulsion; for Ethiopia, the law; and for Chechnya, fear. This is a creative use of the concept of discourse and is a major contribution of this book. There are, certainly, other types of thematic discourse that may be explored.

For the three thematic case studies, semi-structured interviews were conducted with INGO, donor and UN staff familiar with the contexts. A variety of organisations were engaged with – purely humanitarian and multi-mandate. None of the interviews were for attribution. In addition, primary source materials were consulted where possible. Secondary source materials were used for background research. The analysis was conducted in reference to the original research on the applicability of the themes to humanitarian crises and the constructed relations between states and INGOs. My own personal reflections on the contexts, all of which I have personal experience with, were also integrated into the discussions.

With this background in mind, the case studies will be presented in the next four chapters, followed by a discussion on the desecuritisation process.

References

Acharya, A. (2009). *Whose Ideas Matter? Agency and Power in Asian Regionalism*. Ithaca, NY: Cornell University Press.

Bermeo, S. B. (2008). Aid strategies of bilateral donors. Annual Meeting of the International Political Economy Society. Philadelphia.

Biersteker, T. J. and Weber, C. (1996). *State Sovereignty as Social Construct*. Cambridge: Cambridge University Press.

Boll, A. M. (2001). The Asian values debate and its relevance to international humanitarian law. *International Review of the Red Cross*, 83(841), 45–58.

Buzan, B., Waever, O. and de Wilde, J. (1998). *Security: A New Framework for Analysis*. London: Lynne Rienner.

Campbell, D. (1998). Why fight: Humanitarianism, principles and post-structuralism. *Millennium – Journal of International Studies*, 27, 497–521.

Chopin, S. (2011). No go for NGOs? Worrying trends presents new challenges for aid agencies. In Voluntary Organisations in Cooperation in Emergencies (VOICE), Focus: Is independent humanitarian action a myth? *Voice Out Loud: Newsletter of VOICE*, 13 May.

Cochrane, H. (2008). The role of the affected state in humanitarian action: A case study on Pakistan. Humanitarian Policy Group Working Paper. Overseas Development Institute, London.

Davey, E. (2012). Beyond the 'French doctors': The evolution and interpretation of humanitarian action in France. Humanitarian Policy Group Report. Overseas Development Institute, London.

della Porta, D. and Keating, M. (eds) (2008). *Approaches and Methodologies in the Social Sciences: A Pluralist Perspective*. Cambridge: Cambridge University Press.

Dempsey, B. and Kyazze, A. (2010). At a crossroads: Humanitarianism for the next decade. Save the Children, London

Dunleavy, P. and O'Leary, B. (1987). *Theories of the State: The Politics of Liberal Democracy*. London: Macmillan Education.

Dunning, T. (2004). Conditioning the effects of aid: Cold War politics, donor credibility and democracy in Africa. *International Organization*, 58(2), 409–423.

Evans, G. and Newham, R. (1998). *The Penguin Dictionary of International Relations*. London: Penguin Books.

Finnemore, M. (1996). *National Interests in International Society*. Ithaca, NY: Cornell University Press.

Fleck, R. K. and Kilby, C. (2008). Changing aid regimes? U.S. foreign aid from the Cold War to the war on terror. Working Paper, 1. Villanova School of Business Economics.

George, A. L. and Bennett, A. (2005). *Case Studies and Theory Development in the Social Sciences*. Cambridge, MA: MIT Press.

Harvey, P. (2009). Towards good humanitarian government. Humanitarian Policy Group Report. Overseas Development Institute, London.

Harvey, P. et al. (2010). The state of the humanitarian system: Assessing performance and progress. A pilot study. ALNAP (Active Learning Network for Accountability and Performance). ODI, London.

Hausheer, R. (1996). Three major originators of the concept of verstehen: Vico, Herder, Schleiermacher. In A. O'Hear (ed.). *Verstehen and Humane Understanding*. Cambridge: Cambridge University Press.

Hinsley, F. H. (1986). *Sovereignty*. Cambridge: Cambridge University Press.

Hours, B. (2008). NGOs and the victim industry. *Le Monde Diplomatique – English Edition*, 14 November.

Humanitarian Affairs Department (HAD) (2010). A line in the sand: States' restrictions on humanitarian space. HAD Working Papers. MSF-Holland.

Huysmans, J. (2006). International politics of insecurity: Normativity, inwardness and the exception. *Security Dialogue*, 37(1), 11–29.

International Center for Not-for-Profit Law (ICNPL) and the World Movement for Democracy (WMD) Secretariat at the National Endowment for Democracy (NED) (2008). Defending civil society: A report of the World Movement for Democracy.

International Commission on Intervention and State Sovereignty (ICISS) (2001). The Responsibility to Protect. Ottawa.

Kennedy, D. (2008). Humanitarian NGOs and the norm of neutrality: A community approach. Working Paper. University of Minnesota.

Knudsen, O. F. (2001). Post-Copenhagen security studies: Desecuritizing securitization. *Security Dialogue*, 32(3), 355–368.

Lake, D. A. (2008). The state and international relations. In C. Reus-Smit and D. Snidal (eds). *The Oxford Handbook of International Relations*. Oxford: Oxford University Press.

Langguth, G. (2003). Asian values revisited. *Asia Europe Journal*, 1(1), 25–42.

Laski, H. J. (1935). *The State in Theory and Practice*. London: George Allen & Unwin.

McCormick, J. P. (1997). *Carl Schmitt's Critique of Liberalism: Against Politics as Technology*. Cambridge: Cambridge University Press.

McGann, J. and Johnstone, M. (2006). The power shift and the NGO credibility crisis. *International Journal of Not-for-Profit Law*, 8(2). www.globalpolicy.org/component/con tent/article/176/31423.html

Metcalfe, V., Giffen, A. and Elhawary, S. (2011). UN integration and humanitarian space: An independent study commissioned by the UN Integration Steering Group. Overseas Development Institute/Stimson Center, London.

Morgenthau, H. (1962). A political theory of foreign aid. *American Political Science Review*, 56(2), 301–309.

Pempel, T. J. (1992). Restructuring social coalitions: State, society and regime. In R. Torstendahl (ed.). *State Theory and State History*. London: Sage Publications.

Reimann, K. D. (2006). A view from the top: International politics, norms and the worldwide growth of NGOs. Faculty Publications, 4. Georgia State University.

Schmitt, C. (2005). *Political Theology: Four Chapters on the Concept of Sovereignty* (2nd edition). Chicago: Chicago University Press.

Schmitt, C. (2007). *The Concept of the Political* (expanded edition). Chicago: Chicago University Press.

Sorensen, G. (2004). *The Transformation of the State: Beyond the Myth of Retreat*. Basingstoke, UK: Palgrave Macmillan.

Strange, S. (1996). *The Retreat of the State: The Diffusion of Power in the World Economy*. Cambridge: Cambridge University Press.

unattributed (2007). Historical evolution of NGOs: NGO proliferation in the post-Cold War era. *Turkish Weekly*, n.d.

United Nations Development Programme (UNDP) (2002). Human development report 2002: Deepening democracy in a fragmented world.

Uvin, P. and Bayer, L. (2012). The political economy of state-building in Burundi. In M. Berdal and D. Zaum (eds). *Power After Peace: The Political Economy of State-building*. London: Routledge.

Vincent, A. (1987). *Theories of the State*. Oxford: Basil Blackwell.

Voluntary Organisations in Cooperation in Emergencies (VOICE) (2011). Focus: Is independent humanitarian action a myth? *Voice Out Loud: Newsletter of VOICE*, 13 May.

Weber, M. (1946). Politics as a vocation. In H. H. Gerth and C. Wright Mills (eds). *Max Weber: Essays in Sociology*. New York: Oxford University Press.

Weir, K. A. (2003). The paradox of NGO-state relations. Chapter from PhD thesis. University of Connecticut.

Williams, M. C. (2003). Words, images, enemies: Securitization and international politics. *International Studies Quarterly*, 47, 511–531.

2

THE CASE OF MÉDECINS SANS FRONTIÈRES AND THE GOVERNMENT OF SRI LANKA, 2006/7

The introductory chapters laid out the securitisation framework and explored how states view INGOs and INGOs view states. The task for the following five chapters is to examine how the theory works in practice. This chapter analyses the relationship between the Government of Sri Lanka (GoSL) and the humanitarian organisation Médecins Sans Frontières (MSF) in the 2006/7 period, and the next chapter continues the story in the 2008/9 period. As this chapter sets the baseline for the subsequent chapters, this case study is limited to the experience of one organisation in a clear-cut case of securitisation. As the goal of this case study is to set out the basic concepts and introduce the themes that will be discussed in the other studies, it is more deeply described and comprehensive than the latter cases. The following framework was used in the analysis and underpins the presentation:

- *Differentiation*: the creation of difference between the self and others by distinguishing between friends and enemies, instigated by changes in the context.
- *Organisation*: how messages are organised and framed, including thematically.
- *Meaning*: what is meant to be understood by these messages, rather than what they communicate superficially.
- *Action*: what are the actions the messages justified? And what is done – or planned to be done – based on the messages?
- *Practice*: how is the discourse 'done'? And what was the reaction?

This is the basic form of the securitisation analysis as used in this book. It should not be understood to be a clear-cut analytical process, and each stage is not always unique, as will be seen in the next chapters. But as a basic tool for analysis it is useful. Progressively in the presentation of the case studies the structure will retreat into the background while the central logic will be retained.

The next section introduces the context and actors.

Context and actors

Sri Lanka

This section will outline some of the key themes of Sri Lankan history useful to the securitisation analysis. One of the goals of this discussion is to demonstrate the sort of contextual analysis that should be implemented to perform a securitisation analysis. Therefore, the process of analysis as presented in this chapter is as, if not more, important than the content itself.

Although it is hard to generalise how a 'political order' is conceptualised by the elites, it is possible to indicate the tenor of the political ideal in the post-colonial era of Sri Lankan history. It has been argued that the political order is based on the concept of *dharmista samajaya* – a 'just society' (Wickramasinghe, 2006: 246) – and this can be read as the Sri Lankan state's ideology: social justice, but political stability. Leaders are to rule wisely and take care of the population and the ruled are to obey and limit their dissent. This is the predominant political context within which external actors must act. The tensions that are analysed in this case study relate to an external agent struggling to understand and fit into this political environment. More precisely, external humanitarian actors responding to the effects of the civil war struggled to fit into a Sinhalese political order while working predominately in Tamil areas – within the zone of the, at best, 'other', and at worst, 'enemy'.

A pervasive theme in the post-independence period has been the tense and difficult relationship between the Sinhalese and Tamil populations. Tamil dissatisfaction over central policies concerning language usage, access to the civil service and minority rights first developed into a period of low-level violence in the 1970s between Tamil militant groups and governmental security services. This low-level conflict increasingly effected civilians and then transitioned into a full-fledged civil war beginning in the 1980s. Tamil ethnic identity had developed over time from the British period. The 'enumeration' of identities through ethnic labels was first used by the British, and 'in that sense colonial knowledge did not imagine identities or construct them; rather, it opened up a new realm for political identities to blossom' (Wickramasinghe, 2006: 44). These labels became the basis of entitlements and rights as the British colonial administrators systematised the ethnic categories that were used in assigning places in the administration and in deciding on representation in the Legislative Council (Wickramasinghe, 2006: 45). As with many colonial contexts, it is uncertain how politically divisive ethnicity was before the British started to actively enforce the use of ethnic categories in the political process. Regardless, in the post-independence period ethnicity became a dominant political issue.

The Liberation Tigers of Tamil Eelam (LTTE), which became the dominant militant Tamil group fighting for independence for Tamil areas, was established in 1976, though its leader, Prabhakaran, had already created the Tamil New Tigers group in 1972 (Harrison, 2012: xix). The beginning of the conflict proper is often thought to be the occasion of the 1983 anti-Tamil riots, which killed, in wide-ranging estimates, between 350 and 4,000 Tamils and displaced around 100,000 Tamils in Colombo and 175,000 outside the city (Winslow and Woost, 2004: 2). The narrative runs as follows. A reported rampage by Sinhalese troops against Tamils in the north led to a retaliation by the LTTE which left 13 Sinhalese soldiers dead. Their bodies were taken to Colombo for viewing at a cemetery. Mishaps resulted in the ceremony starting late and the crowds that had gathered becoming agitated, and riots ensued. There have been many claims that the riots were pre-planned by the government (Winslow and Woost, 2004: 2). This story is often told in detail, as it has become an important feature of the genesis of the conflict and foreshadowed the violent nature of ethnic relations for the next three decades.

The civil war itself is commonly broken down into five phases, but for the purposes of this discussion it will be broken down into a further two phases (adapted from Weiss, 2011). The period 1983–1987 is known as Eelam War I, and was bounded by the 1983 anti-Tamil riots and the signing of the 1987 Indo-Sri Lanka Accord which marked the arrival of the Indian Peace Keeping Force (IPKF) to the Tamil areas of Sri Lanka. Fighting between the IPKF and the LTTE intensified during the period of its occupation. Once the IPKF left Sri Lanka in 1990, fighting between the LTTE and the Sri Lankan military resumed and Eelam War II began. Peace talks were briefly held in 1995 but quickly failed and Eelam War III began the same year. The year 2002 brought yet another ceasefire which ushered in an uneasy and still violent period of 'peace'. The Indian Ocean tsunami hit the island on Boxing Day 2004, which created its own unique phase in the relations between the GoSL and the LTTE. The final phase of the conflict, Eelam War IV, commenced in 2006 and ended in defeat of the LTTE in May 2009.

Médecins Sans Frontières

Médecins Sans Frontières is an international humanitarian medical non-governmental organisation founded in Paris in 1971 by a group of French doctors and journalists.[1] To a large degree MSF invented and defined the parameters of modern emergency relief, especially in the medical realm. MSF has a dual mandate – medical humanitarian operations and advocacy. Specifically, it will be the Dutch 'section' (nationally identified office) of MSF (MSF-Holland, or MSF-H) that will be discussed in this chapter, although because MSF is a 'movement' the actions and decisions of each individual section are tied to those of the others.[2]

MSF is an international, independent, medical humanitarian organisation that delivers emergency aid to people affected by armed conflict, epidemics, natural

1   The following information on MSF can be found at www.msf.org [accessed 5 October 2017].
2   MSF-Holland (MSF-H) was founded in 1984 and was the third section after MSF-France (MSF-F) (1971) and MSF-Belgium (MSF-B) (1980). Later, MSF-Spain (MSF-E) and MSF-Switzerland (MSF-S) became the final two of the five 'operational sections' of the organisation.

disasters and exclusion from healthcare. The organisation's medical humanitarian action is guided by medical ethics and the principles of independence and impartiality. Principles play a large role in the identity of humanitarian organisations. For MSF, the principles are: independence (assistance is based on an independent assessment of the needs of vulnerable populations); impartiality (assistance is offered to people based on need and irrespective of race, religion, gender or political affiliation); and neutrality (MSF does not take sides or intervene according to the demands of governments or warring parties). And, of course, underpinning these principles is the fundamental principle of humanity, which simply indicates that humans have a responsibility to help other humans in need. Advocacy, or 'bearing witness', is also an essential component of the organisation's identity. To MSF the principles of impartiality and neutrality are not synonymous with silence. 'When MSF witnesses extreme acts of violence against individuals or groups, the organisation may speak out publicly.' Two other key elements in the way MSF defines itself are a commitment to upholding medical ethics and a pledge of accountability for its actions to its patients and donors.

MSF had a long history in Sri Lanka and encountered many constraints over time. MSF-H's relationship with the Sri Lankan government was never easy, although tensions ebbed and flowed as with any relationship. MSF began working in Sri Lanka in 1987 when MSF-France established its first operational presence, based on a memorandum of understanding (MoU) signed with the government in 1986. MSF-Holland first arrived in the country in 1994, although contact had been maintained with MSF-France from the late 1980s concerning whether there existed operational space for another MSF section. The organisation's engagement was strictly related to the war and operations were conducted solely in the north in conflict-affected Tamil areas. MSF-Holland left the country in 2004 because the peace seemed to be holding and humanitarian needs had lessened. In 2005 there was a brief post-tsunami intervention. The final period of MSF-H engagement was between 2006 and 2012.

For both MSF and the GoSL principles, politics and identity were collectively at the centre of negotiations around all aspects of access and helped to define internal compromises. Principles were the reference point for MSF-H, and if any of the themes and concepts could be considered a central point for discussion and decision-making, principles filled that role. As the analysis progresses principles will become increasingly important to MSF-H, as a way for the organisation to both decide on its action and also interpret and react to the behaviour of the GoSL. For the GoSL politics was the most important factor in decision-making, but based on a set of political principles. Implicit in this idea is the existence of the conflict, as the GoSL had to make decisions related to its view of political and military necessity regarding the conflict. Besides the conflict, but intimately informed by it, was an overall sense of identity which influenced political decision-making. This will become clearer as the analysis continues through time and will involve the play of cultural identity in the Sinhalese community in relation to the Tamil minority and the progress of the conflict. Coming full circle, the identity of MSF-H – as understood by itself and the GoSL, informed how it used principles and how it was reacted to by the political structures. As MSF-H was desirous of working in the conflict-affected zones with the minority Tamils and alongside the LTTE, which made the organisation suspect, this forced elements of the Sinhalese elites to push for certain political choices to be made. As can be seen, it was not only a contested relationship but a complex, dynamic and symbiotic one.

Differentiating between friends and enemies: the process 2006

This section will examine the Sri Lankan government's perspective by making a detailed analysis of how the events developed in the July–November 2006 period and how those events were associated with the decision-making of the GoSL in relation to INGOs. A close examination of media reports enables an in-depth understanding of GoSL decision-making, the influence of those events on that decision-making and how the GoSL explained and justified its actions towards INGOs. Securitisation is conducted through discourse, as is the negotiation process itself. These media reports were essential in allowing an INGO to implement its own tracing of events, as a forum for dialogue between the GoSL and MSF-H and as a platform for desecuritisation activities.

While the country was recovering from the devastation of the Boxing Day tsunami of 2004, the civil war with the LTTE was heating up again. Though these tracks are intimately interrelated, for sake of conceptual clarity they have here been divided into two separate discussions to more fully examine how each track developed. The period under discussion is in fact defined by the merging of these two tracks, where INGOs became both political enemies and security threats, necessitating firm handling in a context that could be considered a state of exception.

Politics and war

The political developments in the 1999 to 2006 period can be summarised as the coming to power of the Sri Lanka Freedom Party (SLFP), the political rise of Mahinda Rajapaksa, and the increasing role of the Janatha Vimukthi Peramuna (JVP) (People's Liberation Front) and other Sinhalese nationalist parties such as the Jathika Hela Urumaya (JHU) (National Heritage Party) in the SLFP-led governments. In February 2004, the Sri Lanka Freedom Party (SLFP), the party of the future prime minister and president Mahinda Rajapaksa, negotiated an agreement with the neo-Marxist, Sinhalese nationalist JVP to form a coalition government, what would become the United People's Freedom Alliance (UPFA). In the parliamentary elections of April 2004, the coalition defeated the United National Front (UNF) and Rajapaksa became prime minister. The JHU, a Sinhalese nationalist party newly founded by Buddhist monks, took nine seats. But the UPFA was never able to muster a majority.

In the next steps to power for party and person, Rajapaksa narrowly won (50.3%) the presidential election of 17 November 2005, and in June 2006 he consolidated power by becoming the chair of the SLFP. This government was also based on an alliance with the JVP, which, as will be seen, caused political instability that in critical ways affected the relationship between international actors and the GoSL. As the year 2006 progressed, Rajapaksa increasingly lost support from the JVP and JHU and as such made overtures to smaller parties that had been aligned with the former regime, the UNP. In mid-2006 talks began with the UNP itself, eventually resulting in an MoU being signed with them at the end of October (de Silva, 2007: 104). The role of the JVP by this time had lessened, with important political implications.

President Rajapaksa did not accept the idea that the LTTE were earnest in their negotiations and therefore believed that a military solution would be necessary to settle the conflict. In this view, the effect of ceasefires only gave room for the LTTE to regroup and rearm. In this context, 'cowing Tamils in government-controlled areas, minimizing NGO involvement, controlling the media, suffocating civil society, and keeping political opponents weak and confused' were the conscious strategies used by the Rajapaksa regime to give itself the space to fight the LTTE (DeVotta, 2011: 133).

Sinhalese Buddhist nationalists were the loudest and most consistent critics of NGOs, which were considered to be 'ineffective, extravagant and corrupt' (Amarasuriya and Spencer, 2012: 127). But the concern was not limited to NGOs, as 'NGOs, Christianity, humanitarian agencies, LTTE, global capitalism and moral decline – all mixed together' to form a 'sense of apprehension' in the Sinhalese Buddhist community (Amarasuriya and Spencer, 2012: 130). A common theme of what has been termed 'Sinhalese Buddhist chauvinism' was the idea that international NGOs and Western countries were hostile to Sinhalese Buddhist civilisation (DeVotta, 2011: 135). Humanitarian international agencies were especially open to opprobrium because they were foreign entities and perceived to be solely accountable to Western donors and their publics (Haug, 2001: 22). Anti-globalisation rhetoric was used by both sets of ethno-nationalists, inclusive of opposition to NGOs, foreign interference and fears of Christian conversions (Silva and Hettige, 2010: 13). As an example of the Sinhalese Buddhist nationalist viewpoint, point five of the JHU's political manifesto from 2004 stated that 'the Government should control and monitor all the activities and monetary transactions of the non-government organizations that are in operation in Sri Lanka' (Deegalle, 2006: 391).

There was clearly a 'crisis of legitimacy' concerning NGOs in the eyes of the public, especially when NGOs were engaged in activities related to the peace process (Herath, 2010: 73). Ideological communities such as the JVP and JHU were particularly hostile to what was understood to be a human rights agenda grounded in a Western ideological perspective. The work of international NGOs was particularly open to criticism as they were thought to threaten the sovereignty of the state. '"Internal sovereignty" and "non-interference" [were] key terms in the political rhetoric of Sinhalese nationalists, to be protected at all costs' (Matthews, 2009: 582). As such, members of civil society activists in Sri Lanka had to contend with 'impassioned Buddhist nationalists, LTTE and an aggressive government that can stymie and circumscribe their activities, and their own disconnected agendas' (DeVotta, 2011: 172). The GoSL – and nationalists – often used the media to 'instil fear and suspicion' in the general public about the work of NGOs, creating strong anti-NGO feelings (Herath, 2010: 74).

Wars, especially civil wars, are politically very sensitive phenomena. The involvement of international actors amid a conflict – the external attempting to work in the internal – makes for a politically complex situation. Although humanitarian agencies attempt to remain neutral by not taking sides in a conflict, there are of course political implications to the presence of international actors whose objective is to engage with conflict-affected populations. In this sense humanitarian actors are often seen to be, and are treated as, political actors by host governments.

But clearly there is a third actor to be factored into the equation besides the government and the humanitarian agency, and that is the rebel group that is at war with the government. The humanitarian actor will by necessity negotiate access with the rebel group if it controls territory. This turns a binary relationship into a triangular relationship. Each point on the triangle is not equally weighted, though, as the most significant relationship is that between the government and the rebel group. Humanitarian agencies interact with both but its role is not central to that relationship; not central, but not trivial. As the Sri Lankan civil war progressed, humanitarian international NGOs often found themselves in the middle of a very tense adversarial relationship between the GoSL and the LTTE.

Though both sides of the conflict at times indicated that international aid would be welcomed and even encouraged, it was felt by some international actors that neither side was allowing aid agencies to work. Local and international aid agencies had increasingly become the target of 'threats, harassment and violence' that was prohibiting them from assisting the populations in need (*Daily Mirror*, 23 August 2006). The LTTE also appealed for aid to be given to the north-eastern Trincomalee district by international agencies, but claimed that the government was blocking them from doing so (*AFP* article as quoted in *Island*, 13 August 2006). Yet in this period there were also criticisms in the press that NGOs were negligent by their absence. An *Island* editorial accused the major NGOs of being 'conspicuous by their absence except for a very few' in the response to the displacement crisis created by the ongoing fighting (*Island*, 10 August 2006).

Throughout this period the government expressed alternating views about the role of the international community in relation to the conflict. At times, the GoSL indicated that the international community should leave it to prosecute the war as it saw fit, and at other times it indicated that international actors should be more involved. The latter perspective was often taken when the GoSL was unable, or unwilling, to discuss with the LTTE the rules of conflict, such as when the government stated in July 2006 that it had expected that the international community would have put more pressure on the Tigers to stop using civilians for military purposes (*Island*, 3 July 2006).

In the search for friends and enemies one can see that the friends were the Sinhalese political elites, specifically the political actors guided by security and political concerns: the GoSL – in this period the SLFP government of prime minister and then President Rajapaksa – and the Sinhalese and Buddhist nationalist perspectives of the JVP and JHU. The enemies were those who threatened national security, the existence of a unified state and the political dominance of the government, so both the LTTE and NGOs (both national and international), which were perceived to be linked with the LTTE or at least its undesirable agenda. Note that the self was not a stable entity as it was a coalition government that changed over time – the SLFP had to deal with the JVP and the JHU, and then at a certain point the centre of gravity shifted towards the UNP.

The role of identity in this process of differentiation should be emphasised. The identity of the self was as much an issue as the identity of the other. Each party involved had to reflect on their identity and prioritise action that protected this self-identity. Sometimes also an actor would decide on actions based on an understanding of the identity of the other where it was felt that that identity was threatening. Identity then was a sub-structure which informed the political acts and, as will be seen, a sub-text that permeated the securitisation discourse.

The ACF killings

A major event with serious repercussions was the killing of 17 ACF national staff members in Muttur on 4 August. The workers, trapped inside their Muttur branch office residence because of the fighting in the area at the time, were shot and killed at point-blank range (*TamilNet*, 8 August 2006). The incident was taken seriously by both domestic and international actors and created a cascade of reactions by several Sri Lankan and international actors, all of which informed subsequent GoSL policies on INGO access to the conflict zones. The GoSL's response to any accusation of blame was robust.

Discussions in the press quickly turned to the question of changes to access and security for humanitarian agencies because of the ACF killings. An example is a *Sunday Leader* article which discussed the fact that the government had not yet 'given the green light for unrestricted access to relief workers into LTTE controlled areas'. A government minister stated that 'we have to be extra careful in allowing aid workers into the conflict areas as the situation is very intense'. The article said that the killings had raised serious concerns in the minds of international aid organisations. 'We cannot put their lives at risk', the minister concluded (*Sunday Leader*, 27 August 2006). An opinion piece published six days after the ACF killings in the *Daily Mirror* brought forward several issues surrounding the ACF incident. It was understood that NGOs were increasingly facing security threats, though 'their work represent[ed] a critical component of development activity in the country'. Interestingly, the piece sympathetically noted that NGOs had to obtain work permits, pay taxes, cooperate with the administration when asked to and 'contend with ad hoc strictures such as producing permits from the Ministry of Defence or allied agencies to permit their travel to the North and East'. Such a system had existed before the ceasefire agreement, but the agreement should have 'freed everyone including

NGOs of these shackles'. And now they had to contend with security threats and suffer physical violence against them, such as the ACF attack, abductions, and arrest if they didn't have the proper paperwork. Thus, 'it is as if war has been declared on NGOs too. The perception of their detractors are that INGOs help the LTTE directly or indirectly, are working in an area where war demands exclusion as a policy, are having a good time, [are] dishonest or not too transparent and waste valuable philanthropic resources' (*Daily Mirror*, 10 August 2006). But in the view of the author of the opinion piece this was not the case.

The tsunamis

The central idea to be kept in mind concerning the tsunami and its after-effects is that the political authorities, most notably the JVP and the JHU while in a coalition government with the SLFP, designated who were friends and who were enemies with regard to the Sinhalese nationalist agenda of defeating the LTTE and creating a state dominated by the Sinhalese majority. In this light, the tsunami and its after-effects created a dynamic that had to be politically managed. As is commonly observed there were in fact two tsunamis. The first was the physical wave that hit Sri Lanka on Boxing Day 2004. The second tsunami was the metaphorical wave of INGOs that 'flooded' the island in early 2005. There were several issues of concern for the government resulting from this second tsunami, including the uncontrolled flow of large amounts of aid funding, the perceived interference in Sri Lankan affairs by international actors, the sensitivities of the rehabilitation effort in conflict-affected areas, concerns about corruption and the misuse of funds as well as about monies and materials finding their way to the LTTE, and finally the slowness of the response. These issues and concerns would prejudice the relationship between INGOs and the GoSL in ways beyond the tsunami response.

The massive tsunami that hit Sri Lanka on Boxing Day 2004 caused major damage to many coastal areas of the island. One third of the coastline was affected, 30,000 people died and 20 per cent of population lost their lives or their livelihoods or a substantial amount of income (de Silva, 2012: 176). There were 516,150 displaced, 98,000 homes were demolished or destroyed and 150,00 livelihoods were affected (Grewal, 2006: 9). The south, south-east, east and north-east coasts were the most affected. The tsunami also had substantial political ramifications for Sri Lankan political parties, humanitarian agencies, and Sri Lankan civil society. The government's response was thought to be inadequate by the population, making the government even more unpopular than it had already become (de Silva, 2012: 176). The co-existence of human-made and natural disasters complicated the aid effort. From a relief and rehabilitation response perspective the objective was to get proper resources to the zones most in need as quickly as possible. As the north-east was under LTTE control, a mechanism had to be found for the GoSL, the LTTE and international agencies – the aid triangle – to cooperate in relief distribution. The proposed solution was the Post-Tsunami Operations Management Structure (P-TOMS), which was meant to establish a mechanism to facilitate rehabilitation activities in LTTE-controlled areas. It was an administrative device to ensure funds were shared and distributed equitably. In general Sinhalese nationalist parties did not support it. The JVP were firmly against the LTTE and were thus against P-TOMS, as it was seen to legitimise the LTTE. The JVP threatened to pull out of the government if it went ahead, which it eventually did when the P-TOMS draft agreement was signed at the end of June 2005. P-TOMS, though, was supported by the UNP.

This disagreement over the value and wisdom of P-TOMS is illustrative of the basic political tensions associated with the tsunami response. From a Sinhalese nationalist standpoint, as represented by the JVP, any policy which could be seen to support the LTTE was rejected, as was any policy which encouraged the more active involvement of foreign organisations in the conflict zones. These tensions also pointed to the fundamental instability of the coalition government and the fact that the tsunami response was a politically sensitive issue.

Beyond the political tensions over the constitution of P-TOMS there were more general concerns with how the tsunami funds were being used. In September 2005, the auditor general published a report on the use of tsunami funds and found irregularities, including in how aid monies were collected, distributed and their use monitored (Government of Sri Lanka, 2005). For the most part, the report detailed issues with how the government managed tsunami funds rather than problems with NGO programming (*Island*, 26 September 2005). Regardless, in the press the report was used to paint a negative picture of how the tsunami effort was implemented by all actors, including, and often especially, NGOs.[3] It was an oft-repeated idea that the initial tsunami response had not, in fact, been dominated by NGOs, but by other civil society actors who were the real first responders, such as Buddhist temples (*Daily Mirror*, 19 July 2005). In addition, it was felt that, as political and military authorities and international agencies became involved and took charge of the relief response, the impartiality of the response was affected (Bullion, 2008: 166), marking the later period off from the initial impartial and spontaneous local response immediately after the tsunami. The JVP in particular was concerned about the tsunami response, charging in parliament that the government and NGOs were not following proper procedures in granting houses to tsunami victims, and as a result of this many beneficiaries had still not received new housing while in some cases houses had been given to people whose houses had not in fact been destroyed (*Daily Mirror*, 6 October 2006).

Following on these perspectives, late 2005 witnessed the first indications of the desire of the GoSL to audit NGOs, initially related to the tsunami rehabilitation efforts, but as the war heated up the conduct of NGOs in the conflict zones also became a major concern. A Parliamentary Select Committee (PSC) was set-up to investigate NGOs. The committee's interim report published in 2008 described the

3   The acronym 'NGOs' will be used when indicating a collection of international and national NGOs or when it is uncertain in the sources whether international or national NGOs, or both, were being mentioned.

process of its founding and objectives. On 30 August 2005 a motion was tabled in parliament by Nandana Gunathilake, a JVP MP, based on which it was decided to set up a select committee to look into the operations of foreign and foreign-funded non-governmental aid organisations that were operating in Sri Lanka. The intention of the select committee was to:

> Inquire about the level of transparency of the financial activities of those nongovernmental organizations, identify the manner in which the operations of the said nongovernmental organizations have made an impact on the sovereignty and national security of Sri Lanka, identify the way the operations of those non-governmental organizations have made an impact on national and social well-being and inquire into the manner in which the Government of Sri Lanka should act with respect to these nongovernmental organizations and make the necessary recommendations.
>
> *(Parliament of Sri Lanka 2008)*

The select committee first consisted of 19 members representing all the political parties in parliament. The PSC was formally established in January 2006. Though the impetus of the PSC was the tsunami response, the investigation became more far-reaching over time. Packaged together, the concepts of sovereignty – political autonomy for the Sinhalese political elites, national security (the protection of the state against the LTTE menace) and the social and national well-being of the country (which could easily be read as the continued dominance of the Sinhalese elites unfettered by foreign influences and Tamil terrorist violence) – outlined a particular social-political agenda that left little room for the work of foreign, or foreign-funded, NGOs, which were often seen to be LTTE supporters. This story is, fundamentally, one of the government deciding if, and how, NGOs threatened the Sri Lankan state and nation and what the GoSL should do to counter those threats.

With this as background, the next section will review the critique of the tsunami response. Was there satisfaction with the way in which NGOs had responded operationally?

The response critique

As Sri Lankan political elites had long been concerned with 'foreign interference' and 'neo-colonialism', it was not surprising that the tsunami response was also analysed from that perspective (Weiss, 2011: 302, footnote 54). Some of the criticism was sound as no such massive response is flawless. International NGOs were not always sensitive to the local context and dynamics in how they disbursed funding (Jayasuriya, Steele and Weerakoon, 2006: 16–17). An estimated 300 new INGOs arrived in Sri Lanka within the first month, four times as many as were present before the tsunami; out of these it was estimated that only roughly one half had registered with the Centre for National Operations (CNO), the government clearing house for tsunami operations (Harris, 2006: 1). A major theme in the press concerned the slowness of the rehabilitation response. By August 2006, 20 months after the tsunami had struck Sri Lanka, some 40,000 families were said to be still living in inadequate temporary shelters (*Sunday Nation*, 27 August 2006). The actual numbers were debated, but the press painted a dire picture, though at times using exaggerated numbers. It was often reported that many NGOs had failed to fulfil their pledges to build housing units. President Rajapaksa had indicated that all the promised housing units were to be provided by the two-year anniversary, yet there were real doubts in mid-2006 that the deadline could be met.

The frustration with INGOs in this period was clear: the *Sunday Nation* article from August continued that it was 'sad to note that the International Non-Governmental Organisations (INGOs) have hardly contributed towards meeting the needs of the tsunami victims even after making pledges' (*Sunday Nation*, 27 August 2006). The figures, the article continued, showed that INGOs had 'failed miserably' to deliver assistance and had made 'bogus promises'. There was intense pressure on all fronts for INGOs to act quickly and focus on service delivery. On the surface, this seemed a reasonable approach, but from the INGO perspective 'this meant [that] some equally important aspects of humanitarian assistance, such as accountability to affected populations, the need to prioritize coordination, strengthening local capacity, and basing recovery on a human-rights approach, were side-lined' (unattributed, 2006: 11). It is informative that some INGOs believed that obtaining a 'quick impact' should not always take priority and that there were differing perspectives on both objectives and how to gauge success. INGOs were thought to be unduly influenced by their media profiles. The media, it was claimed, preferred to report 'bleak, simplistic pictures of performance rather than elaborate on the complexities of the challenges involved in promoting equitable and sustainable recovery' (Grewal, 2006: 27). Action was necessary to prove worth on the part of INGOs (Frerks and Klem, 2005: 21). This general climate created pressure on INGOs to focus on quantity rather than quality.

Lack of coordination and competition amongst NGOs was another common theme in the tsunami critique. The context was commonly labelled as a 'humanitarian circus', being defined by over-statement of needs, competition for funding, and poor accountability (Rieff, 2005: 49–51). For agencies with secure funding there were few incentives to coordinate. And it was believed that some agencies were 'openly hostile to any government action that seems to place "controls" on their independence' (Jayasuriya, 2006: 16–17). Insufficient dialogue between NGOs and the government on policy issues was also noted (Grewal, 2006: 32). Added to the criticism that NGOs failed to coordinate properly with the government was the even more serious allegation that organisations had taken advantage of the Sri Lankan government's failure to implement proper accountability mechanisms.

On the topic of tsunami funding, many issues and practices were discussed and criticised. One theme repeatedly discussed was the idea that NGOs had collected money internationally using the suffering of the tsunami victims as a draw but did not use the monies for the victims. A *Daily News* article from late July entitled 'Tsunami Swindlers' (*Daily News*, 31 July 2006), talked about the 'tidal wave of sympathy' worldwide which had helped NGOs to collect millions of dollars for the tsunami response. Sri Lanka hosted some NGOs that were 'name boards' only and existed solely to raise money from local and international sources for humanitarian projects which did not exist. It was often alleged that hundreds of NGOs had quickly been created after the tsunami to take advantage of the generosity of people in the West and in Sri Lanka who had been moved by the tragic events to help. Not all NGOs were in this category, but there was a need for laws to control those that were.

The large influx of funding on one hand allowed for the growth of local civil society organisations but on the other hand fostered the movement of people from local NGOs to INGOs that had more resources. There was a sense that such INGOs were dismissive of local organisations (Bullion, 2008: 166). It was another common theme that INGOs promised that they would implement certain pro- grammes but failed to fulfil their promises, as much of the money was used on themselves or work was prolonged in order to collect as much money as possible. It was also alleged that fake organisations had collected money, and that with pre- existing NGOs they had conducted media campaigns in the West which had implied that the GoSL was not helping its own people. The money collected by these INGOs was then not properly used, and when confronted about not fulfilling their promises, these INGOs had simply charged that the GoSL was not being cooperative. In addition, much of the funding that these INGOs had collected was said to have flowed to the INGO HQs and was not in fact used in Sri Lanka (*Sunday Nation*, 27 August 2006). INGOs were 'drawing on interest' in the words of one article (*Sunday Observer*, 27 August 2006).

In summary, there was a great deal of dissatisfaction concerning the tsunami response shown in both the media and in government statements. The P-TOMS arrangement, though appreciated at the start, was eventually discounted as it was feared that it would legitimise the LTTE. Some dissatisfaction was directed at the government's poor accountability mechanisms, but much of the criticism was focused on the NGO response. The JVP was particularly angered at how NGOs had conducted themselves and their programmes. The procedures for collecting and distributing funds were criticised, as they were seen to be dishonest and ineffective. The response was also thought to be slow, especially related to housing recon- struction. The political response was the establishment of the PSC, backed by the JVP. The Rajapaksa regime took on board much of these criticisms of NGOs, and government officials directly charged NGOs with misconduct. By mid-2006, NGOs were under intense pressure by the political elites and the media concerning the tsunami response. The PSC was also stepping-up its investigation of NGOs. The discourse related to the tsunami response directly, or indirectly, associated the LTTE with humanitarian international agencies. The LTTE and INGOs were both reinforced as enemies and the GoSL was pushed towards a further disengagement from these actors.

The second track to be discussed relates to the war and its effect on how NGOs were perceived and treated by the political elites, inside and outside the government, and by the media.

Securitising the enemy: organisation and meaning of messages

The organisation of the securitising messages can be thought of as a set of dichotomies. These dichotomies are a way to conceptualise the discursive context rather than to assign intention. These are also only examples of such dichotomies and not a comprehensive review of the discourse of the period. Each is based on a pairing of concepts in tension that helped to define the self and the other and explain why the other was worthy of harsh handling. In examining these examples, relevant newspaper articles must be quoted from extensively to demonstrate how language was actually used. The point should be emphasised that it is sometimes difficult to know if the authors or government spokespeople were referring specifically to local NGOs, INGOs or all NGOs, but it is argued that, from the perspective of creating a critical discursive environment surrounding the working of NGOs, it mattered little which sub-set was the target.

In practice, questions can be asked whether the discourse was derived from agreed-upon government policy and discussions or solely reflected the opinions of individual governmental authorities? Was it created by the columnists, editorialists and journalists themselves, perhaps because it was what was understood to be a 'correct' interpretation of events, so governmental authorities would be appreciative? Or were the opinions and language independently derived and then picked up for use by the government? As will be seen through the discussions below, it was a combination of all of the above.

The dichotomies as described below were created based on a careful study of the available discourse of the period. Each dichotomy is illustrated by one or two examples, as much as possible involving direct communications by governmental authorities. Many more examples could be examined for each theme, but for the sake of space only the clearest cases have been chosen for detailed examination and are meant to be generally illustrative of the designated dichotomies. As stated at the top of this chapter, the point is as much to describe a process as to present content. The take-away idea is how to perform such an analytical process. Dichotomies are used as analytical tools, as a way to structure discourse. These dichotomies are the blocks upon which INGOs can construct an understanding.

Principles versus practice: wastefulness and greed

This dichotomy deals with the difference between what NGOs were seen to be doing in practice and what they should have been doing in principle (as this was understood). Many editorials and articles spoke about funding issues, accusing NGOs of not using funds for their intended purposes.

Instead of using collected funds productively to assist with the tsunami reconstruction effort, NGOs were accused of 'feasting' on the funds they had collected (*Sunday Nation*, 27 August 2006). A government spokeswoman who was often critical about NGOs' wastefulness and their 'extravagant lifestyles' was quoted in an interview as saying that concerning housing, reconstruction communities were 'rightfully impatient and often angry' at NGOs, especially when they saw the abundant funds NGOs had collected from developed countries being used in 'living it high, entertaining extravagantly, travelling in luxury vehicles, paying themselves astronomical salaries and lavish allowances'. It was also claimed that such NGOs had spent more than 40 per cent of the tsunami funds on themselves, their travel costs and their own administration (*Asian Tribune*, 24 September 2006).

One common explanation for this phenomenon was simply greed on the part of NGOs. An *Island* editorial entitled 'Humanity, what crimes are committed in thy name!' said it clearly: 'The bogus claims in question point to how NGOs are abusing the concessions they have been given for carrying out humanitarian work in the tsunami hit areas' (*Island*, 8 July 2006). It said that most NGOs were 'having a field day at the expense of the tsunami victims', and that 'some NGO activists thriving on human misery, have the audacity to call the tsunami waves *rattaran jalakande* ("waves of gold")!' There were some good people who were earnest in their desire to help and the state should support them. But most aid was a 'racket', and people in such greedy NGOs were like 'human vultures that descended on corpses and stripped them of gold chains and other valuables in the immediate aftermath of the disaster'. On the peace front it was also a debated whether NGOs were earnest in their desire to work for peace or whether the motivation was related to profit:

> One wonders whether there is money to be made out of this anti-war front. After all conflict, their management and resolution are today's big business. Hundreds of foreign and local NGOs thrive on conflict and conflict related issues. More conflict the better. No conflict, well start one.

Money issues were often brought into the critique as a way of condemning agencies.

Thus, NGOs, even if they said that they were present to care for the people suffering from disasters or the war or were working towards peace, were only out for their own gain. The clear impression left through such discursive practice was that NGOs operated on a profit and gain basis rather than being earnest in their desire to assist people, the underlying assumption (rightfully) being that a truly humanitarian or peace-building organisation would not be interested in profit or extravagant lifestyles. Thus, this dichotomy pitted the principle that NGOs should selflessly help others against the perception that NGO workers were greedy.

Western versus Asian: imposition of Western agendas

This dichotomy relates to Western mental habits versus the 'Asian way' of social interaction.[4] Very often there was an implicit, if not explicit, message that Western organisations did not understand the Asian context. MSF-H demonstrated

---

4   The term 'Asian way' was used by MSF-H in its documentation in this period and meant the perceived ways in which communication and discourse was managed in an Asian context, particularly related to the perceived indirectness of communications.

sympathy for this view as it struggled to understand the 'Asian way' of doing things. The organisation, in fact, considered this understanding vital to properly analysing the context.

One complaint was that Western models were imported by Western organisations to solve local problems when their relevancy or effectiveness had not been tested in the Asian context. Thus, such organisations were not accountable to the people, even though they claimed to speak on their behalf. In one commentator's view, the genealogy of the involvement of Western charity workers started with Christian missionaries in the colonial period who came to Sri Lanka to civilise the natives (Mahindapala, 2006). Modern-day NGOs were a continuation of this breed of Western colonisers. NGOs acted as if they were 'a supra-state, supra-society and supra-people body sitting on top' of local structures. He spoke specifically about what he referred to as 'politicized NGOs', which were those that had come under criticism from 'traditional societies'. 'Despite their claim to be do-gooders they are perceived, rightly or wrongly, as a threat to traditional societies putting their best foot forward to come to grips with the realities of modernity'. Some saw NGOs as intermediaries between the government and communities and this was seen in a positive light as it helped keep governments 'in check'. But others 'consider it [the rise of NGOs] as the invisable hand of Western neo-liberal agencies that haunt the globe' and as 'the behemoth that tends to usurp the powers of the state by dictating national agendas without any responsibility for the consequences of their interventionist actions'. From this viewpoint, these Western agendas were insensitive to the local context and ill-fitted to traditional societies, such as were found in Asia.

Many more examples of Western organisations being labelled as neo-colonialist or acting as representatives of undesirable Western traits could be given, as these were common themes. The perspective as presented in the above example was clear. Western organisations, being foreign, could not understand the Sri Lankan, or Asian, way of doing things. And worse, they tried to impose their own ways of doing things on Sri Lankans. The Western identity of most INGOs was both suspect and detrimental to their ability to fulfil their mandates. It should be mentioned that even local NGOs that were foreign funded were often made to fit into this dichotomy.

LTTE or Singhalese/Muslim: who is supported?

This dichotomy relates to whether NGOs were supportive of the LTTE, and Tamils in general, or were on the side of the Sinhalese, or in some cases the Muslims. In most formulations, it was an either/or choice, as with being a friend or an enemy. You were either with them or against them.

One illustrative article criticised the NGO community as 'these humanitarians who remain stoic when the LTTE is barbaric but can't keep their pants on if by any chance the striped sweethearts get bitten in their behinds; they talk about the government acting too hastily, being too quick to launch military strikes' (*Sunday Nation*, 17 September 2006). And this was no apologist for the government, as the

Rajapaksa regime was described as 'muddle-headed and unprofessional' in most matters. But in the case of not bowing down to LTTE demands, the government was right and the NGOs were wrong in their not taking a tougher stand against the LTTE. Instead of talking about the consequences of the conflict on the population, the NGOs 'talk[ed] about the 17 employees of a French NGO [ACF] who were murdered in cold blood, allegedly, according to them, by the security forces'. But they were also not talking about the 300 Muslims who had been 'butchered in cold blood by the LTTE in Palathoppur'. Being concerned with the plight of the Muslims didn't fit into the Tamil propaganda of persecution so they were ignored and therefore sandwiched in between the LTTE and the government. 'A delicious tidbit isn't it for our terrorism-laundering NGO fraternity.'

The question 'whose side were NGOs on?' was a common question and the answer that NGOs were working in support of the LTTE was a dominant theme. The stories mostly referred to national NGOs with foreign funding, but it is suspected that this distinction was lost on many. In an editorial from the *Island* in September an issue with the Tamil Relief Organisation (TRO) was discussed (*Island*, 4 September 2006). The TRO was officially an NGO but was widely considered to be the 'humanitarian arm' of the LTTE. The editorial explained that the government was determined to 'battle the LTTE on all fronts', including by freezing the funds of the TRO, which was a LTTE front organisation operating 'behind the façade of humanitarian assistance' (*Island*, editorial, 4 September 2006). It is baldly stated, and this is a common theme, that 'there are several other NGO arms of the LTTE, masquerading as human rights or peace-building groups … . For such an organisation [the LTTE] buying some NGO activists and making them dance to its tune is child's play'. The LTTE needs to fight on all fronts, including the NGO front, so the TRO, 'together with fellow NGOs, funded by foreign powers sympathetic to the LTTE, are trying to run a parallel government in the south. They have come to pass as the so-called civil society and spread their tentacles all over society'. Even some members of the press were 'comfort women to their NGO paymasters and help[ed] peddle their not-so-hidden pro-terror agendas' (*Island*, 4 September 2006).

As stated above, it was not always clear whether discourse referred to national NGOs, international NGOs, or both. Often it seems that even the authors were unclear to which they were referring. Most frequently the reference was in fact to a nebulous NGO of uncertain providence. Regardless, these NGOs were assumed to be supporters of the LTTE. This made NGOs suspect from the start, since from the standpoint of the Colombo political elites the LTTE were, quite unreservedly, the enemy. The flip side of this perspective was, logically, that such NGOs were not sympathetic to the Sinhalese cause or willing to provide assistance to the Sinhalese or, at times, to the Muslim population.

Government versus NGOs: who was in charge?

Who was responsible for maintaining humanitarian space? One columnist elaborated on what was described as a 'classic whine' by someone from the INGO world

(*Sunday Nation*, 13 August 2006). The 'whine' was the line of reasoning that the ceasefire agreement (CFA) did not require work permits for humanitarian actors working in the north but work permits were nevertheless were being asked for even though the CFA was still in operation. Then: 'reserve your guffaws for this', as it is explained that the INGO representative was reported to have said, 'this is not justifiable. It is unfair. The government can't say that the CFA is in motion and then do something in violation of the provisions of the CFA.' The writer is incredulous and asks if the INGO people think that 'The CFA is our constitution, just as others of their tribe believed that the tsunami was nothing but the announcement of an open season to do the vini-vidi-vici number economically, politically and culturally?' Whatever the CFA said it did not give 'dubious outfits' with 'dubious agendas' the right to do whatever they wanted. Then the crux of the issue: 'does it mean that governments cannot say "no" to something if they feel it is not in the better interests of the population?' Not all NGOs were engaging in nefarious activities, but then again not all were above board. 'We are talking "national security" here, ladies and gentlemen of the INGO-NGO community. Not all of you are "innocents abroad" and we know that.' And as a conclusion:

> A lot of INGO work in this country makes me want to say 'if you want to help us, give us the money and leave'. If they [INGOs] don't trust the trustees of such funds, then smile, say hello, commiserate with our suffering and leave. If we have recovered to any extent from the tsunami it is because we did what we could for our fellow citizens. If we someday sort out the menace that is terrorism, I am inclined to think it will be on our own.

The tone notwithstanding, the question was a valid one. Was it the responsibility of the government or the NGOs to decide on the parameters of humanitarian action? From the perspective of the NGOs the answer was both, each in its own way and independently of each other. But this idea was not always supported by the government. It was especially galling when what was seen to be an internationally managed ceasefire agreement was used by an international NGO to try to force an action, or non-action, on the formal political authorities of the nation.

Foreigners versus Sri Lankans: who deserves compassion more?

Did foreigners care more for themselves or for the people of Sri Lanka? An editorial directly analysing the significance of the ACF killings is illuminating (*Sunday Observer*, editorial, 13 September 2006). The ACF murder was 'justifiably a traumatic event for the NGO community. The NGOs have taken almost personal umbrage against this act of outrage, which is reprehensible by any standards'. But, 'there is almost a sleight of hand in trying to pass off a horrendous crime without any reference to the broader perspective of the current state of the conflict'. The author talked about the fact that 100 Muslims were 'massacred by the LTTE' the week before [a number which was not proven though often stated], but there was no condemnation by the NGO community, which has however, voiced a collective scream of agony over the death of their aid workers. The rationale may be that their aid workers are kindred – and that the Muslims are but civilians who got in the way.

The article also relates the story of a three-year-old who had died the week before because of a LTTE bomb. The author asked if international aid organisations weren't 'repulsed' by such acts. 'Or is it that aid workers lives are more sacrosanct than the lives of three-year-olds, or those of Muslims fleeing violence?' No life was more sacrosanct or death more venal than another. 'But, all lives are sacrosanct, and all attacks on civilians are reprehensible, and this is a fact that is not brought into perspective in condemning the murders of aid workers alone.' As such, 'the death of the aid workers should be condemned, but not in isolation, but with reference to the broader contours of a conflict that should take into account attacks, counter-attacks and genocidal campaigns, all in proper perspective'. NGOs, therefore, had lost their humanitarian perspective and failed to express compassion objectively.

What is interesting to note here is the importance of condemnation. The bias of an organisation was being gauged through its discursive practices. In this case it was noted that there was more condemnation of the killing of fellow NGO workers than of different types of civilian sufferers, the conclusion seeming to be that NGOs cared more about their own than about civilians, the civilians which they were purportedly there to assist. They did not abide by the author's standard that all life was sacrosanct.

Sri Lanka versus the international community: sovereignty and dignity

What was Sri Lanka's place in the international order? And what was the proper role for the Sri Lankan state vis-à-vis international actors? A fascinating article published in the *Sunday Nation* spoke about sovereignty and the concept of dignity (*Sunday Nation*, 3 September 2006). The theme is outlined by the statement that 'there are some who argue that sovereignty in the purest sense is meaningless in today's world'. The author gives a standard definition of sovereignty and concludes that sovereign states did not exist, if they ever existed at all, given that the definition included the idea that states should have the right and power of regulating their internal affairs without foreign interference. He asked if the term was any longer useful, and answered yes, it still was, as ideal types were useful to determine degrees (in the Weberian sense). Sri Lanka was only an island in a geographical sense. 'We are not just part of a global system of exchange, but a relatively insignificant entity in a complex network of social, economic, political, cultural and military power … . In short, we cannot and indeed are not allowed to do as we please in designing and implementing policy retaining to our internal affairs.' Thus, politicians, regardless of the rhetoric they used, had to kow-tow to representatives of the international community. But, the absence of sovereignty does not mean that a nation or a people are slaves, have no agency, and need to suffer all manner of insults to dignity and self-respect without a murmur. Therefore, it makes more sense to talk about dignity than sovereignty.

It is suspected that the discomfort the author felt may have indeed related to bruised dignity more than an honest fear that sovereignty itself was being eroded, though some commentators did express valid fears of this.

This article went on to say that, though powerless in some ways, Sri Lanka was not altogether without the ability to exercise control:

> While we can and should protest and take measures to deal with the arrogance of certain NGO personnel and other foreign actors and the assumptions they entertain about their roles and jurisdiction, we cannot ignore the fact that they are here and they obtain legitimacy because we don't do what we can and should do.

Though the 'bona fides' of organisations such as ACF should be questioned, 'the fact that 17 citizens of this country were killed in cold blood should be an insult by all of us, individually and collectively'. Summary execution of civilians is 'an affront to the dignity of the very people in whose name the fighting is done', for

> if a country that demonstrated unbelievable generosity and admirable capacity to respond to tragedy when the tsunami struck cannot respond to the inevitable humanitarian crisis precipitated by hostilities, then we as a nation should grieve at how unjust, unthinking and callous we are.

The argument concluded that Sri Lanka did not have the ability to recover its 'absolute sovereignty', but it did retain a sense of dignity. If the political community compromised this dignity it would have compromised on what mattered most 'in terms of nationhood, in terms of being citizens who are heirs to a civilisation and have a right to imagine a different and more benevolent future'. Dignity then should be the focus rather than an untenable sovereignty.

The relationship between the Sri Lankan polity and the international community was a balancing act; a balance between rights and responsibilities; between sovereignty and international obligations; between smallness and largeness; and between sovereignty and the desire to assist. Some thought Sri Lanka had every right and the means to control international actors on the state's territory – the external in the internal – but some were more pragmatic in their views and saw the limitations in a small country's ability to maintain pure sovereignty. And in this view the issue was about dignity rather than sovereignty.

Action in a state of exception

At the end of July 2006, amid the heightened military tensions, there were indications that INGOs were becoming increasingly suspect as reliable actors and new more restrictive administrative procedures were being put into place. As only the two armed actors could substantially influence the development of the conflict, INGOs were at the mercy of the changing situation and had to adapt to survive.

Because of the fighting in the north and east in July and August, thousands of civilians had fled and INGOs had tried to access the affected areas. Access, though, was increasingly being denied. For the first time, the MoD-administered work permits were an operational concern. Security personnel at the Omanthai crossing point (the crossing point between GoSL and LTTE-controlled zones) had prevented NGOs from crossing unless they had work permits. Most INGOs did not have these work permits, and those that didn't were sent back to Colombo. As part of the new administrative procedures,

> on a recommendation by the Social Welfare ministry, the defence ministry has written to the Immigration and Emigration department with a copy attached to the Inspector General of Police (IGP) that the visas of the INGO representatives must be revoked within 48 hours if they failed to produce work permits.
>
> (Sunday Nation, 6 August 2006)

The list of involved governmental agencies was impressive. Any international agency wanting to work in the north and east had to acquire a work permit from the MoD in addition to their normal visas. The question of INGO access to the conflict areas was a developing topic and decision-making by the GoSL, particularly the MoD, was in flux. What was clear was that the MoD was demanding that INGO personnel acquire new work permits from the MoD in order to access the conflict zones of the north and east. INGOs were given until 31 August to comply.

One of the justifications for any added administrative controls in this period of increasing military activity, particularly after the ACF killings, was the need to help protect INGOs. Yet a government statement concerning INGO security by the Human Rights and Disaster Management Minister Mahinda Samarasinghe, reported in the *Daily Mirror*, said that 'NGO workers in the North and East cannot expect security from the government'. He continued, 'while the government was grateful for the valuable humanitarian work carried out by the agencies it couldn't provide protection to the aid workers'. As with the earlier discussion about security, the minister said that the decision to remain in the conflict areas was solely up to the NGO employees operating there, but if any incident occurred the government would carry out an impartial investigation (*Daily Mirror*, 25 August 2006). As if to endorse his statements, a *Daily Mirror* article from the next day reported on a Consortium of Humanitarian Agencies (CHA) (a national grouping of NGOs) statement that more than 2,000 humanitarian workers had decided to pull out of the conflict area and that those pulling out had been requested to hand over their belongings to the military authorities (*Daily Mirror*, 26 August 2006). The picture painted was one of confusion, uncertain regulations, insecurity and massive movement of NGO personnel from the conflict areas, exactly as one would expect in a state of exception. As governments were usually understood to be responsible for humanitarian actors on their territories, whether national or international, it was a disturbing indication of the exceptional quality of the situation that the government was warning NGOs that it was not responsible for their security. Were the new regulations to discourage NGOs from working in the conflict areas? Or were they, and the warning about security, meant to encourage them to leave the country?

So, to sum up, the MoD spokesman said that 'the government has not imposed any restrictions on these NGOs preventing their humanitarian activities. What actually happened is that these NGOs have pledged [fled] the North-East due to the violence situation', and that the MoD is 'aware that some NGOs in the North-East are working with terrorists'. This statement ends with a criticism of NGOs and their tsunami response, saying that after the tsunami struck, many NGOs had arrived and pledged $30 billion, but that not even 15 per cent of the pledged monies had been fulfilled, and that in fact some NGOs were not even still active in Sri Lanka.

At the beginning of September, it was still not clear what the actual regulations were and what the 'price' of access was. It was also not clear under what legal framework the new regulations were being decided. Under whose authority were the MoD actions taken? Were decisions being made by the president, as minister of defence, or were they derived from internal MoD policies? The state of exception was in full flower in this period, with governmental interlocutors tasked with interacting with INGOs seemingly acting in ad hoc ways without any concrete references made to normal legal and administrative procedures. The securitisation process had allowed for action against the designated enemies and this was the result in practice.

To understand the behaviour of the GoSL, 'the security concerns of the government should be appreciated in that the LTTE is dependent on foreigners in its war' (*Island*, editorial, 12 September 2006). The security angle was emphasised, but from the state's perspective: 'The military is of the view that mercenaries could enter the LTTE-held areas under the guise of NGO workers'. The government at this time said that it was to 'call for a more positive role' from INGOs 'in the interest of humanitarian requirements during the present crisis period without succumbing to the pressures of single organisation that prevents them from fulfilling their role' (*Daily News*, 12 September 2006). This brings the narrative back around to the idea of INGOs as being both incompetent and a threat to political order.

At the end of September another actor communicated its intent to become involved in the registration process, the North Western Provincial Council (NWPC), the council responsible at the local level for the conflict areas that were under GoSL control. In fact, as part of the process of obtaining approval for its work, MSF-H had to have the NWPC sign its registration materials. At an illuminating meeting in September, the NWPC discussed the NGO issue and unanimously decided to control the NGOs functioning in the province (*Daily News*, 27 September 2006). There were, so the council believed, 1,400 NGOs working in Sri Lanka – according to one of the UNP representatives – and 'no one knows what they are up to. They perform according to their own agendas'. In the opinion of the UPFA representative:

> We see several NGOs functioning as the agents of the capitalist countries to exploit our resources. Several other NGOs are supporting the terrorists, while some others are converting the Buddhists and Catholics unethically to another Christian Sect. They spend lavishly to achieve their ends. Such NGOs are every dangerous. They endanger the national security and the religious harmony that exists in the country for centuries.

A JVP representative stated that NGOs were 'so powerful that they are able to change even the government's policies'. And of course, most supported the LTTE. Another UNP representative on the NWPC said that several NGOs did good work and they should be commended, but some were indeed threatening national security. The SLMC representative stated that no NGOs were assisting the Sinhala and Muslim populations in the current crisis, but that if it had been Tamils they would all have been active. Finally, another JVP representative said that NGOs 'follow no rules and operate arbitrarily'; 'NGOs play havoc in the country disturbing law and order'. It was a very grave situation to which the council needed to respond.

What is interesting about this discussion is that it was never specified what sort of NGOs were being discussed or whether the criticism concerned national or international NGOs. The council members also fundamentally misunderstood the nature of NGOs if believing that they would act in any way besides based on their own agendas. The last topic on the table during this dynamic council meeting was to decide what to do about the NGOs now that they had been properly characterised as a threat. The provincial minister of agriculture, lands and irrigations said that he doubted if the council could control the NGOs by 'merely passing' a proposed motion to control NGOs. There were no legal provisions in the motion, so he suggested that the council needed to obtain the legal powers to adopt measures to properly control NGOs. One of the UNP representatives agreed and suggested that 'the power and authority of supervision of their activities and auditing their financial transactions [should] be vested under the Provincial Council'. The final word went to the provincial minister of health, sports and youth affairs, who said that the 'activities of NGOs are not second to those of European invaders', and that they had a hidden agenda even if some did good work. The motion was passed that NGO activities should be controlled by the NWPC. As can be seen, this council meeting brings together most of the discursive dichotomies discussed above, and in doing so NGOs were roundly criticised and characterised as a threat which had to be dealt with. It did, though, indicate that in some cases it would be important to clarify the legal basis for NGO control.

One last issue that was mentioned repeatedly in press reports was that NGO expats illegally came into the country on tourist visas. Herath, the head of the PSC, had a meeting in October with Sri Lankan ambassadors/high commissioners to discuss this issue and gave suggestions on how to tighten up the procedures (*Sunday Times*, 8 October 2006). This involved the Sri Lankan high commissioners in the countries where the INGOs were located conducting a comprehensive investigation of the INGOs before they sent visa applications on to the Ministry of Foreign Affairs in Colombo. For 'politically sensitive' areas, such as the conflict areas, the MoD was also to be involved in the vetting process. This is the period when MSF-H, and other agencies also, had particular problems with administrative procedures, and when the PSC was most active.

One of the most intriguing questions related to the narrative as presented above was whether the confusion and incoherence was indicative of governmental agencies hard-pressed to manage a fluid and dangerous situation, or whether it was planned and orchestrated. What is clear is that it was the MoD which took the lead in this, since the MoD was both directly under the control of the executive and the department most intimately involved with the actual conflict zones. The other governmental agencies became involved when other aspects of INGO presence became important, such as immigration issues. When INGOs were thought to have crossed a line, the police could be brought in to give the securitisation process a legal sheen. The involvement at a certain point of the NWPC is interesting as it demonstrates a deepening institutionalisation of the anti-NGO perspective. Each level of government progressively involved itself with monitoring and regulating NGO activities. The engagement in certain ways by the PSC in aspects of NGO regulation and policing that were outside its purview is another demonstration of this. As time passed, the boundaries of action were expanded by an increasing list of governmental agencies – not only in terms of rhetoric but also with regard to action. The general picture is one of sometimes ad hoc and often extra-legal governmental actions by a wide range of departments to severely constrain and curtail the work of INGOs. If the actions taken, or proposed, by the government were confused, contradictory and often incoherently related, the fact of INGOs being considered threats and needing to be managed aggressively was not in doubt.

The MSF story: background

In the period from the end of September into the first half of October 2006, there were several accusatory media reports regarding MSF. At this point it became clear to MSF that there was a serious problem with its relationship with the Sri Lankan authorities. The purpose of this section is to present these accusations. As with the above sections, there will be quotes from press stories since the media was the primary platform for the securitisation process, a process that was implemented through discourse.

The MSF story in fact begins with an incident involving Medicos Del Mundo (MDM), for as will be seen there was much confusion between MDM and MSF in the minds of many local actors. A *Sunday Times* article from late August related the incident (*Sunday Times*, 27 August 2006). The Medicos Del Mundo-Spain (MDM Spain) head of mission had been blacklisted and deported from the country at the end of July. The reason for this was that MDM had issued a certificate to participants at the end of a training programme that had born the emblem of the Government of Sri Lanka alongside an LTTE emblem. To the GoSL this was an unacceptable legitimisation of the LTTE. Though deported at the end of July, the head of mission had returned to the country on a tourist visa and had been deported again, according to the controller of immigration and emigration. This issue of an international agency using the state symbol alongside that of the LTTE was also brought before the Parliamentary Select Committee for review. An official from the Ministry of Health told the PSC that a set of guidelines would be developed for all NGOs 'under the signature of the Presidential Secretary in order to avoid such incidents in the future'. As mentioned, MDM and MSF were often confused in the press and it will be seen how this incident eventually involved MSF.

In late September four INGOs were accused of 'clandestine dealings' with the LTTE and as such they posed 'a threat to national security' (*Island*, 30 September 2006). The Parliamentary Select Committee recommended that the visas for personnel from 'MSS France (sic), MSS Spain (sic), MDM France and Doctors of the World USA' be withdrawn as the members of these organisations had been found to be supporting the LTTE. In addition, the defence ministry had 'confirmed that they had been warned by the select committee about the clandestine activities of these INGOs, who, under the pretext of engaging in rehabilitation work, particularly in the North and the East, had been supporting the Tigers'. Based on the MDM incident the Immigration Department had also warned that those whose visas had been withdrawn could try to return to the country as tourists 'to continue helping the terrorist outfit'. A representative of the Parliamentary Select Committee said that somewhere between 30 and 40 INGO members had already been deported from the country in the recent past. In this report, MSF was specifically mentioned, though it was mistakenly referred to as 'MSS France'. The specific claim against 'MSS France' was that the agency had been critical of the fact that the defence ministry had in the past withdrawn the visas of their personnel and that the agency had even 'sent threatening letters to the Defence ministry officials over action taken against them'. There was, in fact, no basis for these accusations, as MSF-France had not had any staff deported up until that time. This confusion in the press was considered by MSF to be simply a case of mistaken identity.

A variety of other accusations were made against MSF and other French INGOs at this time. Connected with the above confusion was the report that another French NGO, which one was not clear, had been accused of displaying the wording 'the Ministry of Health and Department of Health Services of the LTTE' on a flag flown on their vehicles alongside the emblem of the Sri Lanka government while operating in LTTE-controlled areas. The similarity with the MDM case should be noted. Any visible sign of equity between the GoSL and the LTTE shown by INGOs was aggressively rejected by the government. Another interesting allegation was concerning misuse of 'lifting bags', which were used to retrieve items from the ocean as part of the tsunami response. After the NGOs were finished using the bags they were meant to give them to the navy, though it was suspected many did not. These were apparently bags that could be used by the LTTE to pick up smuggled goods dropped into the ocean. Regarding the accusations, Minister Keheliya Rambukwella said that the government's actions were not 'a grudge against all NGOs operating in Sri Lanka' but were only aimed at those that had violated the law and were 'attempting to meet the needs of terrorists'. Some of these INGOs were 'mercenaries who came as NGOs' to work in the conflict zones. These were in addition to the many INGOs who had come after the tsunami but were now nowhere to be seen despite the massive amount of funding that had been pledged. He concluded with the statement that 'we have to keep a tab on these people. There is no question of pampering them' (*Daily Mirror*, 4 October 2006).

In another statement, Minister Keheliya Rambukwella said that in the case of the six international non-governmental organisations that had had their visas cancelled, the government's decision had been in accordance with immigration regulations as they had violated immigration, customs and defence ministry regulations. The six organisations were Médecins Sans Frontières (MSF) France, MSF Spain, MDM France, Doctors of World USA, Medicos de Mundos, and Solidarities. He described the case of the INGO that had used the LTTE medical department emblem, stating that 'as far as the Government is concerned there is no LTTE medical Department which can deal officially in this manner' (*Daily News*, 4 October 2006). As can be seen, certain stories began to take on a life if their own, continually resurfacing and being melded with other stories.

Quickly following the above reports were those stating that the government had decided to forestall the deportations for a time. The government's Peace Secretariat announced on 3 October that work visas of certain members of the INGOs 'Medicines Sans Frontiers (France), Medicines Sans Frontiers (Spain), Medicos Del Mundo, and Doctors of the World' were being reviewed in accordance with the continuing police investigations, and until those investigations had been completed, the visas of those organisations would remain valid (*Island*, 4 October 2006). A 'well-informed source' said that Medicines Sans Frontiers, 'the France based International Non-Governmental Organisation', could continue to work while it appealed its expulsion. According to the Controller of Immigration and Emigration, visas for INGOs were issued on the recommendations of the defence and foreign ministries and that he had been told not to cancel the visas of Medicines Sans Frontiers until their appeal had been heard (*Island*, 5 October 2006). This article stated that the affected INGOs had pleaded not guilty to 'some of the charges levelled against them', and that they had yet to 'receive any official notification about the reasons behind the ban' (*Daily Mirror*, 6 October 2006). Various designations were given for the organisations, such as: 'MCF France (sic), MSF Spain, MBM France (sic), Doctors of the World USA, Solidarities, and Medicos de Mundo' (*Daily Mirror*, 4 October 2006). Both the press and government statements were not very careful with the names of the organisations. As with the above-described narratives the story was confusing and often incoherent.

MSF was accused of a variety of offences related to alleged support given to the LTTE. The organisation was under criminal investigation and visas for their personnel were (at least for a time) revoked. Their personnel were at risk of being deported and operations had been stopped. Other organisations were also being accused of similar offences, and in fact it was unclear which organisation was being accused of which offence, as even the names of the organisations were confused. MSF specifically was being confused with MDM and French organisations in general. After the initial threats were made concerning the revocation of the visas the government backtracked somewhat and stated that the visas would not be revoked until the conclusion of the investigation. In the proceedings, a number of government departments were involved, including the Ministry of Defence, the Peace Secretariat, the Immigration and Emigration Department and the Parliamentary Select Committee.

Securitisation

As a first step towards unravelling how the relationship between the Government of Sri Lanka and MSF-Holland developed, the preceding section examined the political and military events of 2005/6 and how they influenced the government's positioning towards NGOs. The work and identity of international NGOs, particularly those engaged in humanitarian operations in the conflict areas, was increasingly being questioned by the Colombo-based political elites – political party functionaries, business leaders, influential Buddhist monks, newspaper editors and influential public intellectuals. Both the quickly developing political and military situation and the pre-existing dissatisfaction felt towards NGOs from the post-tsunami reconstruction period informed the government's actions and the political discourse. The environment for NGOs was also increasingly characterised by insecurity as the conflict heated up. Increasingly over 2006 the context of war created a state of exception where the government allowed itself to step outside normal administrative and legal processes to prosecute the war as it saw fit. This was a discursive process of securitisation.

In this case study, the securitising actor was the state, or more properly the government that represented the state, as only a government may enact emergency measures. Yet the instigation for the actions of the securitising actor was as much the responsibility of the political and social elites more broadly, as was witnessed above in the discussion of the domestic political dynamics related to the aftereffects of the tsunami and the prosecution of the war. Identity discussions played a major role in this process, as politics and identity cannot be separated. The referent object – the thing being threatened – was, alternately, national security, the sovereignty of the state, the unitary nature of the country, or the Sinhalese Buddhist identity of the country. In reality, the threats associated with this situation were multi-faceted, but the specific securitised issue this chapter is concerned with is the involvement of INGOs. The audience – the political community that must be brought on board – was the general public and the international community. The audience was also the state itself as well as the political elites at the centre of the political process, as there is often a need for justification to the self in such a process.

Securitisation is a discursive process and therefore these steps as described are implemented through discourse. It should be reiterated that it was not only the government that was responsible for the production of discourse: the Colombo political, social and religious elites also played a significant role in setting the semantic tone of the period. This discourse was often derived from deeply embedded identity beliefs. Indeed, without deep background knowledge it is difficult to understand what discourse was instigated by the government and what was produced by other religious and cultural actors. It is in fact not clear how relevant INGOs felt this distinction to be, though this case study argues that the most nuanced analysis possible enables a better desecuritisation process. The common outlets for discourse as analysed by international agencies were the media, especially the arguments made and language used by editorialists and columnists.

Summary

To summarise the findings thus far, the political and military situation, against the background of the tsunami, the second tsunami and the negative press about the poor tsunami response, created a situation where attitudes towards NGOs had become critical in nature. NGOs were seen to be corrupt, inefficient and more concerned with their wealth and health than the needs of the populations they were purportedly there to serve. For the most part, the performance of these agencies post-tsunami was evaluated negatively. As the war heated up, these agencies were thought to be on the side of the LTTE. These traits were seen to be counter to the identity of the self, which was understood, based on the analysis, to be the identity of the Sinhalese and Buddhist majority. This majority, represented by the Colombo political elites, were strongly nationalist and aggressively anti-LTTE, even in the midst of the peace process. The political elites were not monolithic, though, as there were a number of serious tensions between the SLFP, the JVP, the JHU and the UNP. A triangle was formed between the political elites, dominated by the GoSL, the LTTE and humanitarian international NGOs. As the political and military situation became more tense and difficult, the anti-NGO feelings became stronger and a number of policies were formulated; a number of investigative and monitoring policies, such as the PSC, were then instigated. The killing of the ACF staff again changed the situation for INGOs attempting to work in the conflict zones and another set of restrictions were put into place.

The discourse used to explain and justify such policies became ever harsher in this period as the government securitised NGOs. A process of securitisation was implemented through discourse, which was based on the above understanding of the self and the other. The result of this process was the political definition of who was a friend and who was an enemy. The discourse portrayed NGOs using dichotomies, each of which focused on a particular theme. Principles versus practice: agencies did not follow through with their principles but cared more about themselves. Western versus Asian: Western organisations did not understand the East. LTTE or Singhalese/Muslim: INGOs supported the LTTE and the Tamils over the Sinhalese. Government versus NGOs: INGOs did not support the role of the government. Foreigners versus Sri Lankans: often the foreigners cared more about their own than Sri Lankans. And Sri Lanka versus the international community: the GoSL was a small fish in a big pond but should not accept that fate and should try to take control of its fate or at least protect its dignity.

The next chapter will restart the story at the end of 2008 and discuss a period of 'bare life' securitisation. The response of MSF-H to the events of both periods will be discussed in chapter 7 on INGO response options.

References

Amarasuriya, H. and Spencer, J. (2012). NGOs, the state and 'cultural values': Imagining the global in Sri Lanka. In J. Howell (ed.). *Global Matters for Non-governmental Public Action.* Basingstoke: Palgrave Macmillan.

Bullion, A. (2008). The peace process in Sri Lanka. In M. Chatterji and B. M. Jain (eds). *Conflict and Peace in South Asia.* Bingley, UK: Emerald Group Publishing Limited.

Deegalle, M. (2006). *Buddhism, Conflict and Violence in Modern Sri Lanka.* London: Routledge.

de Silva, C. R. (2007). Sri Lanka in 2006: Unresolved political and ethnic conflicts amid economic growth. *Asian Survey,* 47(1), 99–104.

de Silva, K. M. (2012). *Sri Lanka and the Defeat of the LTTE.* London: Penguin Books.

DeVotta, N. (2011). Sri Lanka: From turmoil to dynasty. *Journal of Democracy,* 22(2), 130–144.

Frerks, G. and Klem, B. (2005). Tsunami response in Sri Lanka: Report on a field visit from 6–20 February 2005. Wageningen University and Clingendael Institute.

Grewal, M. K. (2006). Approaches to equity in post-tsunami assistance. Sri Lanka: A case study. Office of the United Nations Special Envoy for Tsunami Recovery.

Harris, S. (2006). Disasters and dilemmas: Aid agency recruitment and HRD in post-tsunami Sri Lanka (Part 1). *Human Resource Development International,* 9(2), 291–298.

Harrison, F. (2012). *Still Counting the Dead: Survivors of Sri Lanka's Hidden War.* London: Portobello Books.

Haug, M. (2001). Combining service delivery and advocacy within humanitarian agencies: Experiences from the conflict in Sri Lanka. Centre for Civil Society International Working Paper Series, 10. London School of Economics and Political Science.

Herath, D. (2010). Social reconciliation amidst material reconstruction. In D. Herath et al. (eds). *Post-war Reconstruction in Sri Lanka: Prospects and Challenges.* Kandy: International Centre for Ethnic Studies.

Government of Sri Lanka (2005). Interim report of the auditor general on the rehabilitation of the losses and damages caused to Sri Lanka by the tsunami disaster on 26 December 2004, carried out up to 30 June 2005. Government of Sri Lanka Auditor General.

Jayasuriya, S., SteeleP. and Weerakoon, D. (2006). Post-tsunami recovery: Issues and challenges in Sri Lanka. Asian Development Bank Institute (ADBI) Research Paper.

Mahindapala, H. L. D. (2006). What is civil society? Series of articles published in the *Sunday Observer,* 30 July, 6 August and 13 August 2006, collectively entitled: The new salvation army of the NGOs: A Sri Lankan case study.

Matthews, B. (2009). The limits of international engagement in human rights situations: The case of Sri Lanka. *Pacific Affairs,* 82(4), 577–596.

Parliament of Sri Lanka (2008). Interim report of the select committee of parliament for investigation of the operations of non-governmental organizations and their impact, presented to parliament on 8 December.

Rieff, D. (2005). Tsunamis, accountability and the humanitarian circus. *Humanitarian Exchange Magazine*, 29.

Silva, K. T. and Hettige, S. (2010). Multiculturalism and nationalism in a globalising world: The case of Sri Lanka. In Dhammika Herath et al. (eds), *Post-war Reconstruction in Sri Lanka: Prospects and Challenges*. Kandy: International Centre for Ethnic Studies.

Unattributed (2006). NGO impact initiative: An assessment by the international humanitarian NGO community. 31 October, https://reliefweb.int/sites/reliefweb.int/files/resources/267F7CACFEB49C05492572210007001E-NGO_Impact_Initiative-Oct2006.pdf [accessed 26 January 2018].

Weiss, G. (2011). *The Cage: The Fight for Sri Lanka and the Last Days of the Tamil Tigers*. London: Vintage.

Wickramasinghe, N. (2006). *Sri Lanka in the Modern Age: A History of Contested Identities*. London: Hurst & Company.

Winslow, D. and Woost, M. D. (2004). Articulations of economy and ethnic conflict in Sri Lanka. In D. Winslow and M. D. Woost (eds). *Economy, Culture, and Civil War in Sri Lanka*. Bloomington, IN: Indiana University Press.

3

THE CASE OF MÉDECINS SANS FRONTIÈRES AND THE GOVERNMENT OF SRI LANKA, 2008/9

This chapter continues the discussion of the relationship between the Government of Sri Lanka and MSF-Holland and presents the findings from the 2008/9 period. As with the last chapter, the categories of differentiation, organisation, meaning, action, and practice are used as analytical tools to help frame the discussion. A summary of findings from both periods will end the chapter.

2008–2009: securitisation complete, bare life exposed

The 2008/9 period severely tested MSF-H's commitment to the Sri Lankan context. It was a period of crisis for INGOs as well as the conflict-affected Tamil population in the north. The period between September 2008 and May 2009 saw realised a state of unmitigated securitisation of INGOs working in the conflict zone. If in 2006 organisations were, as discussed in the last chapter, treated imperiously and securitised, they were still engaged with by the state as entities considered to be legitimate parts of the political landscape. Notwithstanding the threat of being expelled from the country, which did not actually occur, organisations such as MSF considered that enough 'humanitarian space' existed to negotiate access to the conflict zones, and in the end the GoSL allowed such access. In contrast, following Agamben's revision of Schmitt's concept of sovereignty, in the late 2008–early 2009 period agencies were stripped to their 'bare life' status (Agamben, 1998). INGOs were excluded from the political realm as legitimate actors and dealt with as necessitated by national security requirements – metaphorically 'outlawed'. Yet such agencies were still allowed to remain physically present in the country as they retained a potential usefulness, though as will be seen only on the periphery of the conflict. The key point is that INGOs in the September 2008 to May 2009 period were increasingly sidelined as relevant and legitimate actors and their voices quieted.

2006–2009: building tensions – external and internal

For reasons not as yet well understood, the relationship between the GoSL and MSF-H had improved to the point that the organisation could restart programming in early 2007. The context revolving around the conflict, however, had not substantially improved, and neither had the tenor of the GoSL's relationship with the international community.[1] While the conflict had for all intents and purposes restarted in 2006, the 2002 ceasefire agreement was not officially abrogated by the GoSL until January 2008. Nonetheless, in the 2007 period a number of serious security incidents had occurred which left no one in doubt that the conflict had restarted in earnest. In March 2007, major fighting resumed in the Batticaloa area, resulting in the LTTE losing territory and pulling out of the coastal areas by April (Peiris, 2009: 225). By July the GoSL had retaken control of the Batticaloa and Ampara districts. This period also saw the LTTE 'sea tigers' sustaining severe maritime loses by the Sri Lankan navy (ibid.: 226). The GoSL's Anuradhapura airbase, the second largest in the country, was attacked by the LTTE at the end of October 2007, causing major damage. Fighting occurred in many other parts of the north and east and terrorist attacks continued in the south. This period could be considered as the 'undeclared Eelam War IV'. At the beginning of January 2008, the GoSL officially pulled out of the 2002 ceasefire agreement, stating that the Tigers had to disarm before any future talks could go ahead. The conflict continued to intensify throughout 2008. The final military push began from mid-April.

The human rights implications of the fighting did not go unnoticed by an increasingly concerned, and vocal, international community. As such this period of deepening conflict has been termed by Peiris as the 'human rights onslaught' by external actors, mirroring the military onslaught by the SLA against the Tigers. In Peiris' view:

> The period has also been featured by an extraordinary sharp upsurge of external humanitarian intervention in the Sri Lankan conflict, the intensity of which has had a remarkable correspondence with the tenor and tempo of LTTE failures. There are strong indications of this concomitance representing a causal connection in the sense that the outcry against alleged human rights violations in Sri Lanka is, at least in part, the product of a well-orchestrated attempt to rescue the LTTE from impending doom.
>
> *(Peiris, 2009: 232)*

This passage encapsulates a common view amongst the Sinhalese elites that was mirrored in press reports of the time. It is interesting to note the confusion between the terms 'humanitarian' and 'human rights', a common occurrence not

---

1   The term 'international community' is used to refer to international actors whose nexus was outside of Sri Lanka, for example governments and international human rights and advocacy organisations. Implicit in the term international community is a Western centre of gravity.

only in the Sri Lanka of this period. An overlap can occur when humanitarian organisations engage in advocacy activities, and it has often been the case with MSF that advocacy on humanitarian issues has been confused with human rights advocacy. The misunderstanding of the differing mandates of the two sets of organisations is illustrative of the misgivings in the minds by state officials concerning international engagement in times of conflict. The use of the term 'intervention' is also notable with its implied fear of attack on the Sri Lankan polity. The concept of a humanitarian intervention relates more commonly to situations where states intervene militarily in another state to protect populations in danger and facilitate their reception of humanitarian assistance, interventions which may fall under the Responsibility to Protect rubric, as discussed in chapter 1.

What should be taken away from the above discussion is the increasing dissatisfaction on the part of the GoSL to perceived double standards on the part of the international human rights community in how they approached the conflict. Even if it were admitted that there were legitimate human rights issues to be addressed, the GoSL refused to be considered the sole perpetrator, as the LTTE was also a human rights abuser.[2] The fact of this perceived double standard said something essential to the GoSL about the bias of the international community, which was seen to be against the GoSL and supportive of the LTTE. In many ways international organisations of whichever type – humanitarian or human rights, were lumped together as threats. The message to the GoSL was that it had to protect itself against this fact by taking a strong, proactive, stand. Part of this stand, as will be seen in the next section, was to ensure adherence to international legal norms.

2008–2009: the GoSL reacts to the external in the internal

The September expulsion

The issue surrounding the expulsion of INGOs from the Vanni (the northern Tamil areas) in September 2008 is rather complicated but speaks directly to the discussion of the three Sri Lanka governmental objectives: the need to end the war; the need to respond to the attitude of the international community concerning its prosecution of the war; and the need to deal with the presence of international organisations on its territory which were concerned with the humanitarian response to the war.[3] The three issues of course overlapped and it was this fact that made decision-making a complex calculation. Finishing the war took priority. But as part of ending the war the GoSL had to be concerned with accusations of human rights abuses.[4] The international community also expected that the GoSL

---

2   Such comments of course beg the question of whether the LTTE, as a non-state actor, was legally capable of human rights abuses or whether by assigning such culpability to the LTTE the GoSL inadvertently put them into a category of legitimacy the GoSL had always sought to deny them.

3   See Harrison (2012) for a discussion of the expulsion from the UN's perspective.

4   See Boyle (2010) for a discussion of legal issues from a decidedly pro-Tamil perspective.

would conform to the norms of International Humanitarian Law (IHL) and ensure the proper provision of humanitarian assistance.[5] For this it was necessary that the external agents attempting to operate on their territory be managed properly – to the satisfaction of the international community *and* to conform to internal political and military demands, the greatest of which was to not interfere with the successful prosecution of the war. A solution had to be found to satisfy these conflicting objectives and perspectives. Some clues to the GoSL's thinking can be found in the Lessons Learnt and Reconciliation Commission (LLRC) report which will be describe next.

Within the context of international criticism of the government's conduct at the end of the war, President Rajapaksa instituted in May 2010 the Commission of Inquiry on Lessons Learnt and Reconciliation to study the period between 21 February 2002 – the date of the ceasefire agreement – and 19 May 2009 – the date of the final victory over the LTTE. The commission itself began work in September of 2010 and produced its report in November of 2011. Though written well after the end of the period examined in this chapter, the LLRC report gives a good review of the government's justifications, views, strategy and considerations during the final phase of the conflict (GoSL, 2011). It is useful to refer to the document to find clues to help answer the question of why INGOs, but not the ICRC or WFP, were expelled from the Vanni at the end of 2008.

On the issue of the provision of humanitarian assistance in the period between September 2008 and May 2009, the clear message throughout the relevant sections of the LLRC report was that, since the ICRC and WFP food convoys were allowed into the Vanni, the IHL provisions concerning relief were adhered to (GoSL, 2011: 331). This allowed the GoSL to relocate the offices of the UN and INGOs to Vavuniya, located on the government side of the old Forward Defence Line, where they could, in safety, 'complement' government efforts directed through government channels. The MoD opened the convoy routes to be used (ibid.: 85). The document repeatedly states that the ICRC and WFP supported the GoSL in providing humanitarian assistance. Until March, the GoSL was able to adequately supply humanitarian aid to the conflict-affected civilians but it was admitted that in April relief supplies were less than adequate (ibid.: 87). Food supplies were delivered by sea between February and May by the ICRC, WFP, and the GoSL, as the land route was no longer tenable (ibid.: 124). The similarity to the 2006 period in this regard should be noted, as some patterns remained constant over time.

The report claims that the international community had made no complaints about the supply of humanitarian aid due to conflict or natural disasters until the final phase of the war, which as has been seen was not completely true. In the GoSL's view it had taken 'all possible steps' to deliver food and medical supplies with the support of the ICRC, WFP, and local civil society organisations. These

---

5 For a grounding in International Humanitarian Law, see Roberts and Guelff (eds) (2004), Rogers (2004), Cassese (2001), Henckaerts and Doswald-Beck (eds) (2005a) and Henckaerts and Doswald-Beck (eds) (2005b).

activities were 'in a spirit of international co-operation and solidarity' (ibid.: 126). The MoH was said to have taken responsibility for the provision of medical supplies along with the ICRC. What was not mentioned was the medical aid given by MSF and other INGOs up until the expulsion.

It should be mentioned that the ICRC was the logical agency to facilitate access as it has a formal mandate under IHL – indeed, the ICRC is the guardian of IHL, and based on past performance the GoSL believed that it could be trusted to keep silent about what it witnessed. This last point was optimistic on the government's part, as shall be seen.

Thus, the LLRC report clearly gives a justification for the expulsion and an explanation of its rightful conduct (though not stating this conclusion explicitly). This logic underpinning the expulsion responded to all three concerns as described above: It gave the GoSL as free a hand as possible to end the war without undue interference; it allayed, at least partly, the concerns of the international community regarding humanitarian assistance via its adherence to IHL; and the undesirable agencies were sidelined through an expulsion which was explained as being in their own best interests.

How then was this logic and decision-making explained by the GoSL to both the Sri Lankan public and international actors? As with the securitisation process described in the previous chapter, discourse played an important role in the management of the INGO threats. An *Island* article from 10 September sums up the story. Defence department spokesman Minister Rambukwella was quoted as saying that the GoSL could not assure the safety of NGOs in the Vanni and thus they needed to relocate to a safer zone. The message was clear – legitimate INGOs were at risk and the government was acting responsibly. And, in addition, there was always the risk that they were actually there to help the LTTE. So even in this way the government was acting responsibly by clearing the way for the successful prosecution of the war. There was thus a dual message, which allowed for flexibility in reaction. Again, the similarity between this discourse and argumentation to the 2006 period should be noted, though the outcomes were qualitatively different.

The Parliamentary Select Committee interim report

The Parliamentary Select Committee investigating the work of NGOs was last discussed when it was in the midst of its investigation and it was contributing to the negative discourse surrounding NGOs in the 2006 period. The PSC's 'interim' report' was not in fact published until the beginning of December 2008. A careful reading of the report calls into question whether any substantive investigative work was conducted in the 2007–08 period, an observation which challenges the timing of the report. Regardless, it is constructive to review how the interim report was reported on at the crucial period at the end of 2008. An interview with JVP MP Vijitha Herath, chairman of the committee, serves this purpose (Sriyananda, 2008). The key messages from the interview were that some NGOs were supporting the LTTE – directly and indirectly – and the current laws were not adequate to properly police such NGOs. Herath said that 'no proper bodies' existed to monitor NGOs, their funds were not audited and their activities were not evaluated. Although the NGO Secretariat had been set up to coordinate NGOs, it was not up to the job. In general, he thought that 'most of these NGOs operate in contravention of the law and the state policies', seemingly condemning as illegal and illicit the majority of NGOs. Additionally, he thought that NGOs functioned according to their own agendas and were 'controlled by their mother countries'. As such, some NGOs were a threat to the sovereignty of Sri Lanka and had 'overstepped' their development and humanitarian mandates.

Herath was asked about the fact that NGOs had 'mushroomed' after the tsunami and some had tried to 'indirectly' interfere in state affairs. In his opinion, some had 'strategically' tried to be involved with defence and education matters, and on the whole international interference into the internal affairs of the country had increased. Those engaged with conflict resolution and conflict studies were the most prone to interference. These types of NGOs also voiced most stridently the 'public sector institutions are inefficient' approach to development, thus wishing to bypass the government. And on the humanitarian side, NGOs were helping the LTTE, though it couldn't be said exactly in what way NGOs had assisted the LTTE; nonetheless, it was evident that 'half of these organisations in the North and East have helped the LTTE in some manner'. Some NGOs had also been found to be 'propagating federalism', such as the National Peace Council, which had also 'participated in a protest in Geneva with the LTTE'.[6]

How had such NGOs with 'close links with some of the terrorist organisations' entered Sri Lanka in the first place? Herath responded that legal mechanisms to register NGOs were lacking. 'The vacuum has created a huge freedom for those NGOs', which was of course not the opinion of NGOs as has been seen. Did the country really need NGOs? He couldn't say no, that they were not needed given the conditions in the country, and of course not all were bad: some in fact were genuine and did assist the 'development process'. But, 'some NGOs with devious motives bring disaster to the country', as the 'laws related to forming NGOs are very lenient'. Particularly related to humanitarian assistance, did they actually do any good? 'Some of them are doing an excellent service but those who have links with the LTTE pose a threat'. How should the NGOs doing such damage be punished? 'We need new laws to blacklist them'.

MSF was mentioned specifically in the interview, as it was in the PSC report. Herath stated that 'the Ministry of Defence has reports to show how the Medical Sans Frontieres (sic) (M.S.F.) of France and MSF Spain which is not registered, Medicine du Monde France and Doctors of the World USA have threatened the

6   It should be mentioned, though, that not all opinions were in line with this view. In the words of Basil Fernando (Fernando, 2008) from the Asian Human Rights Commission: 'If the abuse of funds was what the Select Committee was interested in, the Interim Report demonstrates an absence of seriousness. It is perhaps, what in the local Sri Lankan parlance would be called, trying to light a cigar when the moustache is burning. In short, the report borders on being nonsensical.'

national security and the state policies'. In the PSC interim report itself, under the heading 'Threats to National Security', it was stated that 'the Ministry of Defence had received credible intelligence reports with regard to the activities of the following non-governmental organizations. These organizations had dared to act in a way that threatened National Security and state policies'. MSF-F, MSF-E (the section was again claimed not to be registered), MDM-France and Doctors of the World USA were again mentioned. In addition:

> The non-governmental organizations which had met at the office of MSF (France) located at Narahenpita had vehemently criticized the policies followed by the Department of Immigration and Emigration in issuing visas and had discussed a programme of getting the LTTE to send threatening letters as a solution. The Ministry of Defence, having considered this as a very grave issue, even went to the extent of banning the issue of visas.
>
> *(Parliament of Sri Lanka, 2008: 27–28)*

This was a reprise of the old stories from 2006 that had caused so much consternation within MSF. But in contrast to 2006, at the end of 2008 this further mention of MSF in connection to these charges went unremarked by MSF, presumably because this was a period when all access to the conflict zones had been barred and there were more pressing issues to which the organisation had to attend.

It was, clearly, not true that there were no bodies to monitor NGOs, at least from the INGO perspective, as the fact of such bodies was a constant complaint, bitterly made, as was the weight of the administrative burden INGOs faced. It is difficult to reconcile the day-to-day reality of INGOs with this rhetoric. This phenomenon – the misunderstanding of the external by the internal, will be discussed later in this chapter by a MSF-H official. As per both their mandates and their principles, INGOs did, of course, have their own agendas and took seriously the fact that they were *non*-governmental agencies that were independent from the relevant involved governments and neutral concerning political and military controversies. Related to this point, their self-identity was as *international* NGOs, again separate from the local governments with which they engaged. International organisations did not represent Sri Lankan political interests, but neither did they necessarily represent the political interest of their home countries; in fact, for principled humanitarian agencies it was important that they did not.

Two recommendations should be commented upon from the PSC interim report itself. Recommendation number 15 stated that

> NGOs should pay strict attention to national identity, national security, territorial integrity, customs and rituals, values and culture of the country and the commission [to be newly set up to monitor NGOs] should compile a set of guidelines restraining NGOs form taking action to destroy or distort them or to create a sense of dependant mentality in the people.
>
> *(Parliament of Sri Lanka, 2008: 49)*

That INGOs were often insensitive to the local context was commented upon by MSF itself. The misunderstanding of the domestic by the external was not an unreported issued by either party.

Recommendation number 11 stated, in part, that 'Without stopping at extraditing the heads of NGOs against whom allegations are levelled for irregularities/ misconduct, legal provisions should be enacted to totally ban such NGOs' (Parliament of Sri Lanka, 2008: 48). The harshness of this recommendation should be reflected upon, for this was the 'outlawing' provision. In effect, license was given to the internal to place external actors outside the political and legal realm. How, and how completely, INGOs were to be outlawed, is the dominant theme of this period.

In this way the PSC reconfirmed their previous impressions and restated their old accusations – giving further credence to the actions already taken and would soon be taken by the government. It is informative to observe how another orga- nisation responded. In an article in the *Sri Lankan Guardian*, the National Peace Council (NPC) responded to the allegations made against it (*Sri Lanka Guardian*, 23 December 2008). NPC stated that 'we regret that the comments on NPC are unjust, and do not give a proper representation of NPC objectives and work'. They stressed that the NPC was a non-partisan organisation, was independent of political actors, and was not biased towards the LTTE. The NPC hoped that the PSC's final report would be fairer in its evaluation of 'the organization, its mission and its contribution towards ensuring people's participation in a peaceful and just solution to the ethnic conflict'. These comments by the NPC reflects the general NGO response to the PSC interim report.

The confidentiality clause

In April 2009, the GoSL issued a new decree that organisations, in order to renew their Memoranda of Understanding (MoUs) or negotiate new agreements, had to agree to and sign 'confidentiality clauses'. These clauses barred independent public communications by agencies without governmental approval. MSF-H believed that these were a result of earlier ICRC and MSF communications that had embarrassed the government (HAD, 2010: 31). The ICRC had, in fact, and regardless of the trust the GoSL had put into the organisation to remain silent, issued a statement on 28 January saying that hundreds of civilians had been killed in the fighting, a statement the GoSL wholly disagreed with (Weiss, 2011: 127–128). The ICRC office in Colombo was stoned by a mob soon after, reportedly as a result of the statement (ibid.: 177).

For any given organisation, the clause referred to the particular line ministry that supervised the agency. For MSF, MoUs were negotiated with the Ministry of Health (MoH). The MSF confidentiality clause thus stated that

> The partner shall strictly maintain the confidentiality of the information on service provision. All information regarding the construction or service

provision shall be provided to the MoH and no public comments shall be made by the partner, without the concurrence of the Secretary, Ministry of Health.

MSF-H was faced with signing the confidentiality clause in May 2009 as its MoU expired at this time. MSF-F had signed its MoU with the confidentiality clause earlier in April. MSF-H's rationale for signing such a clause will be discussed in the next section. But from MSF's perspective it was clear by April that it had to be increasingly wary of communicating publicly about the conflict.

It will be noted that during this period there were a number of (attempted) visits by international diplomats to Sri Lanka. Carl Bildt, former Swedish prime minister, attempted to visit but was refused entry. David Miliband, the British foreign minister, and Bernard Kouchner, the French foreign minister, both made visits. It should also be noted that at this time there was an active debate surrounding the estimates of the number of trapped and displaced in the zone of fighting, including a statement by the UN High Commissioner for Human Rights, N. Pillay, in March, going against the UN's previously discrete stance on numbers (Weiss, 2011: 205). Although the UN was attempting to be sensitive to the GoSL's dissatisfaction with how the conflict was being reported, particularly concerning estimates of the numbers trapped by the fighting, many international actors felt increasingly frustrated by the lack of clarity. This situation only increased the GoSL's view that international actors needed to be quieted. Part of the way to manage any negative consequences of the presence of international actors was to institute a 'gag order', as MSF-H termed the confidentiality clause. Eliminating the physical presence of INGOs in the conflict area was an important step, but the continued presence of INGOs in the country still risked agencies being able to speak out. Organisations such as MSF-H were still present and attending to the medical needs of those fleeing, if not present in the conflict zone itself.

Framing the successes and failures

It should be stressed that the 'outlawing' of humanitarian international actors was not total and unmitigated. Such actors could not be 'killed' without penalty, and humanitarian international agencies were not permanently exiled into the wilderness. But the outlawing of the affected agencies' mandates and voices was complete, at least as far as the conflict zone was concerned. They were able to remain in the country as potentially useful in the future, but in relation to the conflict they were outlawed as actors to the point where their very voices were muted. This state of affairs was easier to organise and at less cost than expelling agencies from the country. When physical access was undesirable the security card could be used to dislocate the organisations, and when their voices became a liability those could be silenced through administrative means. This type of outlawing did not arise anew in the intense contextual changes and challenges of the end of the war period but was built on a securitisation process already long in progress, as seen in the review of the 2006 iteration. But by May 2009 the securitisation process was complete and INGOs had been stripped to bare life, physically and morally denuded, and devoiced.

The rationale for these acts on the part of the GoSL in 2008/9, as understood by those affected and based on a reading of government discourse, was that the GoSL was fearful that the international community would interfere with the prosecution of the war, as there was little support for it in the eyes and minds of international, mostly Western, actors. But this begs the question why the GoSL and the (Western) international community were not in agreement on the way the conflict should be handled. Why was there such tension between the sides, or, more fundamentally, why were there sides at all? The aim here is not to answer these questions in a broad sense but specifically in relation to the ostracising and gagging of INGOs.

The war had lasted for many years – 2009 was the twenty-sixth year of conflict. The Tigers were a brutal, totalitarian outfit that had relied on terrorism, the killing of rivals and the assassination of political leaders, foreign and domestic, to achieve its goal of Tamil Eelam. The Sri Lankan security services and the paramilitary groups they had supported had also been the perpetrators of brutal acts. The Tamil population had been trapped between the warring parties, and trapped in the conflict zone, long before hundreds of thousands were trapped on the eastern beaches. It was seemingly to everyone's benefit to end the war (notwithstanding the question of what a peace would look like). Where did the communication breakdown occur? MSF talked about not understanding the context sufficiently. What wasn't understood?

The discussion can be centred around the idea of a misunderstanding of drives and a disconnect between perspectives (after Harris, 2006). In this conceptualisation, it can be argued that the GoSL's motivations were primarily based on three themes. The first related to a desire to counter LTTE terrorism and the LTTE as a terrorist non-state actor, a decidedly national security-oriented agenda. The second, a more politically oriented objective, related to being committed to a unified state, which meant a state dominated by the majority, Sinhalese Buddhist, population; a state where the Tamil minority would be subsumed into a unified political entity. To fulfil these two aims the war had to be ended, which meant the LTTE defeated and all obstacles to the formation of a unified state swept away. This informed the third theme, which was the idea that being pro-peace meant being pro-LTTE and anti-unified state. In essence, this was interpreted as threatening Sri Lankan sovereignty.

The international community, on the other hand, had a different set of drives. These were the following. First, that peace was the only way to respond to the social and political grievances that had caused the conflict in the first place. Second, an over-estimated sense of the leverage of what were perceived to be Western political and human rights ideals by the Sri Lanka elites. And therefore third, a seeming rejection of all-out war as the solution to the conflict, and indeed, a deep concern for the human rights of the civilian population who were caught in the midst of the fighting. The outcome of these contested drives was an 'increasingly rigid rejection of criticism over the state's strategy' by the GoSL (Harris, 2006: 2). The basic tension here was between peace and war approaches – ending the war through war or ending it through peaceful means. To the GoSL of the time, the latter view made little sense.

In the midst of this contestation of political and military visions, humanitarian agencies became linked with the agendas of Western political and human rights actors. This was not a new phenomenon, but the end of the war had brought into sharp focus the disconnect between the humanitarian imperative and national security, one result of this being that the state took over humanitarian operations to justify to a suspicious international community what it had already justified domestically, that the war would be ended and in the process the government would take all due care of the affected population. This nicely linked humanitarian operations to the national security agenda (Harris, 2006: 8).

Specific to the relationship of the GoSL with INGOs, some INGOs understood the GoSL's attitude as a way to get rid of witnesses – witnesses to the brutal treatment of the Tamil population – and INGOs saw the GoSL as being pro-war, anti-Tamil, anti-humanitarianism and anti-INGO. The government was nationalist first, meaning Sinhalese, and didn't want anyone to interfere with what it was doing to the Tamils. A dominant interpretation of the GoSL's actions was that INGOs were supportive of the LTTE and were against the conclusion of the war if it meant that the LTTE was defeated. Thus, humanitarian operations implemented by independent Western international NGOs were not compatible with the national security agenda, and thus, the GoSL had to take over humanitarian operations. The ICRC and WFP, though, were allowed to operate to show commitment to IHL and to help argue it was in fact a humanitarian rescue operation. To INGOs this was another proof of GoSL duplicity. It can be argued that INGOs made a moral interpretation of the situation – the 'big bad state', as authoritarian regimes were sometimes known, had stopped the good humanitarians from interfering with their war, a war which was causing massive suffering to the civilian population. On the other side, the GoSL made a political analysis – it was concerned with sovereignty, national security and the designation of friends and enemies.

This clash of viewpoints, clearly not simply a matter of a difference of opinion, was instead founded in identity politics where friends and enemies were designated based on not only political necessity but also profound tensions over self-identities. It was in fact a clash over the expression of norms. Each side had its own views and together these views in tension constructed a dysfunctional relationship.

Putting it all together: 2006–2009 – triangular relationships

This chapter and the last have gone through the Sri Lanka case study in detail. The goal now is to make sense of this story.

Certain structures can be derived from the preceding discussions of principles, politics and identity, and over time these structures were progressively warped until completely breaking down in the 2008/9 period. These structures are triangular in form, in that each of the three nodal points were inhabited by discrete actors who existed in tension with the other nodes. Analysing the changing nature of these tensions, and ultimately the perversion of the very shape of the forms, is a way of comparing and contrasting the two periods and will suggest some conclusions that have been integrated into the theoretical framework. As the previous chapter demonstrated, at the simplest level the war could be described as the military confrontation between the Sri Lankan security forces and the LTTE. But added to the military confrontation were a number of domestic and regional political issues, as well as involvement by the international community, each of which informed the conduct of the war in their own way.

Based on this understanding the first triangle is defined by the relationship between INGOs and the two armed actors – the GoSL and the LTTE. The second triangle traces the tensions between the GoSL, INGOs and the Sinhalese Buddhist nationalist worldview as represented by the JVP and JHU. And the third triangle is delineated by the trilateral dynamic between the international community, INGOs operational in Sri Lanka and the GoSL. As will be seen, these triangles overlap and are mutually reinforcing. This section will explore how the tensions changed over time within each triangle and how the interrelationship between the triangles developed.

One of the key characteristics of the 2006 period was ambiguity concerning the future of the conflict. This ambiguity was caused by, or at least developed within, the context of serious domestic political tensions and the presence of various international actors involved with the ceasefire agreement. The position of inter-national actors seeking to engage with the humanitarian crisis was as a result uncertain. Based on past experience, it was understood that humanitarian agencies would be able to work in LTTE areas, but as there was increasing dissatisfaction with NGOs – as seen through sharper discourse against NGOs as corrupt LTTE supporters – and as the MoD was becoming more controlling of access to the conflict areas, questions were raised in the minds of INGOs about future access. Yet INGOs were still being engaged with as legitimate actors that in theory could fill the space between the two actors, and organisations such as MSF-H did everything possible to widen and occupy this space. It was the existence of this space that is the defining feature that should be noted, as, despite the increasing accusations against INGOs and other international actors that they were LTTE supporters, from early 2007 to late 2008 the triangle as defined by the two armed actors and INGOs remained intact.

In the 2008/9 period, on the other hand, this space had been filled in. The INGO node had been deleted by the GoSL, so that the triangle was reconfigured into a short line connecting only the MoD to the LTTE. On the part of the GoSL there was little room for the interference of international actors as the government instructed the MoD to see to the ending of the war. In contrast to the ambiguity of the 2006 period, in this latter period the GoSL's strategy was relatively straight-forward and led to greater predictive power on the part of INGOs about the access trajectory, which was negative until the end of the conflict.

Beyond the military relationship between the armed actors there were socio-political aspects that influenced both the progression of the war and space available to INGOs. The 2006 period was highly influenced by the GoSL, INGO, JVP/JHU relationship. This relationship affected the space INGOs had to work within. A greater dichotomy was established which conflated military, socio-political and religious aspects to create a polarisation which began to erode the space that INGOs had carved out. After a very rocky period, agencies were able to inhabit sufficient space to work, but the resistance foreshadowed future problems. By 2009 the GoSL–JVP/JHU relationship had been collapsed into a unified view on the conflict, and the GoSL collapsed the triangle down to a dot, again taking the INGO node out of the equation. This is not to say that the JVP/JHU and the Rajapaksa regimes were integrated into one political unit, rather that views of the government and the Sinhalese Buddhist nationalists merged in relation to the task at hand, which was to defeat the LTTE and unify the country under a Sinhalese Buddhist regime. Partly this was a response to the stage of the conflict and partly a reaction to international pressure.

The relationship between the international community, Sri Lanka-based INGOs and the GoSL also highly informed the space within which INGOs worked. The international community had become much more involved in 2009 than it had been in 2006. As the war intensified the international voice became more strident. The international engagement in 2006 had provided relatively little attention and was based on saving the ceasefire, but in 2009 there was massively more critical attention, the fact of war could not be ignored, and efforts had moved towards mitigating the damage the war was doing to the civilian population. The international community's involvement in 2006 was constructive in intent, if not in practice, but in 2008/9 it became more adversarial. This affected the INGOs based in-country as they were again caught in the middle. If the other two triangles had been disfigured over time, this triangle was strengthened.

Why this adversarial relationship between the GoSL and the international community occurred at the end of the war is worth reviewing. There had been a series of misunderstandings between the international community and the GoSL leading up to this period, and there had been clashes over the expression of norms. Misunderstanding as well as securitisation formed a symbiotic relationship, each side had its own views and as seen together these views in tension constructed a broken relationship. A few words are in order to encapsulate what lay behind this. One partial explanation is found in how the context was read by different actors – that is, between an appreciation of the political and sociological context versus a positivistic view that the legal order operates in isolation. The GoSL saw that the sociological and political context helped define its response and this needed to be respected by external actors, yet most international actors did not take into consideration the local circumstances. What was important to most Western actors was adherence to international legal obligations. In fact, the view was that 'the simple legal reality [is] that norms need to be expressed or enforced in order to be realized' (McCormick, 1997: 214). Norms were expressed by the international community, but they were never enforced and thus never realised. The GoSL was the entity which expressed and enforced norms more effectively – the political norm of sovereignty. The juridical norm – and one which was thought of as moral in nature by agencies such as MSF-H – was not realised. The international community acted as the judiciary in the positivistic sense and the GoSL was the guardian of the constitution – the decision-maker. In a context where international actors did not understand the sociological and political context as demanded by the government, it should not be surprising that the GoSL designated friends and enemies sharply and decided that international actors were the latter. It may be wondered how Western, especially humanitarian, actors so failed to understand the dictates of a state of exception.[7]

What can be summarised is that as the war intensified the three triangles changed form, collapsed or were strengthened. INGOs were taken out of the relationship between the GoSL and the LTTE at the same time that the GoSL and the JVP/ JHU nodes collapsed into one, clarifying the geometric pattern into a simpler two-sided confrontation. But concurrent with this process was an increase in the tensions between Western political actors and the GoSL, within which INGOs were again put in the middle to their detriment. The increasingly strident 'interference' of the international community most probably contributed to the reluctance of the GoSL to take a risk with the presence of INGOs, or even the UN. What this meant in the end is that INGOs were the victims of a pincer movement between the internal and the external – caught in a nebulous world of being somehow both yet neither.

David Keen has written extensively on the dilemmas of aid provision in Sri Lanka and elsewhere. Specific to Sri Lanka in the period of 2008/9, Keen discusses differing ways to frame the issue. One way in which to view the relationship between an INGO and a state in the Sri Lankan context is though Arendt's 'lesser evil' concept. This view states that, in essence, one reaction to an unacceptable situation is to try to mitigate the negative consequences by cooperating, if not collaborating, with the stronger force. Keen asks if this is what INGOs do when they have 'argued that they have a duty to provide international relief even if this means quietude on human rights abuses' (Keen, 2014: 2). This sets as a dichotomy silence versus duty of care. This is an intriguing way to frame the choices INGOs make in how they relate to states and is a valid theoretical perspective. This book, though, argues that the relationship is more nuanced than this. Although there is certainly a reaction by INGOs to the actions of states, the relationship may not always be as black and white as the 'lesser evil' formulation frames. Shouldn't the relationship in fact be understood as more of a two-way interaction; a constructed relationship?

As seen in the Keen article, policy discussions and critiques concerning the last period of the war often revolved around the instrumentalisation issue. Another

---

7 Needless to say, these comments should not be inferred as a defence of the government's actions but simply an explanation of differing perspectives.

example of this view is an article by Norah Niland (Niland, 2014), which also includes in its text two reactions in response its thesis. The first is by John Holmes (Holmes, 2014), during this period the UN Under-Secretary General and Emergency Relief Coordinator, and the second by Miriam Bradley (Bradley, 2014), from the Graduate Institute, Geneva. Niland's article begins the discussion by discussing instrumentalisation of aid, the use of Global War of Terror rhetoric and justifications of action based on the concept of sovereignty.

In Niland's view, the international community prioritised geo-political considerations over stopping the 'unrestricted war' (Niland, 2014: 2). As with Keen's argument, this is a valid perspective but overly generalised and needs to be nuanced in a number of ways. On one count, the 'international community' should not be lumped together. INGOs are not the UN, development INGOs are not humanitarian INGOs and the ICRC is unique. Each actor is different, and each organisation has a different mandate. There is a need to disentangle the various mandates, motivations and responses. And what is 'humanitarian'? What is 'political'? And how do the two relate to each other? Niland also speaks of the access versus advocacy tension, calling it a 'false dichotomy' (ibid.). A point of agreement between the perspective of Niland and this book's research is that the relief community needed 'a more effective strategy for coping with narratives and agendas' (ibid.: 13).

John Holmes responded to Niland that there had developed a 'mythology of events' surrounding the end of the Sri Lankan war that was not helpful to the debate (Holmes, 2014: 15). He disagreed with the general idea that the international community had completely failed in its action and responsibility and argued for a more nuanced approach to the discussion. To Holmes 'the crucial question' was whether more good could have been done if the international community had worked 'exclusively on the stopping of the war and the protection concerns of those caught up in it, in the way it has been suggested we should [have]. I do not believe so' (ibid.: 19). Rather, in Holmes' view,

> the government was (and is) highly resistant to public attempts to pressure them, and inclined to ignore entirely those who do this to the exclusion of efforts to work with them in practical ways, and those who focus more on making a public splash than on trying to get their arguments accepted in private.
>
> *(ibid.)*

This is an essential debate and one that deserves more attention. This also brings to the fore the core question of how much INGOs discuss these issues internally as they prepare to react to events. It also brings into play the issue of red lines. Are there red lines? Yes, there are in the opinion of Holmes, but they were not reached in the Sri Lankan case (ibid.).

Bradley provides a more academic response than the practitioner-oriented response from Holmes. Bradley agrees that NGOs do indeed require a more sophisticated political understanding in order to perform their duties, but wonders if this is too much to ask of organisations working in the midst of conflict (Bradley, 2014: 23). Bradley also argues that a deeper understanding of the Sri Lankan case was needed than was provided by Niland, and that comparisons with other conflict situations must also be made. Academic theories were available to assist with gaining this deeper understanding and for use in making comparisons (Bradley, 2014: 25).

These differing perspectives are mentioned in some detail in order to demonstrate that highly politically sensitive periods such as the end of the Sri Lankan civil war will be interpreted in a variety of ways. There is no one answer, no one 'true' narrative. What is important is for humanitarian INGOs to perform an analysis and create a narrative, for without it action becomes ad hoc and potentially counter-productive. Each organisation will develop its own narrative, but this development can benefit from a wider debate. Practitioners of various types, as well as academics, may all contribute to a contextual understanding. This understanding, as is argued in the book, must be formulated using a process that is grounded in a viable theoretical framework.

Summary of findings 2006–2009

Sri Lanka 2006: shadow puppets

The analysis of the 2008/9 period is in some ways more informative than the early period as the exposed tensions were more pronounced, which made the position of each actor sharper. But agencies for the most part work in contexts more similar to the first period, where the space for negotiation is more ambiguous and uncertain, with perspectives and positions less well defined and progress less easily tracked. In such contexts organisations are less able to take a stand as there is less to take a stand against. As with the art of shadow puppetry, audiences see the shadows on the screen but not the colourful puppets themselves.

By late 2006 the conflict was heating up, but it was not yet a fully declared war, giving the crisis an ambiguous status. Publicly, President Rajapaksa maintained his commitment to peace and spoke about the importance of upholding the ceasefire. The political elites were not monolithic, though, for at the same time parts of the strongly nationalist and aggressively anti-LTTE Colombo political and religious class were pressuring the Rajapaksa regime to take a more militarily aggressive stand. Heavy pressure was being exerted on the regime by the JVP and JHU to respond to the sensitivities of the Buddhist Sinhalese majority. By giving legitimacy to the LTTE and Tamil grievances, peace talks and a continued commitment to the ceasefire agreement were seen to be counter to the best interests of the Singhalese and Buddhist community.

The context within which aid actors worked remained dominated by the after-effects of the physical tsunami, the second 'NGO' tsunami and the negative press about the slowness of the tsunami response. NGOs were seen to be corrupt, inefficient and more concerned with their own financial wellbeing than the needs of the populations they were purportedly there to serve. As the war heated up these agencies were seen as being on the side of the LTTE. These feelings were directed as much at local and foreign-funded NGOs as to INGOs, and also at other international aid actors such as operational UN agencies and the ICRC. The influence of domestic political discourse on the socio-political perception of NGOs was substantial. Yet INGOs – the external – were being interacted with as actors with a legitimate standing in the political arena. For without this legitimisation, why would there have been a need to securitise them? If INGOs were not part of the political landscape, why pay them any heed? Yet it was still appreciated by both sides that INGOs were external agents working in the internal. This general view of the place and role of INGOs did not mean that any given INGO was safe in its place. As the political and military situation became tenser and more difficult, anti-NGO feelings became stronger, a number of restrictive policies were formulated and investigative and monitoring mechanisms were implemented. The killing of the ACF staff again changed the situation for INGOs attempting to work in the conflict zones, with additional restrictions put into place. The relationship would change substantially over time both because of domestic political pressures and in response to key domestic events.

The discourse used to explain and justify the increasing securitisation became ever harsher in this period, a result of these tensions between the self and other. The consequence of this process was the political definition of who was a friend and who was an enemy – and why. This discourse portrayed INGOs using thematic dichotomies. In general, the GoSL felt that international agencies did not abide by their stated humanitarian principles but cared primarily for their own wellbeing. In addition, these Western organisations were thought not to understand the Eastern mentality. Foreigners were perceived as caring more about their own people than about Sri Lankans, such as when ACF suffered a security incident and more sympathy appeared to be directed at that organisation than at the suffering population. INGOs involved in the conflict zones were thought to be supportive of the LTTE and the Tamil cause to the detriment of the Sinhalese and thus failing to support the role of the government. In fact, to many, the GoSL was being treated like a second-rate state. The GoSL, though, would not accept that fate, and would try to take control of its own destiny by defending itself against the most egregious practices of INGOs.

MSF-France and MSF-Spain were accused of a number of offences during this period, all of which related to their perceived support of the LTTE and which these MSF sections saw as 'false allegations and insinuations'. The view was that the GoSL was either directly behind these negative stories or at least condoned them. This is the context within which MSF-Holland began the process of re-entering the country and re-registering itself. In MSF's view, who or what constituted 'the government' was not well articulated, but the government was not seen to be willing to normalise MSF's position and accept the organisation's presence – though this would slowly change as the period progressed. As the GoSL attempted to securitise INGOs, MSF attempted to desecuritise itself. MSF thought of itself as a principled humanitarian actor with a long and privileged history in Sri Lanka. In attempting to track the GoSL's discourse, an 'Asian way' perspective was taken by MSF-H, which understood that the GoSL was communicating in an indirect manner.

Given all of the above, in late 2006 humanitarian access was highly constrained. MSF-H faced many administrative challenges, such as delays in the issuance of visas, a slow registration process and blocked MoD passes to the Tamil north. It was not solely MSF that faced such constraints, though, particularly following the ACF killings. The ICRC, although having a good reputation and being considered a reliable neutral facilitator, could still be considered a threat if its actions were not appreciated by the government.

In early 2007 the situation returned to 'normal' – that is, MSF was able to complete its registration requirements and begin work anew. Access was granted to the areas where MSF wanted to work. It is uncertain why this change in attitude occurred. An explanation may come from the reasons the government was so ready to crack down on INGO in the first place. The new regime was under stress, politically and militarily. There were in addition a number of international issues to manage. Such a government was prone to react to domestic political pressure and seek to forestall increased international 'interference'. It is plausible that the Rajapaksa regime needed a pause before letting the situation return to a more 'normal' state, where INGOs were allowed to work but under strict management. The 2006 period was, as it turned out, a trial run for another era when the regime was under even more intense pressure.

Sri Lanka 2008–2009: bare life

From the end of 2008 to the beginning of 2009, the GoSL had to manage a complex, intersecting, set of objectives: to successfully end the war; to avert criticism by the international community concerning human rights abuses and the lack of humanitarian assistance to the civilian populations in the north; and to manage the agencies already operating on its territory. These objectives, and the actions the GoSL took, built on the earlier context. The situation was more straightforward than early periods in that in the common view the end of the war was drawing near and positions had to be taken – a neutral stance was not acceptable to the GoSL. As the GoSL was the perpetrator of the war's end there was no need for nuanced or subtle discussion, much less domestic debate – for the most part the political community was on the same side, and those who were not were set aside. The Parliamentary Select Committee again added its voice to those critical of the negative attributes of NGOs, but in general the GoSL made limited use of discourse as actions could be taken without the need for extensive justification. In the GoSL's view there were too many INGOs, particularly since there was no real need for them – quite the reverse: they were regarded as LTTE supporters and were therefore enemies. It was thus dangerous to allow them to remain operational and able to speak out. Government discourse related more to the international community in general and was tied up with the government's defence of its handling of the war and its human rights record. The GoSL was increasingly dissatisfied with the perceived double standards of the international human rights community in how they approached the conflict. The fact of this perceived double standard said something essential to the GoSL about the bias of the international community against the GoSL, if not its active support of the LTTE. In practice, international organisations of all types – humanitarian and human rights organisations – were lumped together as threats. The message to the GoSL was that it had to protect itself against these threats by taking a strong, and proactive, stand.

The period between September 2008 and May 2009 saw realised a state of unmitigated securitisation of INGOs working in the conflict zone, as they were increasingly side-lined as relevant and legitimate actors and their voices quieted. Humanitarian NGOs were expelled from the north in September 2008 and in April/May 2009 international NGOs, including MSF-H and MSF-F, were required to sign confidentiality clauses in order to remain in the country. These clauses stipulated that all external communications had to be vetted by the relevant line ministry. It was a period of existential crisis for MSF-H, which prided itself on its adherence to humanitarian principles and its dual mandate of medical action and witnessing. In order to fulfil its international legal obligations, the government allowed a certain level of access to the ICRC and WFP. This enabled the GoSL more straightforwardly reject other actors. Securitising physical presence, securitising voice – it was an outlawing of such actors. Yet this was not a total outlawing, for agencies were allowed to stay on the periphery until needed again: they were able to remain in the shadows but in relation to the conflict were side-lined as legitimate actors. These actions were carefully linked to the GoSL's overriding national security agenda, which was to defeat the LTTE and bring the war to a close while simultaneously fending off the increasing international criticism. In this period there were no specific accusations against MSF – specific INGOs were not the issue, but INGOs in general – and the discourse was much more directed at the international community than at operational INGOs within the country.

MSF-H admitted to tactical errors in this last period, but humanitarian space was extremely limited in Sri Lanka at this time, whatever mistakes the organisation had or had not made. Aid actors were allowed to participate in the implementation of the government's plan under strict conditions and would not be allowed unhindered access or the space for independent humanitarian action. As part of its national security agenda the state had taken on full responsibility for humanitarian assistance and was not prepared to let INGOs function. MSF-H also reflected that it had not adequately understood the context, and its history and limited network did not assist it with negotiating access. In fact, its history of being perceived to be on the side of Tamils lost it support with the Rajapaksa regime. Within the organisation there was general displeasure at the acceptance of both the expulsion and the confidentiality clause and the paucity of communications concerning these two issues. Was there a danger of complicity? What would this mean for the organisation in the longer term? Would this become a standard procedure globally?

Conclusion

The Sri Lanka case study, presented in two parts, forms the baseline for the next case studies. The Sri Lanka case is a relatively clear-cut case of securitisation. The case study has been presented in fine detail in order to 'prove the case' and flesh out the theoretical framework. The next three chapters will use the same theoretical framework but will analyse quite different contexts and in unique ways. As the chapters progress, the theoretical background will become less intrusive. The case studies of Chechnya, Ethiopia and Sudan will expand the boundaries of the concept of discourse. It will be argued that there are other, thematic, ways for a state to communicate messages to humanitarian INGOs working in a context of civil conflict or political sensitivity. Once these case studies have been presented, the ways in which INGOs may respond to being securitised will be elaborated upon more fully in chapter 7. It should be mentioned also that the final three case studies will include a wider variety of INGOs in the analysis. While the Sri Lanka case focused on one humanitarian organisation, the next cases will include multi-mandate organisations in the discussion. Politics, principles and identity, the three central themes of this book, will come out clearly as the discussion continues.

References

Agamben, G. (1998). *Homo Sacer: Sovereign Power and Bare Life*. Stanford: Stanford University Press.

Boyle, F. A. (2010). *The Tamil Genocide by Sri Lanka: The Global Failure to Protect Tamil Rights Under International Law*. Atlanta: Clarity Press.

Bradley, M. (2014). Sri Lanka: Limited humanitarian action – or a lesson in the limits of humanitarian action? *International Development Policy*, 6(1), n.p.

Cassese, A. (2001). *International Law*. Oxford: Oxford University Press.

Fernando, B. (2008). Sri Lanka: The interim report of the Parliamentary Committee on NGOs is flawed from the point of view of policy, science and law. Asian Human Rights Commission, 12 December.

Government of Sri Lanka (GoSL) (2011). Lessons Learnt and Reconciliation Commission (LLRC) report.

Harris, S. (2006). Disasters and Dilemmas: Aid Agency Recruitment and HRD in Post-tsunami Sri Lanka. *Human Resource Development International*, 9(2), 291–298

Harrison, F. (2012). *Still Counting the Dead: Survivors of Sri Lanka's Hidden War*. London: Portobello Books.

Henckaerts, J.-M. and Doswald-Beck, L. (eds) (2005a). *Customary International Humanitarian Law: Volume 1: Rules*. International Committee of the Red Cross. Cambridge: Cambridge University Press.

Henckaerts, J.-M. and Doswald-Beck, L. (eds) (2005b). *Customary International Humanitarian Law: Volume 2: Practice*. International Committee of the Red Cross. Cambridge: Cambridge University Press.

Holmes, J. (2014). Humanitarian action and protection: A comment on Norah Niland's 'Sri Lanka: Unrestricted warfare and the limited protective humanitarian action'. *International Development Policy*, 6(1), n.p.

Humanitarian Affairs Department (HAD) (2010). A line in the sand: States' restrictions on humanitarian space. HAD Working Papers, MSF-Holland.

Keen, D. (2014). 'The Camp' and 'The Lesser Evil': Humanitarianism in Sri Lanka. *Conflict, Security and Development*, 14(1), 1–31.

McCormick, J. P. (1997). *Carl Schmitt's Critique of Liberalism: Against Politics as Technology*. Cambridge: Cambridge University Press.

Niland, N. (2014). Sri Lanka: Unrestricted warfare and limited protective humanitarian action. *International Development Policy*, 6(1), n.p.

Parliament of Sri Lanka (2008). Interim report of the Select Committee of Parliament for Investigation of the Operations of Non-Governmental Organizations and their Impact. 8 December.

Peiris, G. H. (2009). *Twilight of the Tigers: Peace Efforts and Power Struggles in Sri Lanka*. Oxford: Oxford University Press.

Roberts, A. and Guelff, R. (eds) (2004). *Documents on the Laws of War* (3rd edition). Oxford: Oxford University Press.

Rogers, A. P. V. (2004). *Law on the Battlefield* (3rd edition). Manchester: Manchester University Press.

Sriyananda, S. (2008). How NGOs threaten sovereignty of state. *Sunday Observer*, 21 December.

Weiss, G. (2011). *The Cage: The Fight for Sri Lanka and the Last Days of the Tamil Tigers*. London: Vintage.

4

FEAR AS DISCOURSE

The case of Chechnya

This chapter will frustrate. Even more than in the Sri Lanka discussion, the Chechnya case study is full of vagueness, uncertainty and indistinction. The nature of the threats in Chechnya to humanitarian actors, Chechen and Russian civilians and the Russian state, coupled with the associated discourse of fear pervasive in such a highly complex socio-political context, make for a rather challenging and provocative analysis. What follows are the results of using the securitisation framework to analyse the relationship between the Russian state and INGOs in the context of Chechnya during the second war and against the anti-NGO political atmosphere developing at the time. Some readers may disagree with the analysis as interpretations will vary between observers, as was discussed in the Sri Lanka case. The fact of conflicting narratives will evoke the critical themes of agency and truth. Throughout the discussion the questions of who and why should be kept in mind.

The Chechnya case study elaborates on the use of fear as discourse. Fear comes in many forms, but for humanitarian organisations working in zones of conflict fear most often relates to insecurity. The ACF attack and murders described in the Sri Lanka case study is an example, where a case of extreme violence perpetrated against humanitarian staff sent shock waves throughout the humanitarian community. Yet some contexts, such as Chechnya, witnessed a far wider-scale and more insidious environment of insecurity. For humanitarian organisations working in Chechnya it was not one incident, or even several incidents, of violence that could be pointed to, but literally dozens over many years and against a background of extreme violence faced by the civilian population. In such a context, concerns about security lead to an overriding atmosphere of fear. This can be considered a situation of indistinction between violence and the law, an important theme explored in the discussion below, as well as in the final two case studies.

Fear is not solely within the purview of violence, of course. Non-violent manifestations of fear, such as administrative rules, regulations and NGO laws that threaten to interfere with the ability of organisations to work, also exist. Such bureaucratic and legal barriers help reinforce an environment of indistinction. The Sri Lanka case hinted at this in the discussion of the MoU negotiations and the work of the Parliamentary Select Committee, and this type of fear appears below in the discussion of the place of NGOs in Russia. This issue will also be prominent in the Ethiopia case presented in the next chapter. Fear of the law emerges as a common theme in the case studies.

A further form of fear is that of expulsion, always in the background as a possibility in any country – and Russia was no exception. A partial expulsion from the areas of conflict occurred in the Sri Lanka example, and this theme will be discussed in the Sudan case, where a whole-country expulsion occurred for an entire set of organisations. Being expelled from Chechnya was a constant fear, although paradoxically, as will be seen, remaining was the greater fear.

The Chechnya case study will focus on two of these aspects of fear: the indistinction between the law and violence, and bureaucratic and legal barriers. First, the political context surrounding the imposition of a new Russian NGO law will be briefly discussed as a way of highlighting some of the key themes defining the relationship between NGOs and the Russian state. Following this is an examination of the politics of fear in Chechnya, the core theme explored in this chapter. But the thematic of fear must first be examined to define a reference point before entering into the case study analysis.

It should be mentioned at the outset that this chapter is heavily informed by my own professional experience in Russia. I managed humanitarian operations in Chechnya and Ingushetia for a major international humanitarian organisation between 2003 and 2007, and was involved with the response to a kidnapping in Chechnya in 2001, as well as a second kidnapping in Dagestan in the 2003/4 period. Integrated into this chapter are also findings from a series of interviews I conducted with several Russian and international organisations during several field trips to Moscow and the North Caucasus between 2008 and 2015. The theme of the indistinction between fear and the law is, therefore, one of personal experience.

Fear as discourse

Fear can be thought of as a form of discourse. It can be manipulative, sub-textual and indirect in nature. Or it can be characterised as menacing, explicit and cautionary. This chapter examines the former view, where orders and directives are not laid down but rather clues provided as to the consequences of non-compliance, however ill defined the rules of the game. The law can be used to explicitly set down the formal rules that one is to follow. Often, however, informally constituted 'prohibited actions' exist outside the legal and administrative norms which other forms of discourse are utilised to 'discuss'. In other words, there are unwritten rules and various indirect ways are found to communicate what they are and the consequences of breaking them. The game itself is political. George Orwell described political speech and writing as being 'largely the defence of the indefensible', and as such, 'political language has to consist largely of euphemism, question-begging and sheer cloudy vagueness' (Orwell, 1968: 136). This definition of political discourse describes well the use of fear, particularly the reliance on euphemism and vagueness – what is meant is something different from what is said, and what is left unsaid is as important as what is stated. Proper interpretation is demanded. The underlying threat, the risks taken for not reading well the writing on the wall, are only vaguely understood, particularly in a context of extreme violence.

A context of conflict such as Chechnya can be considered as a state of emergency, a time of 'indistinction between violence and law' (Agamben, 1993: 62). Such a space of indistinction creates an especially uncomfortable environment of ambiguity for INGOs. In any given case, will proper legal procedures, extra-legal means of persuasion, expulsion or even physical force be used as a method of control? This is, of course, a one-sided question, as the state holds the monopoly of violence, and the only recourse norms-based external actors have is to refer to the law. The state has options, can choose between the two, while the external actors must suffer the consequences of that choice. Laws change – they are not sacrosanct, but malleable, even if embedded in certain domestically and internationally recognised norms of behaviour. How these laws are formulated is unclear from the external perspective. Such a context is a time of pervasive insecurity, where trust in the rule of law fades and levels of fear increase.

From a sovereign's perspective, fear can be a useful, or even requisite, tool. Famously, Machiavelli thought that for the prince there was greater security in being feared than in being loved. In the Freudian view, humans respond more immediately to threats, based on self-interest and self-preservation, than to adoration of a leader or a system. Thomas Hobbes also saw the value of fear: 'Plunged into a civil war by a movement led by bold visionaries, Hobbes regarded the politics of fear as the precondition for the consolidation of order and stability' (Furedi, 2005: 133). Stability is established when the population fears stepping out of the order in which society is embedded. In this way, political leadership can be defined as the management of the politics of fear. This is clearly the case domestically, but also applies to international actors, whether working within or outside the country.

The discourse of fear must be contextualised, as every political environment is different. To a state, discourses of security are 'neither strictly objective assessments nor analytical constructs of threat, but rather the products of historical structures and processes, of struggles for power within the state, of conflicts between the societal groupings that inhabit states and the interests that besiege them' (Lipschutz, 1995: 8). Contemporary events and political struggles are related to historical patterns of behaviour and are embedded in society. These must all be unpacked to fully understand the context of fear. In each of this book's case studies a different context of fear is described.

There are many types of fear – of losing a family member, becoming seriously ill, having one's home destroyed by a calamity, or losing one's job. A more primal fear is to suffer physical or mental trauma through violence, particularly when one cannot defend oneself. This is the case as much for organisations and communities as it is for individuals and families. Social units, of whichever scale, are as affected by trauma as a person. As an example of an affected community, we can reflect on ethnographic research conducted on the survival tactics of Mayan war widows in the highlands of Guatemala in the late 1980s. These women were affected by *la violencia* – counterterrorism operations and repression in the 1970s and 1980s, which included disappearances, killings and rape. Fear is of course a natural response to danger, 'but in Guatemala rather than being solely a subjective personal experience fear has also penetrated the social memory. And rather than an acute reaction it is a chronic condition'. Rather than being a one-off situation or a short-lasting condition, 'the effects of fear are pervasive and insidious in Guatemala'. In such a context 'fear is the arbiter of power: invisible, indeterminate, and silent' (Green, 1999: 55). The memories of violence, the fear they have instilled, and the threat of future occurrences, are all powerful emotions and motivators, yet difficult to articulate, to hear, or to even really see. This is the realm of indistinction, and the Guatemala example should be kept in mind as the Chechnya case study progresses. Fear as an 'arbiter of power' is an especially informative concept, and it is worthwhile to take a few moments to contemplate the significance of the idea.

Violence also comes in many forms – from a mugging with a knife to the use of weapons of mass destruction; from a kidnapping to a mass expulsion of an entire population; from a murder to a genocide. The context of war creates a specific type of all-encompassing violent engagement, set against a background of unique cultural and social relationships (Nordstrom, 2004). War affects society in general, combatants as well as civilians, young and old, civil society as well as governmental institutions. Disruption cannot be avoided, tough decisions must be made by all parties concerned, and action will be forced. One constant in all conflicts is fear of violence and its consequences.

Three important perspectives can be taken from this brief discussion. The first is that fear is a useful tool to be used by governments – fear is an arbiter of power. To be useful, fear must be enacted, and this is accomplished by discourse grounded in ambiguity and based on threats the source of which may not be visible. And second, for the civilians or organisations that are the targets of the discourse of fear and their associated violent actions, there is no possibility for transparent conversation, as the topic is not open for discussion. Yet memories of violence persist and the threat of future occurrences pervades one's thoughts. And third, the context of violence in which fear is felt will be somehow set against the law, as formal rules by which organisations must live will remain in place guiding behaviour. The discourse of fear then becomes an arbiter between violence and the law.

Two manifestations of fear are discussed below. The first elaborates on the political environment from which a new NGO legal framework emerged in the 2005/6 period. The purpose is not to discuss the NGO law per se, but to analyse the politics surrounding the new law and the socio-political pressures that prompted it. Key points will be extracted to elaborate on the background context informing the state–INGO relationship in Russia, against which operations in Chechnya were implemented. The second is to go back earlier into the noughts, to Chechnya during the second war. In this era politics informed the INGO environment in a different way, through the politics of fear. This analysis will concentrate on the role of insecurity in the management of INGOs. The key themes are indistinction and fear, set within the analytical framework as used in the Sri Lanka case study.

It will be remembered that a useful way of structuring an analysis is to review how differences were created, how messages were organised, how those messages were meant to be understood, and what action was being justified. And finally, to discuss the actual practice. In this, as well as the other thematic studies, this basic structure will underpin the discussion, but will not be referred to as strictly as in the Sri Lanka case. It is worthwhile to have this structure in mind, but as comfort levels increase with the analytical process, the steps can be used to inform rather than dictate the structure of presentation.

Indistinction[1]

As with the other case studies, it is important to not 'black box' the internal, but rather to examine how a country interpreted itself and to investigate the 'nature and interrelationship between state identity and security, and the key principles, norms, discourses and parameters within this relationship' (Snetkov, 2015: 4–5). It is within this space that INGOs must manoeuvre, and in practice a much deeper historical analysis would be conducted to situate an INGO within this space, but for the purposes of this case study broad outlines must suffice. The book provides guidance on process rather than a comprehensive set of detailed case studies.

Looking from the outside, Russia is obviously a 'strong state', a self-identity to keep in mind. It is the successor state to the USSR, a nuclear power, one of the five permanent members of the UN Security Council and a major producer of oil, natural gas and minerals. If no longer a global power, it is most certainly a regional power. Confusingly for many INGOs, it is partly in Europe, yet somehow apart, somehow Asian, intimately linked to Europe by political, security and economic interests, although the relationship with the West is ambiguous and challenging. Where lies the centre of gravity in the relationship, and who is weak and who is strong? When discussing potential support on several advocacy themes with a representative from the Moscow embassy of a European country in 2006, the response was enlightening: 'But what can *we* do about Russia? We have no leverage!' The relationship with the West, and its representatives, including NGOs, is contested, possibilities for influence limited and the parameters of negotiation uncertain.

Moving to the internal view, this section focuses on the ambiguity behind the 2006 NGO law and the politics associated with its implementation. The objective

1   This section is informed by interviews I conducted with Russian NGOs in Moscow in the 2008–2015 period, the purpose of which was to discuss the development of the relationship between the state and NGOs, particularly related to the NGO laws. It is also based on my experience managing the process of registration of a foreign organisation in 2006.

is to introduce some of the key components of the relationship between the Government of Russia and NGOs, not to critique the law itself. As is stressed in this book, the political environment is the key factor for INGOs to understand and find constructive ways of interpreting. Administrative regulations and laws do not spring out of nowhere but are manifestations of political decisions. In some contexts, the legal environment, although difficult to manoeuvre, is straightforward, and it is possible to use it to guide how one negotiates access with the authorities. In other situations, inherent ambiguities in the law create an uncertain environment that engenders fear in the NGO community, a useful state from a government's perspective.

Following more than two years of increased tensions in the working environment for NGOs in Russia, the law 'On Introducing Amendments into Certain Legislative Acts of the Russian Federation' came into effect on 15 April 2006. The new law amended four existing laws related to civil society. These amendments enabled the authorities to: 1) deny registration to any organisation whose 'goals and objectives … create a threat to the sovereignty, political independence, territorial integrity, national unity, unique character, cultural heritage, and national interests of the Russian Federation'; 2) prohibit, on rather ambiguous grounds, the implementation of programmes of foreign NGOs or the transfer of funds to local branches; 3) request any information from organisations, including source and purpose of funds, and activities; and 4) insist on the presence of governmental representatives at any NGO event. Annual reports about donations and their use were also to be submitted (Machalek, 2012).

Registration requirements were burdensome – detailed information was requested and roughly a hundred pages of forms had to be filled out. Information on the organisation's founders was requested, regardless of when the organisation was established, including death certificates for deceased founders. The process diverted administrative and managerial resources from programme implementation to the registration file, both in Russia and at the organisation's headquarters. Some organisations had to stop work temporarily until their paperwork could be completed properly, which sometimes took multiple attempts as the process was very complicated. The process made NGOs uncertain about their place in the socio-political order (Kamhi, 2006).

The law allowed the state to divide organisations into good and bad categories – the law would assist the good and deter the bad. As in Ethiopia, which will be discussed in the next chapter, with the 2006 NGO law the 'Russian state sought to reinstate its control over all non-state activity', and conflated domestic insecurities with threats from the West (Snetkov, 2015: 108–109). International human rights, humanitarian, and democracy NGOs were almost all Western and considered to be linked to a Western agenda harmful to Russian interests. Specific to the former Soviet space, a fear of the 'colour revolutions' (the Orange Revolution in Ukraine, the Rose Revolution in Georgia, and the Tulip Revolution in Kyrgyzstan – all taking place between 2003 and 2005) was also in play, revolutions thought to be influenced by the work of Western NGOs. The proper relationship between

Russia and the West was a perennial question, and one that was progressively becoming more sensitive. The law gave the state the ability to sort through who was a friend and who was an enemy. But for the NGOs themselves, the criteria were not very clear.

It should be stressed, however, that there were a great many legal issues for INGOs to overcome – the NGO law was only one of them. The bureaucratic context in Russia was highly complex and administratively burdensome. In the end, the NGO law had little long-term effects on those organisations that had the resources and will to persevere, though it had a winnowing effect on those that did not. But this was the crucial point. To many international observers, the NGO law contravened the principles governments were expected to respect when enacting such laws: laws were to be proportionate, fit for a democratic society, and have legitimate aims. Was, in fact, the actual purpose of the law to decrease the numbers of NGOs through administrative means? Were the requirements too onerous and out of proportion to the needs of the state? And was the state acting 'democratically' by lessening the space for civil society actors? There was also concern that the law had a punitive dimension embedded in its provisions (Human Rights Watch, 2008). Was one of its purposes to punish NGOs that had stepped out of line? The themes of punishment and retribution will resurface in subsequent case studies.

A common explanation amongst the NGO community in Moscow at the time for why the 'repressive law' against NGOs was put into place was that the state, which by consensus was an 'authoritarian regime', was afraid of anyone or any organisation that became too popular and too appreciated. Adulation was reserved for those in power. As a representative of one Moscow NGO put it: 'The same happened in China. When an NGO promoting healthy lifestyle [Feng Shui], which has absolutely nothing to do with politics, gained more members than the communist party, horrible repressions against it were imposed, its leaders were killed and imprisoned'. Others focused on the bright side and observed that there were also some positive aspects to the law. It was true that NGOs dealing with human rights or political issues were under a lot of pressure, but those dealing solely with social issues managed to have fruitful negotiations with the government. For example, the reform of orphanages was highly influenced by NGOs. Therefore, although repression existed, there remained room for manoeuvre for certain types of organisations working on less sensitive issues.

Along the lines of this way of approaching the issue, some NGOs highlighted the fact that there 'were reasonable people in the government, some of which might truly strive to solve social issues and not only use them for propagandistic purposes'. Success or failure depended on the mindset of each person, regardless of the law. But when one started out working with one part of the government, it was unpredictable what kind of person would be in a decision-making post and how he or she would react to one's proposals. As another NGO representative said: 'It's difficult to say where the line is between what is perceived by the power structure as purely social and political, and to forecast how it may react on some of your actions.' But, 'if they see that in your publications you criticise the opponents to Russia, or at least that you critique both sides of a question, I think they would not perceive you as an enemy'. Possibilities existed, but ambiguity persisted.

To many NGOs, therefore, governmental relations were prioritised over public relations, as the government made the key decisions. Yet, was there not still a role for public communications? One view was that any NGO which did a concrete job helping actual people, such as providing medical help, would also understand the causes of the problems they were addressing and have an opinion on the ways to change the system to improve it – not just for the few people the NGO engaged with, but for the whole population. To change the system an organisation should speak out about it. If it doesn't speak it does harm. Raising one's profile in such a way wouldn't do harm if the programming was thought innocuous – on the contrary, it would enable it to get support from the public and the non-profits community and, ultimately, the government. Protecting one's reputation, ensuring positive media coverage and encouraging public support remained viable tools for organisations to continue their work and reach their objectives.

Several key points should be taken away from this discussion, all related to indistinction. First, there is a link between the domestic and the international. The relationship between the government and foreign actors working in Russia was obviously informed by the geo-political context and how domestic politics aligned, or not, with international pressures and norms. This was clearly evident in the Sri Lanka case, and it was equally true for Russia – and in Ethiopia and Sudan, as will be seen. But every country and government internalises and then operationalises these tensions and contested identities differently. A common theme across humanitarian crises is the enactment of tougher new NGO laws, partly as a response to tensions in domestic–international engagement, but the internal political dimensions are unique to each context. At the centre is an indistinction between the role of domestic and international norms. Intensive research is needed by NGOs to understand this uniqueness and to try to shed light on the balance between normative frameworks.

Second, what defines 'political' is ambiguous. What is political is in the eye of the beholder, which is the government, representing a state and its social and historical identity. In this way, the friends and enemies distinction may be the most useful method in determining the parameters of the political. By developing an instinct for knowing who is in which category and being able to articulate why, an external actor may be able to grasp the parameters of the political. And third, related to this, the Russian political order was not monolithic and the approach to NGO programming varied between components of the government and over time. In addition, at lower levels of power decisions were interpreted, and interpretations varied based on the local context. Even if, ultimately, the sovereign decides, it should never be thought that a government is monolithic.

A fourth point relates to the question of how much public opinion mattered in the equation. Was civil society able to influence governmental decisions? In a context of a relatively safe zone being created for certain types of organisations – those seen to be innocuous and doing worthwhile work, did this create more space for advocacy, and if so, how was the public involved with this? Connected to this question, fifth, was the idea that speaking out publicly was generally a risky business, regardless of the answer to the previous question. As many thought, it was the very challenge to the state that prompted the revision of the law in the first place, squaring the circle of indistinction.

The discussion about the NGO law elaborated on some general trends in the relationship between the Russian state and NGOs. International NGOs operating in the North Caucasus, however, faced deeper problems as their work engaged directly with a conflict-affected population. If ambiguities were created through legal means later in the noughts, the beginning of the century had seen a different type of ambiguity, one more appropriate to a context of overt violence.

Chechnya – politics of fear[2]

The law itself was not the most important issue for those working in Chechnya, although the political context from which the NGO law sprang was essential background. Though not yet codified in the new law on registration, legal ambiguities prevailed and extra-legal mechanisms were always available to manage NGOs. The most insidious control tactic was the use of fear, based on a very real context of violence and insecurity. First, fear needs to be contextualised. What did Chechnya mean? What happened?

The modern Chechen wars – for there was intense conflict in the nineteenth century, the 'Chechen problem' was not new – came in two distinct periods, with an anarchic interwar period separating them. The first war took place between 1994 and 1996, the interwar period between 1996 and 1999, and the second war began in 1999; it is left to the individual observer to decide on the end date, or whether the second conflict has indeed ended. It is impossible to calculate the cost of the wars with any accuracy, but it is safe to say that thousands died on the Russian side and potentially 200,000 on the Chechen side.[3] This chapter does not aim to provide a full review of the wars, but presents dichotomies to illuminate some key points.

The first war can be thought of as a 'traditional war'. The primary objective was to re-establish Russian sovereignty over the territory of Chechnya, necessitated by the secessionist movement. The second war is more properly thought of as a counter-terrorism operation, where the goal was less about controlling territory than controlling the Chechen people. The second war 'was an instrument to reformulate Russian nationalism along racist lines that excluded peoples from the Caucasus, depicted as uncivilized and barbarian' (Lacassagne, 2010: 167). The

2 This section is informed by personal experience in being part of the response to two North Caucasus kidnappings and having managed humanitarian operations in Chechnya, Ingushetia and, later, Dagestan, when the kidnapping threat remained high.
3 For detailed discussions of the context, see Babchenko (2007), Gall and de Waal (1997), Gilligan (2010), Le Huérou et al. (2014), Politkovskaya (1999); Politkovskaya (2003) and Tishkov (2004).

second war was an existential threat by the Chechens to the Russian state and people. In this view, the Russian population was slowly convinced of the necessity of the first war, but in the second war there was an active call for a violent response (Wilhelmsen, 2017). What changed was how deeply the Chechens were securitised.

This case study examines the second war, and it is argued that NGOs as well as the Chechen population were securitised. The threat from Chechnya in late 1999 reached the 'existential threat' level in official discourse, while the 'opposition and independent groups, such as the media and NGOs, that were involved with and continued to work on the issue of Chechnya were increasingly securitized themselves as part of Russia's widening security agenda in its domestic sphere' (Snetkov, 2015: 83). As seen in the Sri Lanka case study, on the generic level this process is straightforward. The uniqueness of each situation is in the type of discourse used as part of the securitisation process. In Chechnya during the second war, it is argued that fear was the form discourse took, against a background of intense insecurity.

One of the eternal questions in Chechnya was – why not just kick the INGOs out? Moscow had the control mechanisms to do it, as much as Colombo did in expelling NGOs working in the Vanni, Khartoum in relation to NGOs working in Darfur or Addis Ababa regarding agencies working in the Ogaden, as will be seen in the next chapters. In a state of exception, it is even easier to disallow the presence of organisations. With a robust legal system in place and the ability to expel through administrative means, why let INGOs continue to work in such a sensitive context? As unsatisfactory as it was, one explanation dominated INGO discussions – that it was simply too much trouble for too little gain, or even some loss. INGOs were in some ways useful and could be controlled sufficiently through other means. As stated by one Russian NGO, the Russian government was 'schizophrenic' and had two conflicting thoughts in its mind at the same time. One was that everyone was an enemy and NGOs should be destroyed, the second that there were real problems in the social and healthcare sectors that need to be solved. 'When you deal with schizophrenics it's impossible to make a forecast for the future!' And anyway, does one ever know what the truth actually is?

What, concretely, could be gained from NGOs? Resources themselves were not needed, but the ability of NGOs to work directly with the Chechen population was helpful. The government didn't need to provide services if the NGOs did, which would have necessitated creating a parallel aid structure they were not used to operating; and given the 'tensions' between the Russians and the Chechens, wasn't it easier to let the INGOs implement the work? This was especially the case with the provision of aid to the Chechen IDPs in Ingushetia. Looking externally, there wasn't a great deal of harm to be done by the NGOs if they were properly managed. It was even valuable to be seen to be letting NGOs remain.

In this view, the Russian government tolerated humanitarian NGOs because it saw them as useful, as opposed to human rights organisations, which did not provide any useful services, but only created problems for the government. Humanitarian organisations were considered less politically engaged, or at least had to remain that way to continue to be tolerable. This was the unwritten contract between NGOs and the government. There was concern in the sector, however, that in remaining non-political they lost their chance to influence the situation (Gilligan, 2010: 104–105). But outside advocating for purely technical improvements, was it even possible to influence the situation? For most organisations the answer was no, and so a silent, apolitical stance was justified.

None of this was ever satisfactory as an explanation, but it was impossible to really know, and the consensus was that it was meant to be that way – ambiguity was at the centre of the strategy of control. What *was* unambiguously known was that Chechnya was dangerous for the population as well as for NGOs. Where did the danger come from? Chechnya could be looked at as a matrix organisational structure, where reporting lines did not follow a normal hierarchical structure. The issue was that it was impossible to know who worked for whom, and in what function, at any given time. There were many different types of security services personnel present (local and federal), rebels of various sorts (Chechen nationalists and jihadists), and pro-Moscow local commanders, each of which followed a different trajectory of allegiance. Which side was each on? And was it only one side, or an ad hoc combination changing with the situation? Theories piled on top of suspicions heaped over yet more conspiracy theories. The normal instinct, however, is to look for agency – who was actually in charge? Whoever was responsible for any given incident, it was widely assumed that the ultimate boss – or at least the origin of influence or direction – was various constituencies in Moscow. In the end, it was really hard to tell what was going on, but some sort of narrative had to be constructed.

In this environment of fear and ambiguity, kidnapping was the major issue. Kidnapping is an especially pernicious threat. More than with a murder, a kidnapping traumatises an organisation and the humanitarian community at large. A murder is over with quickly, but a case of kidnapping lasts for an extended period of time, often months or even years. A kidnapping holds not only the hostage captive, but the organisation as well. The unknowns are especially traumatic – the unknown condition of the hostage, or even whether they are alive; the unknown conditions of release; and, of course, the unknown timeframe of release. It is a similar case for the entire humanitarian community in the location, as kidnappings have a damaging effect on the whole community.

It is not necessary to go through the whole sordid tale of kidnappings in the North Caucasus.[4] Suffice it to say that there were dozens of kidnappings of international staff and hundreds more of local aid workers, human rights workers, journalists, and civilians of all types. Kidnapping for ransom had 'spiralled out of control' by 1997 (Gall and de Waal, 1997: 369). Aid workers, journalists, human rights workers, were enemies, especially in periods when the Chechens were winning the propaganda war, as was the case in the first war (Russell, 2007: 111).

4 For vivid descriptions of kidnapping ordeals, see Vincent Cochetel, www.ted.com/ta
   lks/vincent_cochetel_i_was_held_hostage_for_317_days_here_s_what_i_thought_a
   bout/discussion, and Carr and James (2008).

Some, such as Fred Cuny, were never found. Some, such as a group of telecoms workers, turned up beheaded. The kidnappings of Camilla Carr and Jonathan James in Chechnya in the interwar years and Arjan Erkel in Dagestan during the second war lasted for many months – 14 and 20, respectively. Foreign and Russian journalists were kidnapped and the message was clear: don't come here. Aid workers were taken in Chechnya, Dagestan, Ingushetia, North Ossetia and even in Kabardino-Balkaria. Some organisations had multiple kidnappings – MSF had four kidnappings over the years, from Ingushetia, Chechnya and Dagestan.

Explanations for the kidnappings varied. Were they for money, to deny access, as retribution or politically motivated? Or all of the above, mixed and matched differently each time? Definitive explanations were rare, and suspect if held. But whoever was responsible, the result was clear – little reporting about the situation and a less negative image in the media (Roshchin, 2014: 125).

The violence was not limited to kidnappings – one of the most egregious security incidents occurred on 17 December 1996 when six international ICRC workers were murdered at the hospital in Novy Atagi. Regardless of the type, security incidents have a chilling effect. The ACF killings in Sri Lanka, the MSF-B kidnappings in Sudan (as will be discussed in the last case study), clan violence in Somalia or car-jackings in Chad, they all spread fear. Security incidents can be used as a reason to limit access, such as the Vanni 2009, but rarely has a security threat been so dominant in a context as it was in the North Caucasus.

But as is human nature, a narrative was built. The government feared speaking out, so stay away from that. Kidnappings were used as retribution. Threats were used as control measures. There was a 'climate of impunity in Chechnya created by the disregard of the rule of law, the "weapons culture" and the fragmentation of the conflict [all] contributed to a negative atmosphere towards humanitarian actors' (European Commission, 2001). The effect on the humanitarian community was often to leave: on 10 January 2001, all INGOs funded by the European Commission Humanitarian Aid Office (ECHO) suspended their operations due to the kidnapping of an MSF expat. There were limits to the usefulness of narratives in the face of such extreme violence.

As a way of discussing fear as discourse, three themes related to the kidnapping threat should be elaborated upon: indeterminacy, invisibility and silence.

One of the key issues that added to the fear felt by humanitarian organisations was never knowing from whom the threat actually emanated, as it was impossible to ever really know for sure. This is the question of agency. This situation prompted guessing, second-guessing and, frequently, inaction, an often-dangerous tactic. The narrative was that the government always had something to do with the prevailing insecurity, kidnappings in particular, but other actors were certainly involved – criminals, rebels, local warlords. But were the others linked with the government or were they independent? Spin those thoughts around for a while and they lead always to the same place – indeterminacy.

A second key issue was that kidnappings were the definition of invisibility. People were *taken away*, were suddenly gone, were made invisible. As described above, one of the most profound fears concerning kidnappings was the unknowns. You don't see the tank firing at you or go into a bunker to avoid the missile you know is coming. It can happen any time, anywhere, to anyone, and then … nothing but uncertainty and invisibility.

The third key issue is silence. The elephant in the room was not often spoken about, or only in hushed tones. There was surprisingly little direct discussion about kidnappings and the kidnapping risk, and complete secrecy when it happened. Somehow, speaking about the threat made it more real, or increased the likelihood of something happening. Were the authorities listening? Wasn't it bad to even label the threat, as then the perpetrators would become annoyed that the secret was out? Silence was better. Keep the discussions in-house and do not discuss it publicly. Like the bare-life period in Sri Lanka, INGOs on this issue became voiceless.

This case study has not attempted to make definitive statements about the ultimate origin of the kidnapping threat in Chechnya. As with the question of agency, to a large extent objective truth is beside the point. It was the narrative that mattered. As an object of study, the thoughts and perceptions implicit in the narrative, as well as the consequences of these beliefs, are what matters. Fear ruled, and whether purposeful or not, was an effective control mechanism. In this view, fear was the discourse used in the securitisation process. This process will be discussed next.

Fear as securitisation

Applying the securitisation framework as proposed in this book to Chechnya uncovered interesting findings, some of which are at variance to the model as presented in the Sri Lanka case study. As elaborated upon above, when analysing the state–INGO relationship in Russia generally and Chechnya specifically, it was discovered that fear was the most prominent discourse applied to the relationship. There are, however, a few unanswered questions related to this finding, the most pressing of which concerns agency. This question will be addressed before fear and the allied theme of indistinction are integrated into the securitisation framework more generally.

Agency?

Agency has become a catchword in the humanitarian sector and often refers to the capacity of beneficiaries to control their own destinies. Here, agency is used to describe both an actor (an 'agent'), who has the capacity to act, and the manifestation of that capacity – without action agency is not present. Important to this concept is intentionality – the actor must intend the action to occur. Agency therefore should be understood as the exercise of an actor's intention to act. In the securitisation process as argued in this book, the state has agency; without agency securitisation is not possible. A state must intend to securitise, must have the capacity to securitise, and must actually perform the actions that lead to securitisation.

Some of the primary questions posed by the Chechnya case study relate to the question of agency. Was there agency behind the use of fear as securitisation discourse, and if so, who was the agent? In other words, was there a state agent who exercised the intention to use fear as a control tactic? Did a governmental agent either create the environment of fear, or at least consciously use it as an INGO-management technique? And an even deeper question: in the Chechnya case, does the question of agency matter?

The dominant narrative for INGOs working in Chechnya was that, at some level, agency sat at the top of the Russian political structure, actioned by the security services. Somewhere there was a puppet master who used his strings to make various elements of the matrix structure dance. And the audience of the dance was INGOs. Maybe there wasn't direct cause and effect, but in the shadows, one could always, however dimly, see the hands of the puppet master, and he lived in Moscow. Whether this was true or not could not be proven, yet agency was assumed. And, in fact, this conclusion was used to prove the fact itself; if cause and effect could not be demonstrated, it only meant that the puppet master was good at his job. In such a circle of self-referencing logic there was no escape.

Neither this case study, nor any other, is capable of providing an unequivocal answer to the question of whether agency existed or, if it did, where it sat. The only statement that can be made is that that was the belief. Therefore, as to the final question: does it matter if there is truth to the narrative? Well, yes and no. Yes, in the sense that, if INGOs were to properly understand the context, the risks they faced, learn how to operate safely and maybe even desecuritise themselves, 'truth' did matter. But in another sense, it didn't matter, as that was simply the security context, and through trial and error INGOs found a way to work and a narrative – a theory – was developed to explain the facts; a theory which, if rigorously followed, would keep INGOs safe. Whether there was even a conscious sense on the part of the political elites and the security services that this was the operational theory of INGOs did not matter. As curious humans, we want to find the truth, but sometimes we must settle for what works.

For the purposes of the following analysis the narrative will be taken at face value. Agency sat at the highest level in the state and fear was consciously used as a form of discourse in a process of securitisation of INGOs working in Chechnya. The next section will summarise the argument for fear as discourse, relating it to the concept of indistinction, followed by a discussion of the securitisation process in Chechnya.

Fear as discourse

States find different ways to deal with the external. This can be straightforward or ambiguous. Discourse can be textual or sub-textual. In the Sri Lanka case discourse was considered to be governmental statements, the media and editorials. Actions also spoke loudly. What was the case in Russia related to INGOs working in Chechnya?

Indistinction between violence and the law is at the core of the process. The process should not be thought of as creating clear-cut categories, each situation is unique and some are clearer than others. Fear, as manifested in the primary threat of kidnapping, consisted of indeterminacy, invisibility and silence, and this characterisation can be used more generally to describe fear. Threats existed – empirical evidence could not be denied, and although the source was indeterminant, some sort of theory of action was needed, however ill defined. But to a large extent this made discourse invisible, compared with the sort of textual discourse examined in the Sri Lanka case study. Even with a dominant narrative, there was still silence about the core issue, as the sources of fear were hard to talk about openly in a context of indistinction between violence and law.

Securitisation

Putting it all together, how did the securitisation process work in the Chechnya case? The framework is useful as a starting point, and areas of modification will be elaborated on as they appear.

The existential threat involved two layers of analysis. On one level, the existential threat concerned the general background of civil society in Russia. There was a fear of political interference by the West, especially by human rights and 'democracy' groups. The authorities demanded to be at the centre and would not abide others becoming more popular than they were. In the eyes of the state, Russia was more important than the Russians, and the state was the protector of Russia. A threat to the state was an existential threat to Russia, whether from Russians or foreigners.

Against this backdrop, Chechnya created an even more sensitive case and another level of existential threat. Speaking out on what organisations witnessed in Chechnya could not be tolerated by the state. The story was too gruesome for outsiders to hear. Whatever good INGOs did, they were not allowed to do harm to the state through communicating what they saw. The sovereign was to decide on what was proper action without external interference. In Chechnya, also, there was a conflation of the feared Chechens and NGOs and of Chechnya and the West. It was assumed that the West and INGOs were on the side of Chechens, or at least not on the Russian side. The referent object – the object threatened – was therefore the state, as a personification of Russia. Such a view goes a long way to articulating why the threat was existential. Interestingly, the securitising agent was also the state: the centre, the Kremlin, the sovereign. The state was at the centre of everything.

In the second war the Chechens, Chechnya and the associated external actors involved with the conflict were actively securitised by the state through a range of media. The general population had to be convinced to accept the war and the actions of the state in prosecuting the war, a war labelled a counter-terrorism operation. This process was successful and there wasn't as much bad press about the war as there had been during the first war. One method to ensure this continued to be the case was to limit witnesses, including journalists, but also humanitarian NGOs. The open question is, was this smaller securitisation process – targeted specifically against humanitarian INGOs – located within a larger securitisation process following the same rules, i.e. against the rebellious Chechens? It is questionable whether state action against NGOs had to be justified to the general population on more than a cursory level. What was important was to justify state action against the Chechens. In this sense, the discourse of fear this chapter has elaborated upon had no audience outside the intended targets, the INGOs.

Taking the standard narrative at face value, fear was the discourse utilised in the securitisation process. It is argued that fear is always present as discourse and is an underlying component of the securitisation process. But in some cases, fear becomes the dominant theme and an actual form of discourse. In such a context, defining friends and enemies becomes close to being literal. The risks inherent in being labelled an enemy were extremely high.

Another interesting element in the Chechnya case relates to the definition of a state of exception in such a context. Could it be that in some contexts a state of exception is not episodic in nature, as a reaction to an emerging threat, but, paradoxically, a normal state of being? Against what reference point is the designation of a state of exception to be determined? If true, a more permanent state of exception would be an important perspective for an external agent to grasp. The indistinction between law and violence may thus be a constant in some contexts.

Conclusion

The point of these case studies is not to answer contextual questions or to fit empirical evidence into a theoretical straightjacket, but rather to expand the proposed theoretical framework to account for real-world cases. What has been learned in this chapter that should be taken into the others are two main points. The first is that the securitisation process is unique to each context. If there is general value to the concept, it must be modified to fit the realities of each country, each political system and each type of conflict. Regarding the Chechnya case, it had to be modified in relation to the role of agency, for example. The second point is that indistinction and fear are important concepts to be kept in mind, as they were in the Sri Lanka case. Chechnya merely extenuated the importance of the themes. In the next chapters fear and indistinction will occur but other themes will dominate – specifically, the law and expulsion.

References

Agamben, G. (1993). The sovereign police. In B. Massumi (ed.). *The Politics of Everyday Fear*. London: University of Minnesota Press.

Babchenko, A. (2007). *One Soldier's War in Chechnya*. Trans by Nick Allen. London: Portobello.

Carr, C. and James, J. (2008). *The Sky is Always There: Surviving a Kidnapping in Chechnya*. London: Canterbury Press Norwich.

European Commission (2001). ECHO funded non-governmental organisations suspend operations in Chechnya. 12 January.

Furedi, F. (2005). *Politics of Fear*London: Continuum.

Gall, C. and de Waal, T. (1997). *Chechnya: A Small Victorious War*. London: Pan Books.

Gilligan, E. (2010). *Terror in Chechnya: Russia and the Tragedy of Civilians in War*. Princeton: Princeton University Press.

Green, L. (1999). *Fear as a Way of Life: Mayan Widows in Rural Guatemala*. New York: Columbia University Press.

Human Rights Watch (2008). Choking on bureaucracy state curbs on independent civil society activism. Human Rights Watch Briefing Paper, 19 February.

Kamhi, A. (2006). The Russian NGO Law: Potential conflicts with international, national, and foreign legislation. *The International Journal of Not-for-Profit Law*, 9(1). 35–57.

Lacassagne, A. (2010). Controlling the Russian soldiers' mothers and Chechen mothers: The story of a hidden war. *Journal of the Motherhood Initiative*, 1(1), 159–169.

Le Huérou, A. et al. (eds) (2014). *Chechnya at War and Beyond*. London: Routledge.

Lipschutz, R. D. (1995). On security. In R. D. Lipschutz (ed.). *On Security*. New York: Columbia University Press.

Machalek, K. (2012). Factsheet: Russian NGO Laws. *Freedom House*.

Nordstrom, C. (2004). *Shadows of War: Violence, Power, and International Profiteering in the Twenty- First Century*. Berkeley: University of California Press.

Orwell, G. (1968). Politics and the English language. In S. Orwell and I. Angos (eds). *The Collected Essays, Journalism and Letters of George Orwell*, vol. 4. New York: Harcourt, Brace, & Javanovitch.

Politkovskaya, A. (1999). *A Dirty War: A Russian Reporter in Chechnya*. London: Harvill Press.

Politkovskaya, A. (2003). *A Small Corner of Hell: Dispatches from Chechnya*. London: University of Chicago Press.

Roshchin, M. (2014). Kidnapping and hostage taking between the two Chechen wars (1997–1999). In A. Le Huerou et al. (eds). *Chechnya at War and Beyond*. London: Routledge.

Russell, J. (2007). *Chechnya: Russia's War on Terror*. London: Routledge.

Snetkov, A. (2015). *Russia's Security Policy under Putin: A Critical Perspective*. London: Routledge.

Tishkov, V. (2004). *Chechnya: Life in a War-torn Society*. Berkeley: University of California Press.

Wilhelmsen, J. (2017). *Russia's Securitization of Chechnya: How War Became Acceptable*. London: Routledge.

5

LAW AS DISCOURSE

The case of Ethiopia

The Ethiopia case study further develops how states use the law in managing the external. This theme was briefly mentioned in the Chechnya case study from the standpoint of fear and indistinction and in the Sri Lanka case in the discussion of the work of the Parliamentary Select Committee and the tense negotiations over the signing of the new MoU. The use of the law, as will be seen in the next chapter, is taken to the extreme in Sudan. The Ethiopia case concerns the domestic context and will not discuss in detail the applicability of International Humanitarian Law (IHL) or other international laws and norms; although that perspective is important, the focus here is on the creation and use of domestic laws, although international expectations about state behaviour will play a role in the analysis.

A note about terminology. In this chapter 'the law' should be understood to be inclusive of allied administrative rules and regulations. To also closely attend to as the case study progresses are the terms 'state', 'government' and 'regime'. The terms state and government were untangled in the presentation of the theoretical framework, but in this chapter the concept of regime will be highlighted as well. The significance of this concept will be elaborated upon in the closing sections of the chapter.

The law

The law is a tool for states to control the external and can be thought of as discourse used in the securitisation process. The challenges are to understand the impetus for using this tool over others and to interpret the messages the law as discourse is meant to communicate. This perspective turns on its head the idea that in a state of exception a government works *outside* the legal code; in this view, a state tries to bring external actors *into* the domestic legal environment, actors considered to be outside the law. Much of the state–INGO and 'strong states' literature in fact focuses on administrative and legal issues.[1] There are a great many ways in which to understand the law, however, and what is often missing is a discussion of the normative perspective and how laws are socially constructed. The law should not only be taken at face value but must be properly analysed.

The objective of this brief review is to highlight some of the ways a study of the law may assist with better understanding the relationship between states and INGOs. In the process, this chapter will explore an alternative conceptualisation of the state of exception. This discussion is not meant to be an in-depth study of the role of the law vis-à-vis humanitarian action, although the humanitarian sector would benefit from such research as the level of analytical sophistication is currently low in this regard. The focus here will remain on the relationship between states and humanitarian INGOs, using the Ethiopia context as a case study – one of many that could be chosen as the role of the law in negotiating the relationship has become much more important over the last couple of decades.

In a regulatory environment, the law is a system of edicts, backed by authority. 'The rhetoric, if not the reality, of regulation is top-down sovereign control: the legal system (presumably on society's behalf) is taking the initiative directly to modify organisational behaviour' (Edelman and Suchman, 1997: 483). This modification is based on a vision of society as conceived by the state and is not produced out of thin air – cultural belief systems play a large role in how the law evolves (ibid.: 497). The law is therefore not developed in isolation and can be thought of as a product of the interplay between differing cultural norms, a good example of which is the symbiotic relationship between states and humanitarian INGOs. Legal codes are not merely technically conceived institutions, but are instead 'infused with value beyond the technical requirements of the task at hand' (Selznick, 1957: 17). These infused values must be understood by the affected organisations, as the law is a symbolic language signifying a set of normative values, and each legal environment will evolve in a unique way. The law is central to the construction of reality grounded in social norms (Berger and Luckmann, 1967).

There are several ways organisations may fit into a socially constructed legal environment. In a coercive model, organisations simply do what they are told under threat of state sanction. Some states will 'resort to legal instruments, to violence inherent in the law, to commit acts of political coercion, even erasure', a concept termed 'lawfare' (Dunlap, 2008: 147). The law stands in for a violent response, recalling the indistinction between law and violence as described in the last chapter. In this view, the law is a weapon a state may use to force external organisations into conforming to certain domestic norms. An organisation has a choice to abide or not. Organisations can try to evade the law, comply, delay, attempt to co-opt the source of coercion, or even merge with those less affected (Dupuy, Ron and Prakash, 2014). These themes will be more fully explored in the chapter on desecuritisation.

A spectrum can be imagined when considering the indistinction between law and violence. Where a humanitarian organisation rests on the spectrum will change

---

1   See, for example, Edrisinha (2010), International Center for Not-for-Profit Law (2008) and Mayhew (2005).

between contexts and over time in the same context. In the Chechnya case study, the law defined the formal side of control, violence the informal, and fear filled the space in-between the two forms of coercion. Where an organisation stood on the spectrum at any given time was indistinct. In the case of Ethiopia, the law was given a lot of weight and the background was less violent, so as an analytical starting point organisations were assumed to reside on the legal side of the spectrum and were thus less prone to violent retribution. But as the case study progresses the position of humanitarian actors on this spectrum should be closely considered. The closing discussion will return to this question.

Therefore, in a normative view, the view argued for in this chapter, the 'law enunciates social values, ethics, and role expectations which organisations … then elaborate and, to various extents, internalise' (Edelman and Suchman, 1997: 496). This process can lead to the phenomenon of institutional isomorphism, a 'process by which organisations facing the same cultural rules and understandings become both increasingly similar to one another and increasingly congruent with the myths of their shared environment' (ibid.: 496). Social construction is relevant not only to how states and INGOs develop their relationship but within the INGO community as well, as 'myths' explaining the space organisations inhabit are jointly created. This view should be compared with the crucial role of the narrative explanation in the Chechnya case study. Myths and narratives are pertinent to not only individual organisations but the whole INGO community, and can in fact lead to a confluence of narratives. This idea is more graphically represented in the Ethiopia case given the location on the spectrum upon which INGOs resided. Isomorphism is a more likely phenomenon in a context less violent and indistinct than Chechnya. Yet, even in the case of Ethiopia, it is important to consider how important it was whether the narrative was 'true' or not.

In summary, the key idea to keep in mind as the Ethiopia case study progresses is that the creation of the law is a socially negotiated settlement of the parameters of the possible and plays a normative role in establishing a relationship between, and even within, the actors. In this way, the law is a form of discourse and a tool to be used in the securitisation process. There is a message behind the evolution of NGO laws. Organisations have different options in how to respond, but first and foremost they must understand the normative environment upon which the law is based; only then are they able to properly interpret the message. As orientating examples, recall the interpretations given to the Russian NGO law and the work of the Parliamentary Select Committee in Sri Lanka.

The Ethiopian context[2]

The case of Ethiopia involves the process of securitisation in an authoritarian political environment and argues that the law itself can be considered a form of discourse.

2   This section is partly based on field research I conducted on state–INGO relations in Ethiopia as well as field work conducted examining challenges to INGO presence in the Ogaden region.

The Charities and Societies Proclamation (CSP) of 2009 is examined as a form of discourse and the theory of securitisation is situated in the Ethiopian environment. It is not for this chapter to provide a detailed analysis or review of the Ethiopian context beyond the immediate contextual factors that relate to the imposition of the new NGO law. Through the discussion of the NGO law in Ethiopia a specific form of the state of exception concept will be argued.

As opposed to many other areas of the continent, post-colonial borders in the Horn of Africa were not readily accepted, resulting in a series of conflicts over territory and sovereignty in and between Somalia, Eritrea, Ethiopia and Sudan. In a process of building a nation-state in a multi-cultural territory, a government will develop certain tendencies. State formation entails 'an expanding centre of power that radiates outwards to annex territories along its geographical periphery, and then weaves an administrative network to incorporate them and capture their resources' (Markakis, 2011: 7). The periphery is in a marginal position, disconnected from state power. To maintain control the use of political power is the key (Abbink, 2002: 157). It is important to examine how the centre reacts, not only guides, the process of integration, as the periphery's reaction helps define the state's structure. African states do have agency (Brown and Harman, 2003), and can formulate and carry forward nation-building based on their own socio-political trajectories.

In the era under consideration in this chapter, the Ethiopian People's Revolutionary Democratic Front (EPRDF) retained power, having taken control of the state after the fall of the Mengistu regime in 1991. The guiding principle of the newly created federal state was to give each nationality the right to conduct its own affairs, but as time progressed less attention was put on plurality and more on unity. This change in perspective facilitated the implementation of a national development strategy. Irrespective of the ethnicity-based federal construction, a structure developed at the centre that dictated policy in a rigid system of control built on the principle of secrecy (Markakis, 2001: 270). Both aspects have been repeatedly commented upon by INGOs concerning their interactions with the state apparatus. Similar to Russia, in such a political environment civil society was a source of competition, calling into doubt the regime's independence. As a result, the centre delegitimised and criminalised the legal opposition and civil society, and extended state power down to the local level.

A crisis point was reached in 2005, the beginning of a state of exception concerning how the EPRDF regime dealt with civil society. The 2005 federal and regional elections 'represent[ed] the peak of public political pluralism in modern Ethiopia', with 'broad-based civil participation of political parties, media, civil society, intellectuals, and traditional and religious authorities' (Tronvoll, 2012: 269). The joint opposition won one-third of the seats in the House of People's Representatives, but the EPRDF ensured, through various methods of repression, that these electoral gains were not consolidated. The new NGO rules and regulations introduced in 2009 must be considered in light of this political context.

The Charities and Societies Proclamation

Ethiopia has a long tradition of informal community-based organisations such as the *idir* and *iqub*, self-help associations working at the local level. Formal civil society as understood in the West is a recent development, beginning with the work of faith-based organisations in the 1930s and welfare organisations in the 1950s. The famines of 1973/4 and 1984/5 instigated the appearance of INGOs with a focus on humanitarian operations. It was only after 1991, however, that INGO numbers began to increase (International Center for Not-for-Profit Law, 2017). Given the increasingly centralising instincts of the government, relations between the state and INGOs have often been problematic.

The Charities and Societies Proclamation No. 621/2009 (the 'CSP'), issued by the government of Ethiopia in February 2009, had the following objectives: 1) to regulate domestic and international civil society organisations by putting in place standardised registration procedures, 2) to enable and encourage organisations to develop and achieve their purposes, 3) to aid and facilitate the role of organisations in the overall development of the Ethiopian people and make them partners of the government, and 4) to provide a legal framework to facilitate the operations of NGOs and to penalise those who conducted illegal activities.

Within the CSP different categories of organisations were created. Ethiopian Charities or Societies were those formed under the laws of Ethiopia, whose members were all Ethiopian, whose funding was generated solely from Ethiopian sources, and which were wholly controlled by Ethiopians. These organisations could not receive more than 10 per cent of their resources from foreign sources. Ethiopian Resident Charities or Societies were Ethiopian organisations that received more than 10 per cent of their resources from foreign sources. Foreign Charities were those formed under the laws of foreign countries, whose membership included foreigners, or where foreigners controlled the organisation. Organisations of any type were not permitted to spend more than 30 per cent of their budget on administrative costs, a category that was poorly defined.

The CSP established a Charities and Societies Agency with broad discretionary powers over non-governmental organisations, including government surveillance and direct involvement in the running of organisations, as well as the power to suspend licences and confiscate and transfer the assets of any organisation (Amnesty International, 2012).

The activities identified as charitable included:

- The prevention, alleviation or relief of poverty or disasters
- The advancement of the economy and environmental protection or improvement
- The advancement of animal welfare
- The advancement of education
- The advancement of health or the saving of lives
- The advancement of the arts, culture, heritage, or science
- The advancement of amateur sport and the welfare of the youth

- The relief of those in need by reason of age, disability, financial hardship or another disadvantage
- The advancement of capacity building on the basis of the country's long-term development agenda.

Those activities exclusively reserved to Ethiopian Charities and Societies included:

- The advancement of human and democratic rights
- The promotion of the equality of nations, nationalities, peoples, and that of gender and religion
- The promotion of the rights of the disabled and children's rights
- The promotion of conflict resolution or reconciliation
- The promotion of the efficiency of the justice and law enforcement services.

As described above, the ERPDF regime's ideology supported the implementation of restrictive legislation. The ERPDF claimed it was the country's only 'selfless actor', and that in fact NGOs lacked popular support, promoted foreign agendas and were 'inauthentic, undemocratic, unaccountable, or locally illegitimate' (Dupuy, Ron and Prakash, 2014: 7). This deeply frustrated international human rights organisations such as Amnesty International, which described the law as 'a ploy by the government to conceal human rights violations and prevent public protest and criticism of its actions' (Amnesty International, 2008). The Ethiopian government linked NGO activity with spying, and 'according to the government's paranoid and cynical view, foreign NGOs may occasionally provide assistance to Ethiopians in need, but their true agenda is political manipulation' (Center For International Human Rights, 2009). Many organisations had to change their mandates after the passing of the law, as they were no longer able to work on human rights issues (Amnesty International, 2012).

The basic structure of the law appeared to be modelled after the NGO bill enacted by the Zimbabwean parliament (but not signed by the president) in 2004. Similarly, political tensions in Zimbabwe had increased around the 2000 general election when NGOs were accused of political interference. The bill contained prohibitions against the registration of foreign NGOs and access to foreign funding for local NGOs involved with 'issues of governance', which were 'broadly defined to include "the promotion and protection of human rights and political governance issues"' (Human Rights Watch, 2004). Key themes of governmental concern were 'political interference' by NGOs; the promotion of human rights; and foreign sources of NGO funding. In even a cursory review of NGO laws globally, these themes will be commonly found as underlying justifications for the implementation of reinforced legal control mechanisms.

Looking beyond the intent to practice, it is interesting to note that the 'Performance Audit of the Charities and Societies Agency for Fiscal Years 2010–2013',[3]

3   The repost can be found at https://goo.gl/7mgNWJ

performed by the Ethiopian Office of the Federal Auditor General, found many inadequacies in how the CSP was enforced, such as insufficient field and desk based monitoring; low levels of compliance by agencies in submitting audit reports and annual performance reports; and in 2012, 1,250 organisations (81 per cent) had used more than 30 per cent of their annual budget on administrative expenses. The report noted that the agency had not enforced the 5,000–100,000 ETB fine against charities and societies that were found to be in violation. Officials from the agency 'told auditors that they did not opt for a strict application of the directive as they found that to be not feasible (sic); they rather chose to write letters to the organizations asking them to rectify the violations and take responsibility for that'. There was also 'little to no coordination between the Agency and the sector administrators (government ministries entrusted with sectoral oversight and evaluation of projects of charities and societies)'. These findings called into question how effective the law was in practice. As always, it is important to engage with the facts on the ground, as opposed to theoretical consequences.

The response by organisations

International organisations responded to the CSP in a variety of ways. To a certain extent there was isomorphism, as weaker organisations copied stronger ones and convergence evolved. Those working on 'non-contentious' issues such as education, health, agriculture and economic development were usually able to continue their work. Others had to 'rebrand', a process easier if the organisation implemented multiple types of activities. It was an option, for example, to simply remove the word 'rights' from their documentation – 'a discursive shift to an older, 'needs-based' development approach emphasizing service provision and gap filling' (Dupuy, Ron and Prakash, 2014: 17), and carry on as normal.

Several interviews with multi-mandate and humanitarian organisations were conducted as primary research for this case study. As well, internal documentation from a number of organisations was reviewed. The following discussion is based on this research, but, given the sensitive nature of the material, organisations will not be named. From this examination, two views can be articulated which describe how organisations explained the genesis of the CSP. One of these was a charitable view, and the other much more cynical. These views will be presented as imaginary conversations.

The response by a senior government representative to questioning by a country director of an INGO would read something like this. 'Why did the government pass such a law? As an INGO community, we are concerned about what the CSP means to our ability to work.' The response: 'The Government of Ethiopia is the representative of the Ethiopian people. Our duty is to them rather than the foreign aid community or generic international standards. You may do some good, but we mistrust your motives. We have a well-articulated development agenda and we take our responsibility to see it fulfilled seriously. As part of this plan aid activities and actors must be aligned and we demand to be at the helm of this coordination.

Ethiopia needs coherent and consistent action rather than ad hoc work by multiple agencies all deciding on their own programme priorities. If we are to be accountable to the population, we must be able to hold NGOs to account. Putting in place an adequate legal framework is a way to help mitigate against the negative consequences of aid and allows us to control the work of national and foreign aid agencies. This is our right as a sovereign government.'

Now turn to the INGO view, and imagine a discussion over a thick Ethiopian coffee with the same country director. Asked why the government had passed such a law, the country director might say something like this: 'The government doesn't like INGOs, or civil society in general. They are afraid of NGOs. The purpose of the law was to moderate the political effects of INGO action, what the government considers to be political interference. The CSP was simply a way to control INGOs. And maybe it was a way for the government to ensure that more funds were given directly to its budget? Regardless, there is a fundamental difference of opinion about the role of civil society. I don't think the government wants to create a liberal democratic order; they prefer authoritarianism. Meles [the prime minister] is playing the long game, it all fits with the EPRDF regime's ideology. But I guess they can do what they want, they are the government. But in end the population suffers.'

Some NGOs took on board the legitimate aspects of the new laws. Some points were admitted, such as the right of the government to be involved with the functioning of foreign organisations working on its territory. The Government of Ethiopia (GoE) was also given credit for having created a development-oriented state that had been objectively successful, although of course there was a long way to go. But still, the whole business was irksome. It is never nice to be told what one can and can't do, especially when one's motivations were sound.

International NGOs prepared themselves for the fallout of the law in different ways, but most engaged in a similar set of activities. One consolation was that the CSP regulations were not retroactive to ongoing projects, so the task was to look forward. The general approach was one of constructive engagement. Various coordinating groups amongst INGOs and the UN were created to try to create a united front with the government. One group tried to form an advisory board with the GoE, but it was unsuccessful and was shut down by the government, purportedly as it was not useful to pushing forward the government's agenda. More practically, each INGO had to figure out how to model their administrative activities. Importantly, language had to be adapted to conform with the new discursive environment. In particular, as the term 'rights' was no longer to be used, it had to be scrubbed from all documentation. Self-censorship was common. At a fundamental level, each organisation had to identify the acceptable compromises and their red lines, practical and ethical. There was some winnowing of organisations not willing or capable of working in such an environment, but this was not a quick process.

The negative consequences of the CSP were many. Decreased efficiency was a major issue, as considerable effort was required to ensure compliance, while at the same time managers were responsible for ensuring the quality of their programmes. Additional administrative as well as managerial capacity was needed. Staff ratios also had to be kept in mind. Administrative costs, however vaguely defined, had to be kept below 30 per cent, and maintaining correct expat to national staff ratios was vital, as the regulations limited the numbers of expatriates INGOs could employ in-country. This also ate up management capacity, as not every task could be delegated.

To elaborate further on the effects of the CSP on INGOs, take as an example the experience of an international multi-mandate organisation working on development and humanitarian programming related to children.[4] As the promotion of the rights of children was denied to international organisations, the organisation had to review its ways of working to find workarounds. One aspect of this process of adaptation was to review the organisation's working strategies to identify which would put it in conflict with the CSP.

The first strategy of concern was knowledge dissemination and capacity building of local civil society partners as well as governmental agencies. It was felt that it was possible to utilise this method if it complemented the government's long-term development agenda. In other words, programmes had to be linked to agreed-upon development strategies, and this could be done through capacity building of actors involved in the implementation of acceptable development activities through knowledge and skills transfer. Research and analysis activities were possible if aligned correctly to developmental programming, and could still be used for in-house consumption. Advocacy work was clearly off-limits if concerned with children's rights. Local organisations that conducted advocacy activities using institutional funding from Western governments was a particular worry for the government.

The larger concern was that the direct support of partner activities could no longer be based on a rights-based approach. It was possible to provide direct support to partners working in the education, health, livelihood, food security and labour sectors, as well as the implementation of emergency programming, but not children's rights programming specifically. Protection activities were possible with a 'utilitarian approach', that is, in an approach not designed to focus on rights. Ironically, the CSP limited the ability of the organisation to engage with the police, the judiciary, and other governmental agencies; however, psychological, medical and social activities could be implemented in collaboration with the police, courts, prisons, juvenile correction centres, as long as children's rights were not explicitly at the core of the programming.

The overall view was that programming needed to be thought through strategically and that capacity-building efforts, conceptualised correctly, should be encouraged, as there were severe limits on what the international organisation could implement itself. However, an INGO funding local organisations that worked on rights issues could be construed as involvement by the international

---

4   This section is based on an unpublished review of the CSP and its effects on the organisation's programming.

organisation, and there was a cap on the amount of funding Ethiopian Charities and Societies could take from international organisations.

Apart from programming restrictions, financial and administrative procedures were affected by the new law. Under the law a full set of accounts had to be kept which could be inspected at any time by the government and which had to be submitted, and audited, annually. In the view of the organisation, 'from the reading of the provisions, it can easily be understood that the law burdens charities and societies with strict administrative procedures'. As mentioned above, the definition of administrative costs was not clear. A loose definition could seriously affect the ability of an organisation to work, as it would be easy to go over the 30 per cent threshold.

Ways forward included several strategies and options. One solution was to consider entering into a bilateral agreement with the GoE, as then the CSP would not apply. There was no guarantee, however, that such an agreement would be satisfactory to the organisation. As a matter of urgency, increased collaboration, partnership and networking with governmental development actors was indicated. To bolster this strategy, it was necessary to research the government's sectoral policies, strategies and programmes so that the organisation's programming would better align with the country's development agenda. In line with this, more constructive consultation with the government was necessary.

Several points can be extracted from this review of one organisation's experience, albeit one that resonates with the experiences of many other INGOs spoken to for this research.

If the aim of the GoE was to force INGOs to align their programmes to the government's development goals, then this was to a large extent accomplished. As it seems that some organisations were not aware of the details of the government's development objectives, the CSP encouraged INGOs to do their homework and to consider collaboration with the government and its partners. One of the negative consequences, however, and possibly unintended, was to make it more difficult for INGOs to collaborate constructively with government agencies.

Another consequence, a positive development from the government's perspective, was to decrease the 'domination' of Ethiopian NGOs by foreign organisations, accomplished by the cap on foreign funding. From the standpoint of the NGOs themselves, however, this cap did not have a positive outcome in many cases, as some activities would have to cease without this type of funding. For foreign NGOs acting as donors, this restriction also limited their ability to support local civil society organisations.

The biggest change for many organisations concerned the restrictions on 'rights-based' programming. This necessitated a shift of focus to 'needs-based' activities. From the standpoint of the government, non-Ethiopian organisations working on Ethiopian 'rights' was inappropriate, as a concern with rights were best left to the Ethiopian government and people. Foreign interference into such issues was not acceptable. To INGOs that had used a rights-based approach in designing programmes and structuring their support to indigenous organisations, this was a disturbing development. Needs-based programming was an acceptable way to approach programming, but without also considering 'rights', the impact of programming was incomplete, as one of the roles foreseen by many INGOs was to act as a link with international social and legal norms and standards. Programming and advocacy activities were meant to encourage the uptake of internationally recognised rights-based norms. Of course, from the government's perspective, this was exactly the issue: this role was seen as a danger to the socio-political order and had to be aggressively resisted. More than any other element, it could be argued that a state of exception was built around this idea, and the CSP was used as a tool to limit the room for manoeuvre by foreign organisations and the contamination of Ethiopian civil society by these dangerous ideas.

The last point to discuss is the issue of accountability. The CSP made clear the accountability procedures that all NGOs were meant to follow. Arguments could be made that some rules were too intrusive, such as the ability of the government to access an organisation's internal workings without notice. But general rules of accountability could hardly be objected to, such as the annual submission of an organisation's books and their auditing. These accountability mechanisms were seen by many to be arduous, but the reference point was unclear. Were the regulations too burdensome objectively, or only when evaluated against what had been done before?

From the standpoint of a multi-mandate organisation that had historically been engaged with rights-based programming, therefore, there were a number of concerns brought forward by the CSP. But from the perspective of the government the outcome was for the most part positive.

The next example is the experience of a humanitarian organisation that did not concurrently engage with development activities and did not have an explicitly rights-based approach to programming.[5] The organisation was concerned solely with emergency interventions and responding to the consequences of conflict.

First and foremost, the organisation viewed the EPRDF as an ideologically focused regime organised around the principle of 'revolutionary democracy', which held that the party was both the engine of development and the forum for debate and democracy. In this view development and long-term programming was the solution to the needs of Ethiopians, and as such emergency programming was dismissed as a waste of resources and without long-term impact. Humanitarian interventions by foreign agencies outside existing frameworks were strongly rejected, particularly when emergency-focused foreign organisations claimed independence from the structures and mandates of the government.

In attempting to implement emergency operations there were many challenges for foreign agencies. Access to zones of conflict, such as the Ogaden, was difficult to negotiate. Foreign organisations were considered spies and the government did not want INGOs to witness the effects of the prosecution of the conflict.

5   This section is based on field research in Ethiopia conducted by the author during several visits between 2007 and 2014.

Responding to nutritional emergencies was also sensitive, as the government did not appreciate Ethiopia's reputation as a famine-prone country. Other sorts of emergency responses, such as to epidemics, were also sensitive, as the government did not want to be seen as incapable of ensuring adequate levels of public health. It was felt that emergency access was allowed to foreign humanitarian organisations only when the GoE had determined that the cost did not outweigh the benefits. Such a calculation was based on the capacity of the government to adequately respond and also the capacity of the humanitarian actor to play by the rules, the most important of which was to keep quiet about what was witnessed. Advocacy activities and public communications were not appreciated. The government spoke for the population, it was not for foreigners to do so at the expense of the regime.

As with other organisations, the situation as presented by the implementation of the CSP could only be approached in two ways – refuse to be compliant and risk losing access and being kicked out, or try to strictly follow the rules. Committed to staying and responding to humanitarian needs, the organisation decided on the latter option. The task was to decide on what compromises were to be made.

A number of practical difficulties arose once the decision was made to comply. First, there was confusion over the definition of administrative costs, as has been seen with other organisations. Second, obtaining work permits became a major constraint, as, in contrast to development organisations, humanitarian agencies often worked extensively with expatriate staff, especially during large-scale emergencies when large numbers of experienced and specialised staff were needed quickly. Regardless of the preference for international staff, the difficulty with obtaining work permits necessitated the hiring of more national staff. The above-mentioned expatriate to national staff ratios also added to the human resources management difficulties. One knock-on effect was that, when implementing programming in the periphery, the organisation was questioned why so few national staff came from the centre ('highlanders'), as opposed to the local areas. Ratios, formal or informal, were applied at multiple levels.

As described above, there was a thought to liaise better with the government, but it was found that the government authorities often would not readily meet with foreigners. Efforts were made to utilise senior national staff for such networking, based on the experience of other humanitarian organisations that had put resources into establishing such capacity. But, however committed an organisation is to put in place such a structure, it takes time to recruit and develop staff who can perform such autonomous high-level representation on behalf of the organisation. It took time not only for staff member to learn, but for the organisation itself to adapt. One senior international staff members of the humanitarian organisation, in a biting critique, recommended that operational management 'critically question its discourse, reject dogmatism, develop operations in strategic areas with a longer-term vision, address gaps in analytical skills within the organization, preserve institutional memory, and design a more rational institutional setup, including a continuous, coherent and unified representation'. As advised by another international humanitarian agency, survival in Ethiopia entailed a choice of pragmatism over dogma. Be humble, patient, don't overreact, take a long-term view and admit mistakes. In a similar vein, advice from a Western donor was that it was important to be realistic and mature and accept that organisations had to work on capacity building. One must co-operate with the government and give the government credit for successes.

For a humanitarian organisation, humanitarian principles are normally at the heart of programme design, organisational representation and negotiating access. The Ethiopia case was at variance with the norm, however, and the organisation had to come to grips with the idea that negotiations based on humanitarian principles did not work in such a development context; for that matter, neither did negotiating access to a conflict zone such as the Ogaden using International Humanitarian Law. In a conflict zone impartiality could be viewed as working with the rebels.

Regardless of the quality of the internal reflections and the external advice, it is not always easy for organisations to move forward as advised, or as they know they should. Organisations have their own deeply embedded policies and biases with which to contend. By instinct some organisations work towards isomorphism, some towards radical independence. Organisational culture is hard to change. Administrative procedures can be fulfilled and resources put towards compiling all necessary paperwork, but changing in such a way as to flout one's normal ways of working, principles and identity is a more different task.

Organisations of all types had to adapt and change to survive. Decisions had to be made about whether and how to comply and what workarounds were possible. Each type of organisation had its own set of concerns. A multi-mandate organisation had to worry about their rights-based programmes and a humanitarian organisation was concerned about whether they would be granted access to emergencies or conflict zones. Coercion, discretion and compromise were the three modes of analysis (Lockyear and Cunningham, 2017). Would agencies allow themselves to be coerced and accept the dictates of the law? Would agencies choose to collaborate with the government on mutually acceptable programmes? Or would agencies compromise some of its principles and programmatic strategies in order to stay? A full set of choices would find room for all three modes of response. The same process is used in any context where the law is used as securitisation discourse.

All of these potential responses will be more fully discussed in chapter 7, which elaborates on organisational response options.

The law elsewhere

The capacity and desire of states to regulate NGOs has become increasingly apparent globally. Nearly half of the world's states – 86 of 195 countries, or 44 per cent – have passed more restrictive NGO laws since 1955, most of which (69) have appeared after the end of the Cold War (Dupuy, Ron and Prakash, 2014). More research is needed to conceptualise and document this global trend; here, only a few relevant examples can be briefly mentioned.

In this chapter, the influence of the Zimbabwean bill was discussed, and there are of course other examples of the use of the law in NGO regulation in Africa.

Post-apartheid South Africa has gone through a process of centralisation of state power, particularly in the executive, coupled with the exclusion of civil society and citizen's participation (Helliker, 2011: 45). The Zambian government also tightened NGO regulations as it became less enthusiastic about the role of civil society, especially as it related to advocacy activities as opposed to straight service delivery. The process ended with the repressive NGO Act in 2009 (Machina and Sorensen, 2011: 268–269). Aid dependent states are not universally weak in relation to their engagement with external actors. Rwanda is a case of a country with many foreign donors, all with their own agendas, making it difficult for the state to fulfil its own agenda, rather like Ethiopia. Rwanda, though, has managed to take some form of control through the development of good aid polies and a strategic vision. Important has been proactive donor coordination, although joint ownership between state and donors remains in place (Grimm, 2013). The case of Rwanda also points to the idea that states have positive and negative levers to use with donors.

Rwanda is also an example of the regime security approach, where elites react more to threats to the regime than threats to the formal state apparatus. This is particularly the case where the state has been established by a rebel movement, such as in Rwanda, Uganda and Ethiopia. In such an approach, threats to a regime are managed at domestic, regional, and international levels (Beswick, 2013). In the Rwandan case, the Rwandan Patriotic Front (RPF) regime took power at the time of the genocide and established a new government aimed at bringing unity to the country after the civil war and moving the country forward with a development agenda. The comparison with the Ethiopia case is clear. The presentation of the Ethiopian case has highlighted the difficulties in assigning affiliations and locating agency. Certainly, there is an Ethiopian state, and there is a government that is the governing power. But more than this there is a revolutionary regime that took power and thinks of itself as the ideological guardian of the socio-political order. The regime defines the centre that is mandated to establish unity through bringing the periphery into the gravitational orbit of Addis Ababa. The differentiation between a regime and a state will be discussed further when discussing the securitisation approach at the end of this chapter.

These examples can be compared to even more repressive states. In a truly repressive state, the law may not be a relevant concept for analysis as there is complete concurrence between regime, state and government, and civil society is completely absent. North Korea is a case in point, and one of the only examples in the contemporary world of a truly totalitarian state. As Synder (2013) explains, in the mid to late 1990s humanitarian interventions were attempted by a few INGOs and the UN to address food insecurity. Humanitarian assistance and the physical presence of foreigners were considered by the regime to have fundamentally political consequences. The regime rejected the idea that humanitarian aid could be apolitical in nature, as there was no space outside politics. The government was asked to put humanitarian needs above politics, but this was too much to ask of a regime based on the ideology of *Juche* – autarky and putting 'the people' (as opposed to individuals) first. Procedures for the monitoring of food distributions became a point of tension, and contact with the population by foreign agencies was severely limited. North Korea wanted the resources, not the interference. The less they needed resources the more they tried to control the foreigner actors – the UN, INGOs, donors and governments – that the regime thought used the chance of presence to follow through with their political agendas, a belief with some backing in truth. The instincts of many INGOs were developed in areas of the world not comparable to the North Korea context; they came with certain preconceptions, expectations and, sometimes, profound ignorance of the North Korean socio-political order, none of which facilitated negotiations. In the end, most organisations determined that the North Korean context was not sufficiently conducive to humanitarian action and decided to leave the country.

The North Korea case describes a context where there was no pretence of law, only the use of brutally imposed control mechanisms. Regardless of the state ideology, regime security was paramount. It may be argued that Eritrea is a similar context. These cases are outliers in their management, but not in their fundamental structure, which is shared by many political systems. These all benefit from the use of the securitisation framework to analyse how they function.

The law in the securitisation process

Based on the analysis of the legal arena in Ethiopia, a narrative can be built. INGOs were socially mediating actors who stood at the nexus between the international order, the state and the population. Much of their work was interpreted as political interference by the government. They were therefore considered threats to the established order, particularly in relation to the rights-based agenda of many agencies. A focus on independence and emergency interventions by humanitarian agencies over aligned development activities were also danger signals. Such a situation created the sense of a state of exception that characterised the relationship between the regime and international NGOs. In the terminology of this book, the external was being rejected by the internal until modifications were made on how the external engaged in the internal. Instead of acting outside the law the state reinforced the law. The law, as a discursive element in the securitisation process, sets down a normative pattern of behaviour. The Ethiopian case, however, brings with it a number of challenges to a securitisation analysis and the concept of the state of exception.

The existential threat was the perceived political interference by foreign agents that challenged the ideological agenda of the regime. Fundamental disagreements existed between the external and the internal about how the polity should be constructed and managed. There was not room for two visions of how the socio-political should develop, and civil society, especially foreign organisations, threatened to compete with the government. Critical issues related to the fear of rights-based agendas and perceived interference with the development agenda as envisaged by the government.

As with Russia, the referent object, which in theory should be easy to articulate, may not be that easy to determine in the Ethiopia case. Certainly, it was the

Ethiopian people, as represented by the state, which was threatened. But the government was also under threat as it was the governing power that was responsible for the development of the country. In many ways, however, the EPRDF regime was the political entity most threatened, as was seen in the Rwanda example. And in fact, Meles, the prime minister of Ethiopia in the period discussed, was often compared to Kagame, the president of Rwanda, in discussions with INGOs. Regime security, if not articulated as such, was often in the background in INGO discussions as a driving force in the government's actions.

Clearly the government was the securitising agent, but the differentiation between the regime and the government clouds this judgement. The regime was the custodian, the revolutionary agent, acting on behalf of the people, while the state apparatus was used as a tool. Ethiopia is not North Korea, but the concurrence between the government and the regime causes conceptual difficulties. Who was the sovereign? And again, as with Russia, the question of agency was a key consideration.

The audience of discourse were those actors who were the threat as well as the international community more generally. If the discourse was the law, then the audience was clear. Through the imposition of the law a series of messages were communicated about how the socio-political order was to be constructed and how it would not be. INGOs attempting to work in the country, as well as interested states and other international political actors, were put on notice. The parameters of foreign involvement were clearly set out.

The state of exception may at first glance not seem the best way to conceptualise this situation. If a state of exception implies that a government will work outside the law in order to respond to an existential crisis, how does the concept fit the Ethiopian case? The state of exception, as has been argued, was linked to the existential threat to the developmental process and regime security, and the law was used to protect this process and the centre against interference by the international order. But as reinforcing the law only made the state's formal position stronger, where was the exception? It is argued that the law was outside established norms only in reference to *international* norms. The law was outside accepted international norms that guided how states and international organisations should relate. The rhetoric by many organisations could be simplified to the statement: 'Yes, they have the right, but that's just not the way these things should work … .' The international community held at the same time the conflicting views that the GoE had the right to reinforce its laws but that these laws broke international norms of behaviour. The Government of Ethiopia well understood this phenomenon, and in fact producing such a reaction was part of the message that INGOs were to understand. Such a response by INGOs helped highlight the fact that the GoE would not tolerate the imposition of foreign norms. Who were friends and who were enemies was clearly categorised, and the enemies would be legislated out of the picture. In its own way, this form of discourse also instilled fear, as the full weight of the law threatened punishment to those who would not cooperate.

The law was therefore a form of discourse, one that combined control with fear. The law needed to be interpreted – there was meaning behind it and clear messages were being communicated by the government. As each of the case studies show, organisations must be able to perform this interpretation if they are to be able to properly respond to the actions of the government. In a clear clash of identities, such as between humanitarian organisations and state development agendas, Ethiopian/non-Ethiopian, state responsibility/foreign interference, INGOs must understand where they stand. The law is a political issue and is often in tension with the principles upon which international organisations base their behaviour and thinking. These tensions must be understood before they can be managed.

Finally, a few words on where the Ethiopia case falls on the continuum between law and violence. We began from the starting point that in the case of Ethiopia, more weight was placed on the formal side of coercion and less focus was placed on violence. This supposition held true, as the context of violence against INGOs was much less severe than in any of the other case studies. But using the lawfare concept, it can be wondered how much the aggressive use of the law can be metaphorically compared to insecurity (without establishing a moral equivalency). Looked at this way, there is a similar spectrum that can be visualised with violence at one end and the law at the other. Complying with the law, and staying well away from clearly unacceptable behaviour and rhetoric, ensures a decreased state of 'violence'. A certain amount of fear is implicit in this tension between the law and violence. The law then is a coercive force backed by a credible threat.

One important difference between the Ethiopia and Chechnya cases – besides the fact that in one case violence was metaphorical and in the other it was real – concerns the questions of agency and truth. In the case of Chechnya, who the agent was could never be confidently stated and the truthfulness of the narrative could never be confirmed. In the Ethiopia case, however, the agent and the truthfulness of the narrative could be much more confidently stated. Indistinction remained evident in the Ethiopia case, however, resulting from confusion surrounding the concept of regime security.

Conclusion

Implicit in the use of the law is the threat of expulsion from the country, but this did not happen in the Ethiopian case, although it did periodically from the Ogaden, such as with ICRC in 2007, and access was denied to organisations from certain areas of the country on occasion, as happened with emergency organisations over time. INGOs, however, were never forcibly kicked out of the country. What factors go into a decision to actually expel an organisation? The law was available to remove organisations, as it was in Russia. But for the most part this tool was not used. It may be that modification of the behaviour of organisations was a sufficient outcome, and organisations reacted in ways that ensured they were not forced to leave. But this is not always the outcome. The next chapter turns to Sudan and the Darfur crisis, when organisations were forcefully expelled from the country.

References

Abbink, G. J. (2002). Paradoxes of power and culture in an old periphery: Surma, 1974–1998. In D. Donham et al. (eds). *Remapping Ethiopia: Socialism and After*. London: J. Currey.

Amnesty International (2008). Ethiopia: Comments on the Draft Charities and Societies Proclamations. www.amnesty.org/download/Documents/52000/afr250082008en.pdf

Amnesty International (2012). The 2009 Charities and Societies Proclamation as a serious obstacle to the promotion and protection of human rights in Ethiopia's written statement to the 20th Session of the UN Human Rights Council (18 June–6 July). www.amnesty.org/en/documents/afr25/007/2012/en/

Berger, P. L. and Luckmann, T. (1967). *The Social Construction of Reality: A Treatise in the Sociology of Knowledge*. London: Penguin Press.

Beswick, D. (2013). From weak state to savvy international player: Rwanda's multi-level strategy for maximising agency. In W. Brown and S. Harman (eds). *African Agency in International Politics*. London: Routledge.

Brown, W. and Harman, S. (2013). African agency in international politics. In W. Brown and S. Harman (eds). *African Agency in International Politics*. London: Routledge.

Center For International Human Rights (2009). Sounding the horn: Ethiopia's civil society law threatens human rights defenders. Northwestern University School of Law, November.

Dunlap, C. J. (2008). Commentary: Lawfare today: A perspective. *Yale Journal of International Affairs*, 3(1), 146–154.

Dupuy, K. E., Ron, J. and Prakash, A. (2014). Who survived? Ethiopia's regulatory crackdown on foreign-funded NGOs. *Review of International Political Economy*, 22(2), 419–456.

Edelman, L. B. and Suchman, M. C. (1997). The legal environments of organizations. *Annual Review of Sociology*, 23, August, 479–515.

Edrisinha, R. (2010). Special section: Restrictions on foreign funding of civil society, Sri Lanka. *International Journal of Not-for-Profit Law*, 12(3).

Grimm, S. (2013). Aid dependency as a limitation to national development policy? The case of Rwanda. In W. Brown and S. Harman (eds). *African Agency in International Politics*. London: Routledge.

Helliker, K. (2011). Land reform and marginalised communities in the Eastern Cape countryside of post-apartheid South Africa. In K. Helliker and T. Murisa (eds). *Land Struggles and Civil Society in Southern Africa*. London: Africa World Press.

Human Rights Watch (2004). Zimbabwe's non-governmental organizations bill: Out of sync with SADC standards and a threat to civil society groups. 3 December. https://goo.gl/Uaa8Bh

International Center for Not-for-Profit Law (2008). Defending civil society: A report of the World Movement for Democracy. http://unpan1.un.org/intradoc/groups/public/documents/un-dpadm/unpan045561.pdf

International Center for Not-for-Profit Law (2017). Civic Freedom Monitor: Ethiopia, 11 May. https://goo.gl/LWs5gw

Lockyear, C. and Cunningham, A. (2017). What is your constituency? The political engagement of humanitarian organisations. *Journal of International Humanitarian Action*, 2(9). https://doi.org/10.1186/s41018-017-0024-1

Machina, H. and Sorensen, C. (2011). Land reform in Zambia and civil society experiences. In K. Helliker and T. Murisa (eds). *Land Struggles and Civil Society in Southern Africa*. London: Africa World Press.

Markakis, J. (2011). *Ethiopia: The Last Two Frontieres*. Woodbridge, Suffolk: James Currey.

Mayhew, S. H. (2005). Hegemony, politics and ideology: The role of legislation in NGO-government relations in Asia. *Journal of Development Studies*, 41(5), 727–758.

Selznick, P. (1957). *Leadership in Administration: A Sociological Interpretation*. New York: Harper & Row.

Snyder, S. (2003). The NGO experience in North Korea. In L. G. Flake and S. Snyder (eds). *Paved with Good Intentions: The NGO Experience in North Korea*. Westport, CT: Praeger.

Tronvoll, K. (2012). The 'New' Ethiopia: Changing discourses of democracy. In K. Tronvoll and T. Hagmann (eds). *Contested Power in Ethiopia: Traditional Authorities and Multi-party Elections*. Boston: Brill.

6

EXPULSION AS DISCOURSE

The case of Sudan

This chapter explores the use of expulsion in the securitisation process. The last three case studies described situations where INGOs where securitised but still allowed to remain in the country. Even in the 'bare life' era of Sri Lanka in 2009, INGOs were not expelled from the country, although they were temporarily denied access to the Vanni. Organisations were periodically denied access to the conflict zones of the Ogaden in Ethiopia, as well as to other sensitive areas affected by disasters, yet organisations were not kicked out of the country in the period under study. Rather, the law was used to control international NGOs and delimit their areas of presence. Even in the darkest days of fear and indistinction, INGOs were allowed to remain operational in Chechnya. The power of a government to control foreign organisations, however, can be taken further. Against the backdrop of the war in Darfur, this chapter examines the securitisation process in Sudan in 2009 when a set of INGOs were expelled from the country. Focus is placed on the international–domestic political nexus as one explanation for why INGOs were expelled. After a review of the political background of the expulsions, the reactions of the organisations expelled will be discussed before the expulsion as discourse concept is situated within the securitisation framework and the challenges of desecuritisation are elaborated upon.[1] First, the theme of expulsion will be introduced.

Expulsion

In considering the relationship between a state, the internal, and an INGO, the external, the state has the option – if not the capacity in cases of truly failed

---

1   This chapter is partly based on insights gained from working on the Darfur file for a major international humanitarian organisation. Primary research was also conducted, including interviewing INGO and UN personnel involved with Sudan during the expulsions.

states – to force an international organisation from its country. This chapter engages solely with the fact of expulsion – why states would take this action and how INGOs react to being forced to leave. The first challenge is to conceptualise the idea of 'being kicked out'. What is the best label to use? Besides expulsion, other options include exile, ostracism or deportation. Each has its own perspective, but the common theme is the convergence of power and politics. Three interlinking concepts will be explored – deportation, expulsion and exile. The first two are paired and will be dealt with as a set. Concerning this set, two specific ideas and terms will be examined: the removal of a set of like actors – corporate expulsion – and the removal of individuals – deportation. A discussion of exile will follow. The point of this discussion is not to provide a deep sociological analysis of the themes, rather it is to draw out several important points concerning why states may decide to kick out INGOs.

A corporate expulsion is the removal from society of a set of subjects with similar characteristics (Walters, 2002: 271). Corporate expulsions have often affected religious groups. An example was the use by Louis XIV in the seventeenth century of the law and maltreatment to force protestant Huguenots from catholic France. Using the tactic of *dragonnades* – the billeting of poorly disciplined soldiers ('dragoons') in Huguenot homes, protestants were effectively terrorised into either converting or fleeing. Orthodoxy, and therefore the power of the centre (in the person of the king of France), was challenged by an outsider group, one that would not conform. In such a case, the corporate entity was reviled by the majority to the point that it was to be violently removed from society. It should be noted the mix of legal and violent tactics – harassment was not based simply on brute force, but grounded to a certain extent in the law. Fear, obviously, also played an important role in the process. As it should be clear at this point in the review of the case studies, this fits an established pattern. Violence, the law and fear form an intimately linked set.

Other characteristics than religious identity can prompt corporate expulsions. Stalin's violent relocation of ethnic groups suspected of disloyalty during the Great Patriotic War (WWII) can also be thought of as a corporate expulsion.[2] Several ethnic groups from the North Caucasus, including the Chechens, Ingush, Karachay and Balkars, were expelled from their homes to the Central Asian republics of Kazakhstan and Kyrgyzstan in 1943/4. In the process, a substantial percentage of the populations perished. They were finally 'rehabilitated' in the mid-1950s and allowed to return home. In this case the suspect ethic groups inhabited the borderlands of European Russia, geographically as well as metaphorically. A long history of rebellion by various groups in the Caucasus fomented fear in Moscow. In this situation, 'ethnic conflict, civil war, and foreign intervention' combined to create a threat to the centre (Rieber, 2003: 139). The groups were already considered troublesome, and a new external threat increased Stalin's suspicion of their

2   It should be noted that these actions are commonly referred to as 'deportations' in the historical literature, but for the purposes of this discussion they are conceptualised as corporate expulsions.

trustworthiness – were they, as a group, reliable? Such cases have not been uncommon is world history; this is but one particularly egregious example.

In these examples, suspect minority groups that were considered a threat to the majority and the centre were expelled. Whether related to religious or ethnic persecution, corporate identities were the target of expulsion. Expulsions were a mix of legal and violent tactics, and were based on fear of the other. Needless to say, fear was also generated in the targets of persecution. Expulsions must always be viewed in their political context – corporate identities cannot be delinked from a domestic, and international, political context. Each case will have a different genesis, method of execution and response. But the power of the centre – the sovereign – to decide is always critical. Power, politics and identities are intimately linked.

The corporate expulsion concept can be compared to the use of ostracism by the Greeks, a method used to expel a disruptive individual from the group. An ostracism – ten years in exile – was in fact a democratic process to which there was no defence, although there was no confiscation of property or social disgrace attached to the individual (Finley, 1977: 80). Ostracism could be considered a pre-emptive measure, protecting the polity from potential harm, but without doing irreparable harm to the man ostracised. In the modern world, the practice persists in the form of deportation, although the administrative apparatus behind it is quite different as is the discursive environment within which it takes place. Deportation is most often talked about in terms of immigration policies, and this is a useful concept to explore further through an example.

In the context of deportations from Canada early in the twentieth century, 'the legal framework served an administrative imperative to rid the country of the unwanted' (Miller, 2000: 70). The rationale for deportation was based less on the discovery of offence than the search for an offence to justify deportation. Judgements were made about the ability of targeted persons to become 'good citizens'. If expectations of good citizenship were not met, then the person should not be allowed to remain, as they were a threat to the socio-political order. In such a context deportation was a 'disciplinary process', where 'power resided in the lessons it taught and in the conformity it generated' (Miller, 2000: 83). If an external – an immigrant – wanted to become part of the internal – a citizen – then they had to demonstrate their commitment to upholding the accepted social order. Anyone else was considered a liability and therefore a political danger that needed to be neutralised.

A more contemporary example of deportation as social control comes from the United States in the 1990s, when criminal and deportation law began to converge. Deportation of long-term legal residents for post-entry crimes became a form of punishment, incapacitation, deterrence and retribution (Kanstroom, 2000: 1894). In such cases, infractions would be punished by deportation, which both incapacitated the threat and acted as a deterrent to others. A sense of retribution was also present, purportedly against the individual, but also potentially towards the group from which he or she came; or, possibly, against the very idea of external agents attempting to inhabit the internal. Punishment, retribution and deterrence will be recurring themes in this chapter.

Remembering the friends and enemies designation as being at the heart of the political, a deportation – and, it is argued, a corporate expulsion – can be thought of as 'an instrument to be used against those who can be defined as political enemies of the state', and as such is intimately linked to sovereignty (Walters, 2002: 278). Whether referring to a set of organisations or individuals, the state has determined that they are a threat and should be removed from the socio-political order. A state protects its sovereignty by deciding whom should, and should not, remain on its territory. Whether regarding an expulsion or deportation, Agamben's 'bare life' concept is conceptually useful to interpret the meaning behind the action. Sent away, a person's or a group's existence is transmuted to the barest form of life, which can be equated with 'civil death' (Walters, 2002: 269–270).

The above discussion uncovers several key points about the process of exclusion and deportation. The first is to differentiate between individuals and collective sets. For the purposes of this study, a case of individuals, or even individual organisations, being expelled is less illuminating than cases where a set of humanitarian organisations was kicked out. Whereas an organisation may have particular reasons for being expelled, unique to itself, a case of mass expulsions says something more fundamental about the interaction between international actors and the domestic political order. Analytically, the task is to figure out what the common characteristics are that were so repulsive to the centre.

A second question is to zero in on what is being threatened – the socio-political order in general, the government, a regime, sovereignty, or even the sovereign himself? Is it suspicion of the borderlands or fear of international interference that is behind the decision to expel? In the case of evaluating whether someone, or even an entity, is a 'good citizen', how is this concept defined? A 'bad' citizen is defective in some way and therefore a threat – but in what way? Most probably, more than one entity is being threatened, and intertwined are many threats and threatened objects. Analytically untangling this question is an essential step and challenging to perform. And third, the roles of punishment, deterrence and retribution must be elucidated. What is the purpose of the expulsion, besides removal? Is an expulsion pre-emptive, based on an excuse or justly caused? Is it punishment of one actor for a mistake or, worse, retribution against a set of actors? And is there room for rehabilitation after the punishment?

Another way of looking at this theme is through the perspective of the actor being expelled or deported. The state of having been deported or expelled can be characterised in different ways. Here the concept of exile is elaborated upon. Edward Said defined exile as the 'unhealable rift forced between a human being and a native place, between the self and its true home: its essential sadness can never be surmounted' (Said, 1984). An exile longs for home but is incapable of returning. It is perhaps unwise to personify organisations, but using this as the basis for discussion, how do organisations react to being exiled, where the 'homeland' is the humanitarian crises that they are meant to inhabit?

Importantly, exile should be thought of as a social role, 'scripted not only by local cultural conventions', but also by external agents (Lumsden, 1999: 32). Exile is a negotiation between the homeland and the exile. It is important to examine how one reacts to being thrown into this role, and what sort of 'negotiation' is conducted. Various responses are possible. Some exiles from Nazi Germany, for example, lead successful lives abroad, using their skills in their new homes. But some lost their identity and direction, and some committed suicide as a result (Evans, 2003). Organisations too have identifiable personalities and identities and will react in unique ways. An expulsion of an organisation will lead to some sort of negotiation between it and the 'homeland' it was expelled from.

Based on this very brief outline of the many facets of the concepts of expulsion, deportation and exile, the case of 13 international organisations being expelled from Sudan in 2009 will be examined. From this point on only the term 'expulsion' will be used, with the understanding that it refers to a case of corporate expulsion. The term, however, will also include some of the aspects of the deportation and exile concepts described above, such as punishment, incapacitation and retribution, as well as the idea that there will be a negotiation between the exile and the homeland. In the case of an expulsion a set of organisations are determined to be 'bad citizens' and a threat to the centre and as a result are kicked out. The analysis below will try to determine who was being threatened and evaluate the government's reaction in order to situate expulsion as discourse in the securitisation framework. The reaction of the organisations – the exiles, will be examined to glean lessons about response options.

Sudan 2009

As previously indicated, contrary to the conscious belief or unconscious bias of many in the aid community, African states do have agency (Brown and Harman, 2013). Much of the rhetoric in the humanitarian sector, as reviewed in the introduction, suggests that states are 're-asserting' their sovereignty as if they had previously abandoned the concept. In all periods, but most particularly in times of crisis, governments will make decisions which they feel are in their best interest, often against the interests of external actors. Here it is necessary to suspend judgement about the moral issues involved, or the expectations held by external actors about what is correct state behaviour, and engage with the 'facts on the ground'. INGOs must deal with the political realities they are exposed to in the field. The threat of being kicked out is always there, and although cases are rare, the risk is real. The challenge for INGOs is to formulate a response to these harsh political actions that is in keeping with their principles. The Darfur crisis, and the difficult relationship with the Sudanese government, presented a particularly tough set of challenges for humanitarian organisations.

It is hard to pin down the identity of Sudan, present or past. A multitude of identities have been contested over time: Sudanese, African, Muslim, Arab, Islamist. Since the Omar al-Bashir-led Islamist coup in 1989, the Islamist and Arab identities of the country have been particularly at issue.[3] Much of this period has seen rule by decree and emergency laws. The emergency focused on in this chapter is the conflict in Darfur, the westernmost province of Sudan. The conflict began in the late 1980s as a regional civil war, was militarised by the ongoing civil war in Chad, and reached a critical level of humanitarian crisis in 2003, spurred by the open rebellion of the Sudan Liberation Movement (SLM) and the Justice and Equality Movement (JEM) rebel groups. The Government of Sudan (GoS), along with the Janjaweed, a local militia group, was accused of oppressing Darfur's non-Arab, although Muslim, Fur, Zaghawa and Masalit ethnic groups. In the ensuing conflict, the government was accused of carrying out ethnic cleansing against Darfur's non-Arabs. Estimates vary widely, but in the order of hundreds of thousands of civilians were killed through violence or as a result of the displacement crisis.

As a result of the violence, President Bashir was indicted by the International Criminal Court (ICC) for war crimes and crimes against humanity. As a reminder, the remit of the ICC, in operation since 2002, is to prosecute the crime of genocide, crimes against humanity, war crimes and crimes of aggression.[4] The ICC charged President Bashir with 1) racially polarising Darfur into 'Arab' and 'Zurga' or 'black' groupings, 2) using the 2003–2005 counter-insurgency operations as a pretext to expel these groups, and 3) using the internally displaced (IDP) camps to 'kill off' the non-Arab populations through malnutrition, rape, and torture (Mamdani, 2009: 271).

The ICC issued an arrest warrant for President Bashir on 4 March 2009. Later that day and into the next, the Government of Sudan expelled 13 international NGOs and revoked the licences of three national NGOs. The 13 international NGOs were Action Contre la Faim (ACF), CARE International, Cooperative Housing Foundation (CHF), the International Rescue Committee (IRC), Médecins Sans Frontières Holland (MSF-H) and Médecins Sans Frontières France (MSF-F), Mercy Corps, the Norwegian Refugee Council (NRC), Oxfam GB, Planning and Development Collaborative International (PADCO), Save the Children UK and Save the Children US, and Solidarités. The national NGOs were the Amal Centre for Rehabilitation of Victims of Violence, the Khartoum Centre for Human Rights, Development, and Environment and the Sudan Social Development Organisation (SUDO). In total 7,610 aid workers were affected, of which 308 were expats and 7,302 national staff, or 40 per cent of aid workers involved with the Darfur response. The affected organisations were delivering roughly half the total amount of aid for Darfur. As was commonly stated at the time, 'assistance to Darfur's 2.7 million-plus displaced people has been severely compromised' (Pantuliano, Jaspars and Ray, 2009). The initial reaction was that 'all signs point to an extremely well-planned response by the regime to a judicial decision that was universally expected' (Reeves, 2009).

3   For a good review of these contested identities and how they have played out over time, see Mamdani, 2009: 171–205.
4   See www.icc-cpi.int/Pages/Main.aspx

The ICC indictment was 'a new era of domination and infringement upon the independence and sovereignty of Sudan', President Bashir stated at the time.[5] The sovereign, President Bashir, was both he who decides as well as he who was threatened. This set up an interesting dynamic, with the existential threat personified in not only the position but also the person of the sovereign, as an ICC indictment is against a person, not an office. In the case of a president, this makes for a complete overlap between the sovereign and the individual indicted. This of course follows a clear logic, as the president – the sovereign – is ultimately responsible for the actions of a government and is the one who decides.

The standard explanation in the international community for the expulsions was that they were in reaction to the ICC arrest warrant. Expulsion was only one method, albeit extreme, of control, which was the principle of behaviour underlying the engagement between INGOs and the government. The government had long made it a policy to control aid agencies to limit their witnessing and political involvement. Tight control over INGOs was implemented by the HAC – the Humanitarian Affairs Council. Visas and internal travel restrictions had been used to control access, which for a time was easier than expulsion or deportation, although there was the constant fear on the part of international organisations of being kicked out (Cockett, 2010: 246–47).

Another way to control INGOs was through fear, as illustrated by the MSF-Belgium kidnappings on 11 March, when five workers were kidnapped for three days and released unharmed. Common wisdom within the INGO community thought that the motive for the kidnappings was to create a sense of untenable insecurity that would force organisations to leave Darfur. The three sections of MSF present (Belgium, Switzerland, Spain) withdrew, leaving no MSF section operational and primary and secondary medical programming in Darfur reduced (Reeves, 2009). Security incidents had, in fact, long plagued humanitarian operations in Darfur, creating an environment of fear. This environment of fear can be compared in many ways to the Chechnya context as discussed in chapter 4.

Many examples could be used to illustrate the debates around the functioning of the ICC, sovereignty and the work of international organisations in Sudan, but one opinion has been chosen as representative. Ahmed Hassan (2009),[6] in a blog for African Arguments, thought that crises such as Darfur have at their foundation political rather than humanitarian issues, and NGOs should never have mixed humanitarian action with politics. This arose from a cultural misunderstanding. The West was ill prepared to deal with Africa. 'Simply, coercion and threats won't work here.' President Bashir was visibly unaffected by the ICC decision, and travelled outside the country five times over the next weeks 'in a daring sign of total defiance'. In fact, 'that is how the leadership reacts to threats in this part of the

---

5 See 12/30/2016 *Taipei Times*, www.taipeitimes.com/News/world/print/2009/06/13/2003446013
6 Ahmed Hassan is a Sudanese peace activist and international humanitarian worker with work experience of over 22 years, covering more than ten countries in East Africa and South, Southeast and Central Asia.

world, the more you press them, the more they push you and strike back'. The Sudanese government was out to show that NGOs were 'overrated' and 'useless'. The expulsion of the 13 aid agencies wasn't going to cause the IDPs to die. The cost, in fact, was an opportunity cost paid by the humanitarian agencies. They should have left conflict management and politics to human rights organisation, advocacy groups and governments. 'I guess that is what I understand from humanitarian neutrality and the humanitarian code of conduct.' As he understood it, 'political advocacy is not part of the original humanitarian charity work.' If there was more suffering because of the expulsions, the agencies were morally responsible for it. The rights-based approach, mixing humanitarian and human rights perspectives, faces justifiable criticism. INGOs and donors cared less for the populations than their own political agendas. In the end, 'the act of the government was a mere retaliation over the ICC interference'.

A number of issues can be extracted from these views, views that were by no means unique to Hassan. One intriguing idea is that the increased suffering, if any, caused by the expulsions was the fault of the INGOs themselves, as they inappropriately mixed politics with their humanitarian action and did not abide by their own principles. The government had every right to retaliate against such interference. As it will be remembered, a similar rhetorical argument was made in the Sri Lanka case study – INGOs were held up to their own metric and were found wanting. Another similarity to the Sri Lanka case is the insinuation that Western INGOs did not properly understand the context. The corollary in the Sri Lanka case was the idea that Western INGOs did not understand Asian values.

In this period there was broad suspicion that the work of the expelled organisations were somehow linked to the ICC indictment and many INGOs were accused of active cooperation with it. For example, the American organisation the International Rescue Committee (IRC) was accused by the GoS of signing an MoU with the ICC, which the IRC denied. There had been a proposition to do so, but it had been rejected: 'The policy that was later adopted specifically directs IRC staff members not to communicate in any way with the ICC and not to support ICC investigations' (Charbonneau, 2009). Having once discussed the idea of cooperation, however, was enough to tar the organisation as an ICC collaborator. Even without having actively cooperated with the ICC, there were consequences to implementing any sort of advocacy activities in such an authoritarian regime, and being kicked out was one of the most serious. Were INGOs, as some believed, simply too inexperienced and too ready to take a 'partial view of the conflict', engendering distrust by the government? (Walton, 2015: 7). As some argued, it was not the job of humanitarian organisations 'to advocate for a global moral order based on judicial punishment and just war' (Weissman, 2009). These views should be compared with those expressed by Hassan. There was certainly an indistinction between politics and humanitarianism in both the behaviour and rhetoric of humanitarian INGOs.

To explain how humanitarian organisations got to this place, a standard narrative amongst the external community traced the background political context that led to the events of 2009.[7] It was generally felt that access to Darfur had been easiest during 2004–2005, but conditions had by 2009 reverted to previous norms established at the beginning of the conflict. In the period of better access, negotiations were taking place between the Khartoum government and the Sudan People's Liberation Movement (SPLM) concerning ending the civil war in South Sudan. The Comprehensive Peace Agreement (CPA) was signed in January 2005. In this view, the Government of Sudan had given access to aid agencies in an effort to get into the good graces of the West to moderate any negative consequences of the peace agreement. INGOs were also useful as service providers to stop people from dying on TV – the government then could be seen to be doing something constructive. Cooperation with the West, however, hadn't brought the expected benefits and a new calculation had to be made concerning how to deal with INGOs and their Darfur response. Reverting to difficult access conditions in 2009 therefore was a political message sent to the West. Against this background, the ICC indictment was the final straw and demanded strong action by the government.

Interestingly, many in the humanitarian community believed that the organisations chosen to be expelled were selected at random – that in order to most effectively communicate the message of dissatisfaction, a combination of British, American and French organisations should be expelled. If there were criteria beyond this, it was to choose those that already had bad reputations or those with which key government actors had personal grudges. In this view, the focus was on communicating the message, rather than punishing particular organisations, beyond a couple of especially troublesome INGOs.

Oxfam's rhetorical response to the expulsions was typical for the sector: 'We strongly refute the government's accusations that we have acted outside our humanitarian mandate' (IRIN, 2009b). Regardless, for the expelled organisations it was not for them to decide, as the Sudanese state had the power to make its own decision. But what of the organisations not expelled, what was the appropriate response? There were tough debates at the time about the dangers of staying:

> Simply trying to continue operations as before sets a dangerous precedent in terms of humanitarian space. If the UN and other NGOs rush to replace the expelled and disbanded agencies, the Sudanese government may well conclude that it can act against aid agencies with impunity, confident that others will step forward to fill the resulting gaps. This is of particular concern given the Sudanese government's longstanding antipathy towards those agencies that address issues around gender-based violence, and protection more generally, and agencies that speak out publicly about the situation.
>
> *(Kleinman, 2009)*

---

7   Taken from interviews 2016/17 with staff from humanitarian organisations working in Sudan at the time.

As such, there was a need for close co-ordination between the remaining organi-sations, as well as proactivity setting of parameters within which to work.

Against this political background humanitarian actors searched for explanations for the expulsions and wondered if there were an overall strategy at work. As it was literally only a few minutes after the announcement of the ICC indictment that INGO compounds were surrounded by security personnel, the conclusion was that the response was well and meticulously planned. If not the 'excuse' of the ICC indictment, then there would have been something else to justify the crackdown. The ICC indictment, given the already tense relationship with the Western inter-national community and humanitarian INGOs, was a perfect justification for the expulsions, but some other event would have been either engineered or capitalised on to implement the expulsions.

An open question, however, was, faced with an arrest warrant, why choose to increase tensions with the international community? Was it simply that, as Hassan stated, a sovereign state could not let itself be pushed around without pushing back? A number of response options were available to the government. Perhaps it was easiest to lash out at vulnerable targets, such as INGOs. Such action showed that the government was still in control, and a message was also being commu-nicated that such foreign interference was counterproductive as it decreased the quantity of aid actors responding to the crisis in Darfur. Retaliation – to punish agencies that colluded with the ICC – and to get rid of the witnesses were also viable explanations. INGOs had, through their reporting, unwittingly colluded with the ICC by generating material useful to the ICC indictment, and it was commonly assumed that there were intelligence agents working for INGOs, also unwittingly on the part of the INGOs. All of this contributed to the government's opinion that INGOs were fundamentally dishonest. Expelling such unwanted organisations would send a clear signal that the indictment was not going to be accepted and there was a price to pay for it.

On a more practical side, getting rid of aid workers could also give the govern-ment more leeway in managing the IDP camps in Darfur, camps that contained 2.7 million people (Aly, 2009). Although the UN and others warned about the consequences to the vulnerable populations if the agencies were not allowed to provide assistance, on 8 March Bashir said that Sudan would cover the work of the expelled agencies (IRIN, 2009a). In the end, the UN stepped in to hire national staff to enable programmes to continue or quickly restart. For the most part, the implementation of these programmes was not hindered by the GoS and bureau-cratic impediments did not worsen. A situation of indistinction was created – had the crisis actually been large enough to necessitate the size of the pre-expulsion response? Would the departure of the 13 INGOs have massive humanitarian con-sequences? From a government's standpoint, an argument for expulsion could be made easier if it were doubtful that the presence of organisations was justified in the first place.

A common analysis made by humanitarian organisations working in conflict zones is that governments often use INGOs as 'political footballs'. INGOs are kicked down the pitch in an effort by the government to gain political advantage. In this metaphor, being kicked around is less about the INGOs themselves and more about how they can be instrumentalised to achieve political and security goals, domestically and internationally. The INGO view of the Sudan context fits this mould. The conflicts in Darfur and South Sudan, the relationship between Sudan and the West and the role played by humanitarian organisations were all linked and intertwined. International humanitarian NGOs were somehow caught in the middle and kicked down the pitch by the various political actors involved, against a backdrop of changing rules.

What of the exiles themselves? Some organisations did not try to return to Sudan out of principle. They did not accept the decreased humanitarian space or the compromises that return would have necessitated. Some had burned their bridges sufficiently that the likelihood of return was low. But many returned within a few months, after the dust had settled. One method of return was to change the name of the organisation or to let another national section of the organisation register in its stead. For all organisations, it was difficult to stay away, as Darfur was where humanitarian organisations were meant to be.

The Sudan case can be compared with other such incidents in the other case studies. Sudan 2009 was a case of total expulsion from the country of 13 organisations. This can be contrasted to the case of the expulsion of organisations from the Vanni as described in the Sri Lanka case study. In that case, at least discursively, the organisations were not so much forced to leave as told that staying was too unsafe. Regardless, this was also a case of corporate expulsion, albeit framed in quite a different way. It was clear from the Sri Lankan government's perspective that they did not want witnesses and that INGOs were considered enemies. Clearly a state of exception was in place and the government was acting outside normal procedures to manage INGOs. However, the government did not frame the issue so bluntly. Rather, through discursive manipulation organisations were required to leave. The expulsion was a temporary affair and organisations were not kicked out of the country.

Another case of in-country expulsion was that of humanitarian organisations being periodically denied access to the Ogaden in Ethiopia or other zones afflicted by disasters. In the case of the ICRC their expulsion has lasted for many years. These cases relate to individual organisations and how their relationship with the Ethiopian government developed, and therefore could be considered as deportations. Also, as with Sri Lanka, the organisations were not expelled from the country but only denied access to specific geographical areas of the country. These areas, however, were important to the organisations and denying them access was, in effect, punishment. This sort of internal exile reminds one of cases in Russia and the USSR where politically unreliable people were sent away to remote parts of the country as punishment of the individual, incapacitation of his or her ideas, and deterrence to others.

What these two cases have in common with Sudan is that, once expelled, the organisations became exiles, hoping for re-entry. Although remaining in the country, they were still exiled from their 'homes'. Without access to the Vanni, the Ogaden or any other zone of conflict or disaster, the organisations themselves were thrown into their own existential crises, a period of indistinction. In all of these cases, fear was chronically present: will we be denied access?

The connection between the external, the internal and the external in the internal differs between place and over time. But some generalisations can be drawn from the Sudan case in how expulsions can be seen as a form of discourse in the securitisation process.

Expulsions as discourse and the securitisation process

Were INGOs 'good citizens'? This can only be answered by first defining what good citizenship meant to the government. Being a good citizen would entail a critical mass of the following characteristics: being from and of Sudan; not being beholden to foreign governments, donors, or intergovernmental organisations; not being representatives of international norms; being embedded within the Sudanese government; and being politically reliable. International organisations did not exhibit these characteristics, almost by definition in many cases, so it was unlikely that INGOs could ever be considered good citizens. Useful, perhaps, but not good. This fact, known by both sides, put INGOs into a certain category, similar to that of an immigrant, without permanent status, always suspect and caught in an era of increased deportations – or, worse, a period where infractions were actively sought to excuse deportations. In such a context, punishment, incapacitation, deterrence and retribution were the norm and corporate expulsions from the country became reality.

Against this backdrop, the general theme of expulsion must be situated in the securitisation framework. Similar to the other case studies, the standard framework will be used to present the case.

Expulsion as securitisation

The existential threat in the case of Sudan at first glance seems clear: the threat of the ICC indictment. The president of the country – the head of state – was being threatened with arrest by an international court. Outside of a serious threat of invasion, few threats would be considered graver to a state. Such a threat also impacted the functioning of the regime, the centre of political power and the associated elite structures. Particularly in the Sudanese case, the Khartoum regime was the nexus of power that held the country together, albeit through, paradoxically, threatening to break the country apart. The referent object, therefore, was not the Sudanese people so much as the sovereign and sovereignty. In this case, it was the actual sovereign himself, the president, who was threatened. Sovereignty in such a case is also a tricky concept, as much of what can be labelled sovereignty at the practical level is protection of elite status and the benefits accrued from being at the centre of power. Sovereignty, really, was simply where the sovereign, and the elites surrounding him, resided.

The securitising agent was clearly the government, the executive, which mobilised the bureaucratic apparatus to implement the expulsion orders. But as with the other case studies, it should be asked how far there was a convergence, or divergence, between the government and the regime. The audience of discourse was the international community – the West in particular. The GoS had a number of messages to send related to the humanitarian context – INGOs were interfering with the socio-political order, they weren't needed, the humanitarian crisis was overblown – but these were beside the main point, which was that the government would not be threatened. It is plausible that the choice of response to the ICC arrest warrant – to target INGOs for expulsion – was arbitrary, albeit convenient; it could have been another symbol of the West.

The threat by the ICC certainly challenged the sovereignty of the state and could be considered a state of exception – the situation demanded firm action. The expulsions were not outside the law, but did contravene normal expectations of how states engage with INGOs, especially in the midst of a humanitarian crisis. Such a corporate expulsion is highly unusual. Proper due process was lacking and no warning had been given to the organisations. As it was clear at the time that there was a link between the ICC arrest warrant and the expulsions, a sense of unfairness was felt about the collateral damage done to the humanitarian operations the INGOs were implementing.

Expulsion as discourse

In the Sudan case study, the argument for expulsion as a form of discourse has been completed. In the case studies, a distinction has been made between a single agency deportation, within country, such as seen in Ethiopia; corporate expulsions, within country, as seen in Sri Lanka; and the corporate expulsion from the country as witnessed in Sudan. In each example, the expulsion was a form of discourse and messages were being communicated, each unique to the time and place. The Sudan case reinforces the idea that corporate expulsions can be used as discourse when the primary audience was *not* the agencies themselves but rather the Western political community in general. In the Sudan case, the INGOs expelled remained secondary targets of discourse, as was the case, to a certain extent, in the Sri Lanka case study. However, this is not to say that individual agencies, even as part of a corporate expulsion, may not be targeted for specific reasons, as was the case in Sudan, as the choice of organisations was not completely random.

Conclusion

Expulsions are a drastic measure that sends a message in a brutal way. Organisations and the international community will take notice, and as such expulsions are an effective form of discourse. Such discourse makes clear how the securitisation process is enacted and effectively defines the state of exception. Now that this final form of discourse has been examined, the next chapter will put together the lessons from the case studies to formulate a general view on the response options available to humanitarian organisations when securitised. The various forms of securitisation as described in the case studies will each entail specific responses, but some general statements can be made about the response options.

References

Aly, H. (2009). Kidnapping aid workers: Part of Sudan's strategy? *Christian Science Monitor*, 16 March. https://goo.gl/vMvsdq

Brown, W. and Harman, S. (2013). African agency in international politics. In W. Brown and S. Harman(eds). *African Agency in International Politics*. London: Routledge.

Charbonneau, L. (2009). NGO expelled from Darfur considered ICC cooperation. *Reuters*, 16 March. https://goo.gl/5iKKXm

Cockett, R. (2010). *Sudan: Darfur and the Failure of an African State*. London: Yale University Press.

Evans, R. J. (2003). *The Coming of the Third Reich*. London: Penguin Books.

Finley, M.I. (1977). *The Ancient Greeks*. London: Penguin Books.

Hassan, A. (2009). Politics of aid in Darfur: The NGO expulsions seven months on. *African Arguments*, October 16. https://goo.gl/ojQcDu

IRIN (2009a). NGO expulsion to hit Darfur's displaced. 9 March. https://goo.gl/gmdKAg

IRIN (2009b) Oxfam appeals against expulsion. 15 April. https://goo.gl/AKjWcN

Kanstroom, D. (2000). Deportation, social control, and punishment: Some thoughts about why hard laws make bad cases. *Harvard Law Review*, 11, 1889–1935.

Kleinman, M. (2009). Tough choices for agencies expelled from Darfur. Humanitarian Policy Network Report, 6 May. https://odihpn.org/blog/tough-choices-for-agencies-expelled-from-darfur/

Lumsden, D. P. (1999). Broken lives? Reflections on the anthropology of exile and repair. *Refuge*, 18(4), 30–40.

Mamdani, M. (2009). *Saviors and Survivors: Darfur, Politics, and War on Terror*. New York: Pantheon Books.

Miller, F. A. (2000) Making citizens, banishing immigrants: The discipline of deportation investigations, 1908–1913. *Left History*, 7(1), 62–88.

Pantuliano, S., Jaspars, S. and Ray, D. B. (2009). *Where to Now? Agency Expulsions in Sudan: Consequences and Next Steps*. London: HPG/ALNAP.

Reeves, E. (2009). Khartoum's expulsion of humanitarian organizations. *Sudan Tribune*, 25 March.

Rieber, A. J. (2003). Civil wars in the Soviet Union. *Kritika: Explorations in Russian and Eurasian History*, 4(1), 129–162.

Said, E. (1984). *Reflections on Exile and Other Essays*. Cambridge, MA: Harvard University Press.

Walters, W. (2002). Deportation, expulsion, and the international police of aliens. *Citizenship Studies*, 6(3), 265–292.

Walton, O. (2015). Humanitarian NGOs: Dealing with authoritarian regimes. Bath Papers in International Development and Wellbeing, 42.

Weissman, F. (2009). *Humanitarian Aid and the International Criminal Court: Grounds for Divorce*. Paris: CRASH.

7

RESPONSES TO SECURITISATION

International humanitarian NGOs have several options available to them in responding to a securitisation process. This chapter presents and discusses these various options. Organisations also have different perspectives on the adequacy and appropriateness of the response options given their differing mandates and political orientations, and these variations will also be discussed. The Sri Lanka case study is used as the baseline, and lessons from the thematic chapters are integrated into the analysis to provide nuance and depth to the discussion. The chapter ends with the development of key findings concerning how INGOs respond to being securitised.

The response matrix

Organisations have at their disposal several options when faced with being securitised. These are summarised in the chart below.[1]

Of course, these are idealised constructs. In practice, an INGO will combine features of more than one option. The chart should therefore be considered a matrix, rather than a list of discrete options.

Desecuritisation, accommodation and counter-attacking all imply remaining in active dialogue with the government. Withdrawal and concealment result in removing oneself from active negotiation – the former by removing oneself from the country, the latter by remaining in the context but trying to remain invisible. Even if an organisation chooses the desecuritisation option, there may be elements of accommodation included in the response. This will particularly be the case when heavy administrative requirements are demanded to gain access. Therefore,

---

1   Compare these INGO reactions to securitisation to Labonte and Edgerton's typology of denial, particularly the discussion of INGO options to respond to these denials, such as collaborate or turn away (Labonte and Edgerton, 2013: 51).

TABLE 7.1 Humanitarian INGO reaction options in a securitised context

	Description
Desecuritisation	To desecuritise oneself is to proactively respond, through one's own discourse, to the securitised discursive environment and the actions of the government. The goal is to moderate the negative consequences of the securitisation process, allowing for greater operational leeway. Desecuritisation demands a careful reading of the state's securitisation discourse. Targets of an organisation's desecuritisation discourse may include the government, the political elites, the general population or even other international actors.
Accommodation	To accommodate means to fulfil most, or all, of the government's demands. Accommodation entails at least partially admitting to the legitimacy of the securitisation discourse. If accommodation is depended upon as the primary response, then there will be little effort put into desecuritising oneself.
Withdrawal	To withdraw is to give up on the possibility of working in the securitised context and to leave the country. This decision may be due to the unwillingness or incapacity of the organisation to desecuritise, accommodate or counter-attack and where concealment is not an option. Withdrawal may be accompanied with an advocacy campaign or public statement.
Counter-attacking	To counter-attack is to attempt to securitise the securitising agent. This is a high-risk tactic that forgoes the defence and relies on the offence. The goal is to reach a point of securitisation equilibrium where neither party has the advantage.
Concealment	To conceal oneself is to hide away from the government as completely as possible. This can be considered an internal withdrawal. All engagement with the government ceases. Concealment lasts until the organisation is discovered or the situation improves.

prioritising the desecuritisation option does not preclude the inclusion of some elements of accommodation, nor does it take withdrawal off the agenda. But if an organisation chooses accommodation as the first and primary response, this may severely limit the organisation's ability to desecuritise, as inherent in accommodation is a tacit admission of the legitimacy of the securitisation discourse.

A note about the counter-attacking and concealment options. These are theoretical possibilities and have been included in the matrix of options for the sake of completeness. But as will be recalled from the case studies, neither option was utilised, for reasons elaborated upon below. This is not to say, however, that these options will never be used; they remain available, if only rarely used.

Sri Lanka: 2006–2007 desecuritisation

MSF analysed the GoSL discourse and made a choice to try to desecuritise itself. This process entailed an active use of its own discourse to counter the securitising discourse directed at the organisation. But as will be seen, elements of accommodation were included in the MSF response related specifically to administrative requirements. This section will trace the process MSF used in deciding on this strategy. First, MSF's analysis of the context will be presented, followed by a discussion of the internal MSF debates during this period that were based on this analysis. Next, MSF's discursive responses and the discursive indicators it used to track the GoSL's meaning are reviewed. A final section speaks more generally about the process of desecuritisation MSF used. This narrative is based on an analysis of many hundreds of MSF-H documents and a number of key informant interviews. The story told is a composite understanding gleaned from this primary source material. As such, unless pertinent or unique, the sources are not cited, however where possible a sense of which types of documents are being referred to is provided in the narrative.

MSF's understanding of the context

This section reverses the angle used in the securitisation analysis and begins the story anew from MSF's viewpoint.[2] Chapter 2 presented and analysed the GoSL's handling of the events of 2006 in relation to international humanitarian actors. The confused and at times incoherent nature of the discursive environment and of the government's actions has been noted and demonstrated. This discursive environment has been characterised as a context of securitisation. This section will examine how MSF reacted to the government's actions, and analysed and responded to the general discursive environment.

As discussed previously, MSF-H had been operational in the country continuously from 1995 until the beginning of 2004, when it left the country because the peace agreement seemed to be holding and humanitarian needs had decreased. The organisation returned at the time of the tsunami, but, as it was a short and light intervention, MSF-H did not suffer from many of the problems experienced by organisations that had remained operational or worked on development issues such as housing reconstruction. This brings the story to mid-2006, when MSF-H decided to return to Sri Lanka given the renewal of conflict.

At this time MSF-E and MSF-F were already present in the country. MSF-F had begun operations in Port Pedro and Jaffna and MSF-E was interested in starting up operations in the Mannar area. The focus of attention for MSF was on the conflict-affected populations in the north, although all sections wanted to also be

2   It will be recalled that MSF is a movement comprised of five 'sections' (headquarters), which are responsible for operations. Though this narrative is focused on MSF-Holland the presence of two other MSF operational sections – MSF-Spain (MSF-E) and MSF-France (MSF-F) – informed the thinking and action of MSF-Holland. This somewhat complicates the narrative, as it also complicates the advocacy and operations of individual MSF sections in locations where more than one section is present. But as these 'inter-sectional' dynamics were important to the decisions made by MSF-Holland, they will also factor into the retelling of the tale. As far as is feasible the following designations will be used to differentiate between the MSF actors: 'MSF' will refer collectively to the three sections present and individual section designations will be used where appropriate, i.e. MSF-H, MSF-F and MSF-E.

present in the east, specifically in the tense Batticaloa and Trincomalee areas. Gaining access to areas where active fighting was occurring, however, was extremely difficult. Complicating matters even more, at the end of September MSF-F and MSF-E were accused of vaguely specified crimes and were in the process of being expelled from the country. MSF-H, however, was told that it could remain.

As the case study analysis showed, there were several political factors, agendas and personalities behind the aborted expulsions. In MSF-H's analysis the ground had been well prepared for an 'attack' on INGOs by the GoSL and all that was needed was a 'trigger' – and this was provided when the Spanish section of MDM gave out training certificates which used the insignia of the LTTE alongside that of the GoSL Ministry of Health (MoH). MSF-H was convinced that the MSF problems began when MSF was mistaken for MDM. A high-level MSF-H official working in Sri Lanka at the time was told during this period that the government did not differentiate between the various organisations as there was 'really no difference between them', so in effect MDM and MSF were considered the same organisation. The discussion of a trigger recalls the analysis of the role of the ICC indictment on the expulsions from Sudan.

For MSF-H, there were three explanations for why it was not also threatened with expulsion. The first related to timing, as MSF-H had returned to the country too late to be involved with the trigger event. The second related to the residual good relations MSF-H had with the authorities from its former operations. And the third was simply the fact that MDM, the organisation that MSF had been mistaken for, was French and the MDM section that was involved in the incident was Spanish, and therefore MSF-France and MSF-Spain were more naturally implicated than the Dutch MSF section. To heighten this difference, MSF-Holland at this time used the Dutch designation for the organisation – Artsen Zonder Grenzen – rather than the French name.

MSF-H documentation from late 2006 paints the following picture of the thoughts and intentions of the Government of Sri Lanka and the general Sri Lankan population. MSF collectively thought that segments of the public believed that MSF was partial to, and supportive of, the LTTE, and was also part of a conspiracy by the international community to both undermine Sri Lanka's sovereignty and perpetuate the conflict through its humanitarian programming. It was felt that these perceptions created a real security risk to its staff.[3] The specifically anti-MSF stories in the media were viewed as a sub-set of the general anti-NGO sentiment as espoused by the government and communicated through the media, and which MSF saw as being 'false allegations and insinuations'. It was felt that the GoSL was either directly behind these negative stories or at least condoned them. Interestingly, the media itself was thought to be open to publishing corrections. Who or what constituted 'the government' was not well articulated, but the government was not seen to be willing to normalise MSF's position and accept the organisation's presence. Questions were asked about how to respond to this situation:

3   MSF document: 'Risk Analysis annex', 1 November 2006.

Whether by design, intense bureaucracy, coincidence or whatever, the space for humanitarian action – at least for MSF – has decreased to 1–2%. Long discussions about the whys and wherefores but the bottom line remains that we have little room left. Also agreed (but less certainly) is that, barring major and significant changes in tangible results (as opposed to good news/bad news stories in the press), MSF should not simply sit back and allow external actors to determine when we act; there has to come a time when we decide when action is needed.[4]

It was agreed by all involved that the government needed to clear up the allegations about MSF, especially as insecurity had increased due to the allegations and the 'government's ambivalence'. Although each section was in a different stage in dealing with the bureaucracy, all felt that there was an unacceptable time delay in the processing of permits and visas. It was noted that the government did not talk with one voice. For example, concerning the charges made against MSF-F and MSF-E, the Immigration Department first said that there was a police investigation, but the health minister said that it was up to the Ministry of Defence (MoD), which itself refused to give any comment on the matter. But later the controller of immigration and emigration said that the MoD told him to revalidate the organisations' visas as the investigation had been concluded. It was difficult for the MSF sections involved to understand where they stood and which department had the true story. This was thought to be partly due to excessive bureaucracy, but also partly due to unexplained antipathy the MoD felt towards MSF, which was a serious issue as the MoD was in control of all governmental decisions concerning the work of INGOs in the conflict-affected areas.

MSF of course read and analysed the same discourse as reviewed in the case study examination. In general, it was felt that there was a 'misinformation campaign' against INGOs to encourage them to leave and be replaced by Sinhalese NGOs. The MSF analysis was that the '1500 NGOs' that had arrived since the tsunami had necessitated the government rationalising the situation. In MSF's view, subjects of concern to the government were: corruption, illegal activities, misappropriation of funds and lack of respect for promises made. Another concern was that INGOs were trying to recolonise Sri Lanka. The government was also missing out on funds because of NGO tax exemptions.[5] Reports from this period reiterated that 'the government will shortly introduce an amendment to the Voluntary Social Services Organizations (Registration and Supervision) Act to ban NGOs and INGOs that act contrary to national security interests'. This was related to recommendations made by the Parliamentary Select Committee (*Daily News*, 6 October 2006). All sections considered this to be a highly unfortunate situation as Sri Lanka was a context where fighting was becoming more intense and there was a 'lack of

4   Extracted from notes from inter-sectional discussions from the beginning of October 2006 as preparation for a press conference.
5   MSF document: 'Communications report', October 2006.

medical and surgical services for civilians in conflict areas', but at the same time access to the populations in need was nearly impossible.[6] The concern for potential changes in the law should be noted and compared with similar concerns in the other case studies.

Internal debates: 'Clearing our name' and access

MSF was in 'crisis' mode in September and October 2006. In this period MSF was waiting for meetings with high-level officials in the government to try to negotiate an end to the crisis. At this point the exact status of the affected sections was still uncertain, although through various informal contacts it was understood that the government didn't have any serious issues with MSF. However, government officials could not say so formally, supposedly for reasons of 'face'. The MoD had downgraded the 'crisis' to a visa issue and from their perspective the problem had been adequately dealt with. But from MSF's perspective it had not yet been adequately dealt with without a formal, public statement on the part of the government. For all of the sections the main objective was to 'clear our name' – however, there were different views about how this was to be done. The primary objective was to ensure the security of the organisation's personnel, especially those involved with the programmes that were progressively being closed down due to the crisis. The secondary objective was to return to implementing field operations. The initial response was in two parts: first, the removal of the perception that MSF was partial to the LTTE, and second, a public announcement by the government was hoped for which would state that the charges against MSF had been dropped and the organisation had been cleared of all accusations of illegal acts. Only on this basis could access be properly negotiated.

The sections agreed that it was highly unlikely that there would be 'an overt public retraction' by the government. Crucially, MSF-H felt that it was necessary 'to be sensitive to reading a string of subtle hints, rumours and signals akin to the wall posters in Mao's China signalling a mood change – this is something we are not used to, and is alien to our occidental culture'. It was also felt that MSF collectively had missed such signals in mid-September, before the crisis had erupted, and that it was important not to miss such signals again. There was much debate about what could be expected: maybe not an official public statement but something more in the 'Asian way vein'? Or preferably something more than this, such as a public statement by an official mentioning MSF by name, if not an official retraction or apology. The government had allowed, or condoned – MSF never knew which – the publishing of the fact that MSF was allowed to stay in the country during the investigation, and this was a good start, but MSF was looking for at least one more story, even if only a statement by the police or a report in the 'police beat' section of the papers, anything which clearly stated that MSF was no longer a suspect in any ongoing investigations. It was agreed that the 'clearing our name'

6   MSF document: 'Communications officer report', October 2006.

story in principle needed coverage equivalent to the coverage given to the allegations in the first place. But in considering what sort of response to expect from the government a consensus formed that it was important to try to see the situation from the government's perspective and to be realistic. In the words of one MSF-Holland official, 'I agree that the climate is hostile to NGOs. I do not agree it is impossible to work here, it requires patience, a willingness to progress in small steps, not sledgehammer tactics and an understanding of Asian cultures'. Regardless, the frustration with the situation was clearly stated:

> We acknowledge our impotence to change this situation solely through a face-to-face strategy with the authorities (until now our public communication has been weak and limited to a small number of local journalists) … we have reached the limits of the silent advocacy strategy and our lack of public communication is bordering on complicity with a policy of hindering humanitarian access to civilians in need.

Ideas to respond to this situation were varied. One option discussed was to launch an aggressive lobbying campaign with the GoSL as well as through 'normal' NGO channels such as the Consortium of Humanitarian Agencies. Another response discussed was to put pressure at the international level, involving the Western diplomatic corps and the international press. On a domestic level it was thought that there should be more positive stories about the organisation in the local press, including open letters to the MoD. But with the notable exception of the press briefing discussed in the next section, the dialogue through the press was a 'one-way street', as MSF did not effectively use the press to communicate. MSF was 'passive in reading the papers but not reacting' to the stories, and this was thought a mistake by key MSF-H informants.

Interestingly, during this period MSF strove to accommodate to all administrative requirements. Regardless of the focus on desecuritisation, the organisation did not argue with the need to fulfil the bureaucratic requirements demanded of it to remain in the country and gain access to the areas and populations of concern. These administrative requirements related to visas, residence permits, MoUs and permissions to access the conflict-affected areas. In fact, it was the government's delay in completing these administrative tasks that created the 'crisis' in the first place. In this narrative, the existence of these parallel tracks must be understood.

Related to the above, much of the internal MSF debates revolved around the implications of the situation to MSF's current and future access.[7] Regardless of whether the delays were intentional or caused by excessive bureaucracy, the consequences were the same, and that was the inability to access the populations in need. A central (rhetorical) question was,

---

7   This section is based on 'Communications plan for Sri Lanka, Draft 18 Oct. 2006' and 'Risk Analysis annex', 1 November 2006.

if by playing the game we get access to thousands in a few months, is it worth the lives of the hundreds in the meantime? In which case we are no longer an emergency organisation but [a] development [agency]: Rebuilding broken infrastructure and building coffins not performing surgeries.

In the end, the MSF assessment of the context was that it would be a long-term conflict and therefore MSF assistance would be needed even more in the future. The 'logical conclusion' was that the organisation should not consider leaving, 'so long as there are potential victims who need our help and so long as there is even a remote possibility of accessing them then we have to keep the channels of communication open'.

Yet it was important to avoid complicity with the GoSL policies on limiting access, and red lines had to be determined. As such the question of withdrawal became increasingly more prominent in the debates. Some voices argued that 'without significant changes to access, we should decide upon withdrawal'. There were many discussions about how long to wait to make such a decision. Initially it was decided that 19 October would be the decision day (although for undocumented reasons this deadline would not be adhered to). If there was no progress by that date there would be an international media press conference in-country and outside and a posting on the MSF websites stating that 'MSF decides to leave Sri Lanka due to lack of humanitarian access'. However, there was room for flexibility depending on the circumstances. If MSF-H were able in the meantime to get its MoU signed and the first visas issued allowing access to Vavuniya, this would then allow moderation of the coverage. Some voices thought that it was too short a time to give to the government, especially given that the government was preparing for new peace talks with the LTTE on 28/29 October. At times, the MSF discussions were highly introspective and did not take into account the general political context or the fact that NGOs in general were being securitised and it was not only a problem with MSF. In the end the period of trying, waiting, debates and desecuritisation lasted well into December, at which time progress was finally made on obtaining the needed paperwork to be able to stay and work (discussed in more detail below). Regardless of the periodic arbitrary decision deadlines that were set, a final decision to withdraw was difficult for the organisation to make.

Although the feeling of crisis in the documentation from this period is palpable, a retrospective MSF-H report written at a later time admitted that 'the issue may have looked more important to us than to the rest of Sri Lanka, in other words, our concerns may have been exaggerated by paranoia/egotism' and 'the effects of the slanders in the press – at least in terms of risks to our staff and programmes – [were] much less than originally thought'. But most interestingly, the report also stated that in the future 'what we should *not* do is to put improving our public reputation (beyond that needed for security) before struggling for access – our energies should be focused on getting the programmes running'. Thus, the very choice of the desecuritisation option was questioned. Was desecuritisation a necessary concern? Did it assist the organisation in gaining access in any way? Were other choices available and worthier, even those not considered at the time?

Regardless of the after-the-fact questioning, the discussions from this period paint an intriguing picture of the options under consideration, or not under consideration, to respond to the situation.[8] Withdrawal before attempting other options was never on the table, though withdrawing if all else failed was repeatedly discussed. Accommodation without priority being given to desecuritisation was never discussed as an option, being outside the bounds of MSF thinking during a period of crisis. And lying low was also not seriously considered – quite the contrary, as it was felt that it was necessary to do more to actively promote a positive image of the agency as well as battle the negative images. Counter-attacking was never seriously considered as an option. In the final analysis, a desecuritisation (with some accommodation) approach was decided upon. The targets of desecuritisation were both the government and the general population. The next section will review the actual discursive responses utilised by the organisation.

Discursive responses

During the crisis period, several attempts were made to desecuritise the organisation and hopefully in the process create the space for operations. These attempts included letters to the government, press work and advocacy activities with international actors. This section will review a number of these efforts. It should be understood, however, that desecuritisation activities happened on a daily basis and this discussion will only review a select number of activities.

A collective MSF letter written on 29 September to the minister of human rights and disaster management is illustrative of both the type of dialogue MSF had with the GoSL during this period and the themes under discussion. The letter stated that MSF had arrived back in the country in June and was working closely with the MoH in assessing needs, and 'to facilitate the implementation of new activities, MSF has undertaken the usual procedures to obtain necessary permissions and clearances'. However, MSF had been 'verbally informed' that 'along with other NGOs, [we] will be denied further visas and asked to leave Sri Lanka. The reasons for this are unclear at this time, but we feel strongly that it may be due to some misunderstanding'. As far as MSF was concerned, the organisation had always acted appropriately and with transparency. MSF wondered if it wasn't possible that the activities of another agency had been mistaken for those of MSF and that expatriate personnel working for another agency had been mistaken for MSF staff. The message at this point in time was that MSF was uncertain why it was being targeted but was sure that it was a mistake. This letter also gives a clear indication of the important role administrative requirements played in the negotiations with the government.

8   This section is based on the following documents: 'Internal MSF discussion notes', 14 Oct. 2006; 'Sri Lanka: Situation Analysis and Response', 16 October 2006; and 'Report by the Heads of Mission of MSF Holland, Spain & France' (undated).

When such letters did not have the desired effect, other options had to be considered. One activity as part of the response in the beginning of October was to hold a press conference to give MSF's side of the story.[9] Senior MSF officials from Europe were in attendance. Prior to the press briefings, the following main points were outlined for discussion:

- MSF has assisted many people in an impartial manner.
- MSF is in Sri Lanka because the needs are acute but the organisation will leave when this is no longer the case.
- MSF supports and works with local health structures.
- MSF believes that if the authorities do not recognise the value of our work, then our value is diminished.
- Security of MSF personnel is of prime importance and the organisation believes that security is reduced when the population and authorities do not acknowledge the organisation's neutrality.
- If insecurity rises too much then MSF will reconsider its continued presence despite the recognised needs.
- The unfair and inaccurate allegations against MSF must stop and a clear statement is demanded from the government whether they value MSFs work or not.
- It will be the people of Sri Lanka who will suffer if MSF cannot remain.

As a result of this press conference the MSF narrative was put into the public sphere and various articles relating the MSF side of the story appeared over the coming days. A *Sunday Nation* article paraphrased the MSF message as saying that 'working in Sri Lanka during the last few months had been difficult due to increased violence in the North and the East and the hostility aimed at them by certain facets in the civil society' (*Sunday Nation*, 8 October 2006). The focus on *civil* society should be noted. Interestingly, the *Sunday Nation* contacted the French Embassy and 'learnt that the MSF considers the situation as grave and they are planning to issue a media brief early this week'. In another story MSF was described as 'one of the INGOs accused of having acted contrary to national security interests', and MSF was summarised as saying that 'it expects a swift resolution to the problem and stands committed to alleviate suffering in an unbiased manner' (*Daily News*, 6 October 2006). A story in the *Island*, 'Tell us are we welcome or not – MSF', also described the press conference (Gunaratna, 2006). The sub-headline was that MSF had 'appealed to the government to tell whether they are "welcome here or not" at a hurriedly called briefing'. MSF was also reported to have said that the government didn't 'speak with one voice'. MSF was quoted as saying that they had been 'put into the basket of wrong-doers'. The basic issue from MSF's viewpoint involved the negative media reports concerning the organisation and its desire for 'the government to clear up these allegations, one way or the other'.

---

9   MSF document: 'MSF Core Messages for Press Briefing' (undated).

Although MSF had been told by various officials that a police investigation was ongoing, MSF was said to have stated that the police had not yet visited the organisation. Ironically, during the press briefing itself, officers from the Criminal Investigation Department (CID) actually arrived at the MSF office related to the police investigation. The police did not bring any formal charges against MSF and the visit was described in an internal MSF report as 'a polite investigation'. Intriguingly, MSF noted in another internal report that the details about the actual accusations against it were only confirmed during the police visit and that the charges had been changed from the originally reported 'conspiracy to assassinate senior government officials' to 'merely criticising the Department of Immigration'.

A letter[10] to the president three weeks later gives a more comprehensive view of the situation. After stating that MSF had been in the country providing medical assistance since 1986 and, as always, stood ready to respond to a crisis, the organisation complained that access was being denied: 'Administrative and bureaucratic obstacles [were] resulting in a lack of permits and permissions' and were preventing the organisation from being able to work, even though 'the media reports that people need assistance in these areas; the MoH requested help in these areas. The needs are clear'. The letter ended with a plea:

> Your Excellency, you have on many occasions publicly called for support of humanitarian causes and care for the people of this country. We urge you to allow MSF to help your people by facilitating our access to those in need. A prompt decision on your part will see MSF medical teams working alongside MoH personnel helping to ease the suffering of hundreds, if not thousands of Sri Lankans.

Not through MSF's instigation the letter also appeared in the *Island* on 20 October 2006. In the accompanying story MSF was said to have offered to help the government to treat the war wounded 'in the backdrop of reports' that government hospitals were unable to cope with the large number of war wounded. As the *Island* was considered to be a sensationalist newspaper, one more likely to be read by the general population (at least by those who could and would read the English language media), MSF was uncertain why it would have reprinted such a letter, especially when it was framed by the government's lack of capacity to deal with the medical needs of the war wounded. Or was this itself the reason? Using the MSF-H view on signals, was this an Asian way signal to indicate that MSF was indeed welcomed?

Whether the analysis of the signals was correct or not, MSF's administrative problems began to subside in November. As such a whole series of letters were sent to GoSL contacts thanking them for their assistance. An example is a letter sent on 9 November to the minister of foreign affairs. MSF acknowledged and appreciated

---

10 MSF document, 'An Open Letter to His Excellency Mahinda Rajapaksa, President, Democratic Socialist Republic of Sri Lanka, October 19, 2006'.

the efforts of the ministry and the minister 'in facilitating the granting of approvals for Médecins Sans Frontières in Sri Lanka'. The organisation had in fact seen results of this facilitation, and it was 'clear that there has been a general shift in attitudes towards the value of MSF to the people of Sri Lanka'. MSF expected that 'the final hurdles' were to be cleared over the next few weeks, at which point 'the first teams should be in the field, aiding those in need'. The letter closed with the line 'on behalf of MSF, and the people of Sri Lanka, our thanks to your Honour and your staff'. One cannot help but wonder how such a statement was interpreted by a government official, but it does speak volumes about the often paternalistic attitude INGOs have towards the populations for whom they work.

However, the above optimism was short-sighted as the administrative issues were not resolved in the envisioned timeframe. The visa issue had in fact not been solved and expatriate staff could still not enter the country. It was thought to be the MoD which was holding up the process. In an attempt to rectify the situation – namely, to speed up the process – the three MSF sections agreed upon the following tactics.[11] First, release an update of the current situation to all interested parties (non-public) including selected Sri Lankan diplomats outside of Sri Lanka. Second, meet with key embassies and high commissions to see if they would intervene with the MoD and request it to issue work permits as soon as possible. Third, meet with relevant ministries – the MoH, the Ministry of Human Rights and the Ministry of Foreign Affairs – to give them the message directly and in person. Fourth, discuss the MSF situation with UNOCHA and 'the apparent contradiction of having us on the list to access un-cleared [conflict] areas while not being allowed to bring staff in'. And fifth, send letters to the MoD with the above messages. It was envisioned to allow two-and-a-half weeks (to 15 December) for the above activities to produce notable results. The minimum acceptable result was MSF expatriates being granted residence visas without special exceptions. As was discussed earlier in the year, it was decided that without such concrete progress a public campaign would be implemented. For such public communications, the common themes would be:

- MSF cannot work in a continuous state of delay and procrastination; it is not possible for us to constantly put qualified medical personnel on standby for months on end.
- MSF calls for someone in authority to inform us how much longer we must wait before expatriates will be allowed to work in Sri Lanka.
- We do not know why the process is slow, however, the overall delays are unacceptable; MSF no longer accepts the minor excuses for each trivial delay of a few days without looking at the bigger picture: months have gone by without the ultimate target being achieved, namely the provision of medical assistance to those in need in Point Pedro, Mannar and Vavuniya.

11 'Sri Lanka Communications, November 28, 2006, MSF-all sections'.

At this point in time MSF still did not know how much of the delay was excessive bureaucracy, how much was internal politics ('had little to do with MSF itself') and how much was 'deliberate blocking' and 'had a lot to do with MSF itself'. All sections had received verbal encouragements by government officials and theoretically MSF's presence was welcomed. As far as MSF could tell there were 'no objections to our interventions at any level'. In fact, all sections had received a letter from the MoH stating that they would 'be able to work at [their] relevant projects and should proceed with getting expatriates into the country'. Yet this was not the case in reality. MSF's main concerns at this time (the end of November) were:

> The constant delays in the system that seem too long to be simply a matter of excessive bureaucracy; actions that should take days take weeks or months. The lack of certainty; procedures and rules change constantly seemingly with new requirements added with each visit. The subsequent inability to forecast how long the process of getting staff into the field will take (if ever!)

The next step, in December, was to send a series of letters to external actors, including to a wide variety of embassies and UN agencies, as well as the ICRC. A letter to the American ambassador is a good example of these. It stated that, although formal indications had been given by the MoH that the administrative problems would be solved soon and remembering that such formal, written communications were considered to be much more ironclad than Asian way verbal communications, 'paradoxically, our efforts to get expatriates into the country are currently blocked by the MoH'. The letter continued to remark that

> MSF's main concern at this time is the simple fact that despite the months of endeavouring to meet all the bureaucratic hurdles thrown at us and despite the support of some able people in the government, we are still no closer to our main objective of helping patients in the North.

MSF asked for support in calling for the Sri Lankan government to:

- speedily process all outstanding memoranda of understanding, applications for visas and associated papers, and other permissions needed to get qualified and experienced medical personnel into those areas identified as in need;
- actively assist MSF to set up their interventions to assist Sri Lankans;
- make time commitments to MSF regarding how long it will take to get permission for personnel to start work (from time of application) so intelligent plans could be made for staffing without depriving others in need around the world.

The next step if such diplomatic support was not helpful was to start a public campaign. Finally, though, the problems were solved before it was necessary to 'go public'. For an unknown reason, but possibly as a result of the diplomatic pressure, the dam had broken and by February 2007 the situation had gone 'back to normal' according to an article on MSF in the *Island* ('MSF returns to the north', 20 February 2007). In this article MSF stated that it had obtained clearance from the MoD and signed an agreement with the MoH to open surgical programmes in Point Pedro, Mannar and Vavuniya, and on 21 December 2006 a MSF team had returned to the Jaffna Peninsula to start the programme there. The article goes into detail about the programme. Without knowing the background, anyone reading the story would have thought that starting the programme had been a relatively unproblematic endeavour.

A retrospective report on the September to December 2006 period sums up MSF-Holland's experience during this period:

> In the post-tsunami period, there is some suspicion of NGO's and their activities in general, with reports of NGO's supporting LTTE. Regulations and restrictions on activities and access to populations in the north and east of the country have been tightened. MSF suffered directly from this, with MSFE and MSFF being at one stage 'banned' and asked to leave the country. This was eventually resolved with the intervention of several higher up and key actors from both MSF and the international community. All approvals must ultimately go through the Ministry of Defence (MoD). The high level of suspicion combined with the increased levels of bureaucracy and unclear government procedures have led to long delays in processing of visas and to get MoU to allow projects to commence.

From MSF-Holland's perspective the administrative crisis was over and it was time to re-engage with the humanitarian context.

Discourse indicators

The next question to be addressed in this chapter is how MSF read the discursive environment. What discourse analysis tools did the organisation use to track changes in the discursive context? In the difficult September to December period MSF-Holland was concerned about (again) missing the 'Asian way' signals communicated by the government. These 'signals' were thought of as messages indirectly communicated to the designated recipient via means other than face-to-face or written (official) communications, allowing for 'plausible deniability' on the part of the government. But more than being messages to specific actors, such as MSF, or types of actors, such as humanitarian INGOs, these signals were also thought to be directed at certain segments of the population, such as the political elites, or even the population as a whole. In the case of the political elites the objective would be to give indications about how the actor, or actors, should be engaged with. In the case of the general population the objective would be to justify the policies and behaviour of the government.

In an effort to understand the changing nature of the government's attitudes towards humanitarian INGOs, MSF-H used various indicators to mark discursive changes, such as media stories and speeches by government officials. The aim was to locate sources of discourse that would allow signs to be read. But beyond the need to gauge the government's attitude, knowledge of which would inform the organisation's approach to negotiations, there was a secondary objective to the monitoring of discursive practice. This objective related to MSF's desire to know what information the general public was receiving, as it was considered important that there was also a change in the public's perception of INGOs. The organisation felt that some of the security risks its staff faced were derived from the negative attitude towards INGOs held by the general population, and as such it was vital to understand what sort of information was directed at them. Therefore, the concern was not limited to what the government thought; the organisation was as interested in what the general population was thinking. The viewpoint mirrored in an interesting way the government's securitisation objective. This section will review what some of these sources of discourse were, how they were used as indicators, and the analysis MSF-H had of them. To do so a few of the sources will be reviewed in detail.

Referring back to the timeline of negative media stories presented above, it will be recalled that the timeline also marked contextual events which were on MSF's radar, particularly political events that were occurring at the time. The domestic political situation was watched closely as the political manoeuvrings were considered to be relevant to the changing status of INGOs. MSF expected that a change in the attitude towards INGOs would coincide with the arrival of a 'new political environment', such as the JVP losing their influence in the GoSL and the subsequent rise of the UNP's political fortunes. As seen in chapters 2 and 3, the JVP played a leading role in the anti-NGO rhetoric and policies. The JVP was behind the Parliamentary Select Committee on the role of NGOs and much of the negative discourse concerning NGOs came from JVP representatives or from newspaper editors sympathetic to the JVP and JHU agendas. Therefore, if the political weight of the JVP was lessening this might have a positive impact on how INGOs were perceived. Other political events were also investigated by MSF for signs of a changing attitude to INGOs, such as speeches given by President Rajapaksa that mentioned NGOs, of which there were many. Three of these speeches are analysed below. Two of these were made at key international events which took place in September – the Non-Aligned Movement (NAM) summit in Havana, Cuba, and the yearly UN General Assembly debate in New York.

The NAM summit was held in mid-September and President Rajapaksa played a prominent role in the meetings (*Island*, 17 September 2006). The NAM at that time was composed of 118 member states. One of the key issues at the NAM summit, as well as for the UN General Assembly meeting which closely followed it, was the fight against terrorism, and one in which Rajapaksa stressed in his speech: 'All of us together need to find innovative means and ways to combat terrorism, as it poses a grave threat to the political and economic well-being, sovereignty and territorial integrity of nation-states' (*Island*, 18 September 2006). Rajapaksa chaired the opening session of the final day. But it was a side meeting that drew the interest of MSF (*Island*, 17 September 2006). Rajapaksa had a one-to-one meeting with UN Secretary General Kofi Annan in which he stated that 'the Sri Lankan security forces had been compelled to take measures to defend themselves in the face of widespread provocations by the LTTE'. This statement was necessitated by the repeated calls by the international community to the GoSL to decrease the level of violence in the conflict with the LTTE. President Rajapaksa also

> noted that access to areas of conflict had been given to the ICRC and UN agencies for relief work. However, the government would provide such access only to internationally recognized NGOs as there were some NGOs that did not perform a useful function.

This was viewed by MSF as a positive statement on access, even if conditional in nature. It was important that it was a public statement and that it was reported in the Sri Lankan media. This story followed closely on another reference made on access in an article in the *Island* (14 September 2006). Notwithstanding so much criticism of NGOs in the press, the President's Office had 'invited national and humanitarian international aid agencies to join with the government to support internally displaced persons in Muttur and Trincomalee'. Such a statement was understood to be primarily a rhetorical device for international consumption, but it was still a positive indicator for those watching for indicative signs of improvement.

The final communiqué of the summit itself contained a few relevant points for INGOs seeking to understand the general perspective of developing states vis-à-vis INGOs (*Island,* 14 September 2006). Four paragraphs were of especial interest. In the first the NAM condemned the increasing attacks on humanitarian personnel but also stated that 'humanitarian agencies and their personnel should respect the laws of the countries they work in and the principles of neutrality and non-interference, as well as cultural, religious and other values of the population in the countries where they operate'. Such a statement was indicative of the two-sided nature of the relationship between INGOs and states. INGOs should not be attacked, but INGOs should also remember to work within certain political, legal, and cultural parameters. In addition, a warning was given that

> The provision of humanitarian assistance must not be politicised and must be in full respect of the principles of humanity, neutrality and impartiality as set forth in General Assembly Resolution 46/182 and its annex as providing the guiding principles for the coordination of humanitarian assistance, and emphasised that all UN humanitarian entities and associated organisations must act in accordance with their respective mandates, humanitarian international law and national law … . In this context, they stressed that humanitarian

assistance should be provided under the principle of request and consent of the affected country.

As such the Non-aligned Movement rejected 'the so-called "right"' of humanitarian intervention, which has no basis either in the UN Charter or in international law. These were clear signals to humanitarian INGOs that there were limits to humanitarian assistance. As an organisation that was associated with this 'right of intervention' and even contained the idea of 'without borders' in its name and identity, MSF was well aware of this perspective, which was held by most states. In the Sri Lanka context consent was being requested by MSF and the fact that it was not forthcoming was the major issue to be addressed. The GoSL's perspective on this very question – was consent to be given to MSF? – was in fact the core of what was being tracked by the organisation. As it was understood that decisions came down from the top, the president's perspective was especially important to monitor.

Immediately following the NAM summit, the 61st United Nations General Assembly debate took place in New York at the end of September. The theme was 'Implementing a Global Partnership for Development'. Discussions were also held on the UN Comprehensive Global Counter-Terrorism Strategy.[12] As was the tradition, every head of state or government made a speech, and President Rajapaksa's speech was given on 20 September. In his speech Rajapaksa characterised Sri Lanka as having been 'influenced by the core Buddhist values of non-violence, loving kindness, compassion, equanimity and mindfulness'. Related to the discussion of the conflict the president made reference to Sri Lanka being chair of the Ad-hoc Committee on Measures to Eliminate International Terrorism and said that all involved with this issue would 'spare no effort to realize the international legal framework to facilitate our common struggle against terrorism'. The speech touched on a number of issues related to the humanitarian situation in Sri Lanka. A clear statement was made on access to humanitarian agencies which was very similar to that made at the time of the NAM summit: 'As a responsible government, we will continue to provide unhindered access to conflict-affected areas to the ICRC, to UN Agencies and to other recognized humanitarian agencies'. Concerning the actual humanitarian situation, it was characterised in the following way:

> Over 53,000 Muslims were evicted from their homes by the LTTE, following the recent violence. They are the innocent victims of the LTTE's ruthless policies. Following government counter measures, almost all of these have now returned to their homes. The government has assumed responsibility to

12 See the statement by H.E. Sheikha Haya Rashid al Khalifa, President of the United Nations General Assembly, 19 September 2006. www.un.org/webcast/ga/61/pdfs/kha lifa-e.pdf [last accessed 25 March 2015].

provide medical supplies, food and other essential items to the Internally Displaced Persons living in the affected areas.

In any such setting it is of course understandable that a government will advertise its role in responding to a crisis. In this case the government was making clear that it was responsible for attending to the crisis and the needs of the affected population and that it was the legal entity responsible for deciding on the parameters of access for humanitarian agencies to the conflict-affected zones. As with the NAM statements, international actors were welcome as long as they played by the rules as set down by the state. Such a statement, though, was still considered by MSF to be a positive indication of governmental attitudes towards humanitarian organisations as it did provide potential space for negotiations.

Other international bodies were also monitored by MSF. The Tokyo Donors' Conference was a post-ceasefire agreement on reconstruction funding mechanisms and the Co-Chairs – Norway, the European Union, Japan and the United States – met periodically. In the midst of the developing crisis the co-chairs issued a statement of concern about the humanitarian situation. As part of his response to these concerns, President Rajapaksa agreed to the formation of a consultative committee chaired by the minister for human rights and disaster management and comprising key government officials, inclusive of the MoD. Importantly, the committee was 'to meet key NGOs and their representatives on a regular basis to address matters of common concern'. In a statement the president 'emphasised that the GoSL would continue to facilitate humanitarian access to the conflict-affected areas keeping in mind security considerations', and expressed his 'appreciation of the contribution that many NGOs and humanitarian agencies were making towards assisting the Government's efforts to provide essential services to conflict-affected areas' (*Island*, 10 October 2006).[13] As this statement was aimed at the Sri Lankan audience it was thought particularly indicative of the government's attitude by MSF.

Press articles were characterised by MSF on how 'intellectual' the audience was that read the different newspapers. There was strong debate between different MSF officials about the benefits of 'intellectual' over 'sensationalist' newspapers. The *Mirror*, for example, was seen to be targeting the intelligentsia, as opposed to the more sensationalist *Island*. Some thought that editorials in an 'intellectual paper' should not be considered reflective of a position of the government and in fact would not contribute to the clearing of MSF's name. In this view, what was needed was 'some news in the newspapers where the common public can have access and easy understanding of the situation', rather than articles, editorials or books that would not reach the general public. This fits the agenda of desecuritisation introduced above, which focused on how the GoSL was thought to be communicating with the common person rather than the political elites. However,

---

13   See also 'Sri Lanka Co-Chairs Call For Immediate Cessation of Hostilities', Press Statement, Sean McCormack, Washington, DC, 11 August 2006. http://2001–2009.state.gov/r/pa/prs/ps/2006/70312.htm [last accessed 25 March 2015].

not everyone within MSF agreed with this analysis, and some in fact argued the contrary view. Regardless, a reading of the internal documentation shows that the former view won out. In this discussion, it should be remembered that the news- papers mentioned were English-language publications and so were not read by the less educated segments of the Sri Lankan population.

Asian way desecuritisation?

The above analysis shows that the process used by MSF-Holland to analyse and react to the situation mirrored that of the GoSL's, in the true sense of being the mirror opposite. Whereas the GoSL challenged the presence of NGOs and through discourse attempted to securitised them, MSF-H examined the actions and discourse of the GoSL and tried to improve their relationship through a process of desecuritisation. One of the prime audiences for both parties was the general population. The GoSL wished to justify its actions in restricting access to INGOs and MSF-H wished to convince the general population that it was not a security threat, therefore decreasing its insecurity. Of course, this was not the whole picture as MSF-H's relationship with the GoSL was constructed in other ways as well. There were many communications – direct and indirect – between MSF-H and the GoSL, particularly related to MSF-H's request to the authorities to de-restrict its activities. But in each case the objective of the GoSL was to portray MSF-H as a threat and the hope of MSF-H was to convince relevant actors that it was not a threat. In this light, the intellectual/sensationalist debate was informative. But in practice the population was not substantially engaged with, and other international actors, especially diplomatic actors, were in fact relied upon to provide leverage with the GoSL.

One aspect missing from the attempted desecuritisation process, interestingly, was principles, particularly given how important principles normally were in negotiations and locating the organisation's identity. The identity as presented by MSF was that of a medical organisation; the humanitarian norm was poorly represented in MSF's thinking and action. To MSF the core problematic was that there were needs, a lack of access, and something had to be done to rectify the situation. MSF also did not frame the situation in terms of dichotomies in the same way as the GoSL did, except for the Asian–Western pairing. To MSF the Asian way perspective was important in defining how the organisation approached the discursive practices of the GoSL. The other dichotomies used by the GoSL were barely represented in MSF's discourse analysis.

It cannot be concluded if the desecuritisation process as implemented by MSF was fully, or partially, responsible for the organisation's success in achieving access in early 2007. As it is clear that not only MSF was affected during this period – all organisations had problems with access and administration, and NGOs in general were securitised in the press – it is uncertain whether MSF's actions had more than a minor effect, particularly since most organisations were able to return to a 'normal' situation in early 2007. This question, though, needs more research. If the return on the desecuritisation investment is low, it may not be a worthwhile response option.

Sri Lanka: 2008–2009 desecuritisation

The MSF-Holland response[14]

This section will move on to the 2008/9 period, as this era was the next major test for INGOs. While the 2006 period was dominated by domestic issues, the next crisis point saw international influences increasing in importance. If the extent of the securitisation process can be questioned in the 2006 period, with the situation 'going back to normal' by early 2007, it will be seen that there was no question about how far securitisation went in the 2008/9 phase, when bare life was exposed.

The expulsion and fall-out

It will be remembered that almost all humanitarian organisations were, in effect, expelled from the area of active fighting in September 2008. The key question to be examined here is why MSF-H chose not to denounce the expulsion. The organisation fully expected, as did all other observers, that the conflict would escalate, and as such there would be a future role for an emergency humanitarian medical organisation. At issue was whether speaking out about the expulsion, or more precisely the denied access to the Vanni, would improve the likelihood of gaining access or would hinder a successful negotiation. In the end MSF-H decided that speaking out would not in fact help the situation and therefore decided not to speak out publicly about the lack of access. The rationale for this conclusion can be summarised in the following explanation from a senior manager's after-the-fact evaluation of the organisation's decision-making during this period: 'If Ban Ki Moon, Obama, Milliband [the British Foreign Secretary at the time] and Kouchner [one of the original founders of MSF and at the time the Minister of Foreign Affairs of France] couldn't get INGOs access then MSF wasn't going to be able to influence the situation'.[15] This was a humble, yet realistic, appraisal of the organisation's lack of leverage to influence the decisions of the government concerning access to the conflict zone. In addition, if diplomatic representatives of the international community were often accused of being LTTE supporters at heart, then MSF understood that 'NGOs like MSF that [had] only worked on one side of the conflict (with the Tamil population) were viewed as being less than neutral'.[16]

14 This section is based on internal MSF documentation as well as interviews with senior MSF-Holland managers who held positions of responsibility for the Sri Lankan mission, in the Amsterdam headquarters and in Sri Lanka, during the 2008/9 period.
15 MSF-Holland General Director (MSF-H GD), 'Chrono, Negotiations & Outcomes of MSF's Serendib Negotiations', MSF-Holland, Amsterdam, February 2010.
16 HAD, 'Sri Lanka: Context Analysis and Strategic Direction', MSF-Holland, Amsterdam, 28 May 2009.

Notwithstanding this pessimistic assessment of the organisation's position, there was also a hopeful side to the analysis. Though MSF felt that it had been grouped together with the rest of the international community in the minds of the Sri Lankan authorities, and negatively at that, it was also believed that MSF had through its history established for itself a unique space that could be leveraged in negotiations. For, unlike most other NGOs, MSF had not newly arrived in the post-tsunami reconstruction phase and its presence had always been related to the conflict. While this fact had meant that the organisation had often had a tense relationship with the government and, as mentioned, there was a residual impression of a lack of neutrality, MSF had also been 'responsible for the bulk of the delivery of healthcare to the LTTE-controlled area during the worst of the conflict, and we did so responsibly and in ongoing dialogue with the government'. This history of cooperation, relevancy and usefulness was considered an asset when entering into negotiations over access.

The organisation's history was therefore a two-edged sword – the operational history was viewed as a potential drawback in that the focus on the conflict-affected Tamil population probably called into question the organisation's neutrality, but that long history was also a positive era of negotiation and operational relevancy which had been respected by the government. Although probably a fair assessment of the impact of the organisation's history, for the September 2008 to May 2009 period the negative aspects of this history won out as far as accessing the Vanni was concerned. The government was adamant in how it portrayed the situation and its prosecution of the war was to continue in the same vein until the final defeat of the Tigers. This was a period when the conflict was being labelled a humanitarian rescue operation by the Sri Lankan military and there was heavy use of 'war on terror' rhetoric to justify the military's actions and nullify the Western critique, a critique that was neither respected nor appreciated. Residual positive memories of previous periods may have assisted certain organisations in regaining access after the conflict was over, but during the heart of war the very status of INGO was enough to make such organisations fundamentally suspect and a threat.

MSF-H's characterisation of the GoSL was realistic and far from naïve. The government was not a 'gentle or benign one', but this could not be expected of a government that had been faced with a long-term civil war. The GoSL had been 'willing to undertake harsh actions of questionable legality in pursuit of their military agenda', and had tried, often quite successfully, to manoeuvre the international community away from criticism of its conduct. As part of this strategy the government had tried hard to show that it respected IHL and human rights law and was attending to the needs of its population. As such the government had been 'meticulous' in at least appearing to follow the internationally respected norms of conduct in times of civil conflict.

MSF-H also desired to remain correct in its behaviour. Communicating about the humanitarian conditions within the Vanni was discussed, but the idea was discounted as the organisation had no presence and thus no operational credibility upon which to witness and communicate. Additionally, the ICRC was present and was communicating the conditions they saw. The issue was not as much that information was not getting out about what was happening, rather that no subsequent positive actions were seen to be taken by the GoSL, at least in the view of most international observers. Another voice was therefore not needed and in the organisation's view it would not have assisted in MSF-H's fight for access or aided the situation of the conflict-affected population. It was repeatedly stated in MSF-H documentation that the objective of communicating was to improve the conditions faced by the population, not to make MSF-H feel better for having spoken out.

From September 2008 until January 2009, then, MSF-H, along with many other organisations, waited on the sidelines, silent, expecting the worst but unable to respond in any meaningful way to those caught up in the fighting in the Vanni. MSF-H anticipated the time it could assist the displaced flowing out of the Vanni. Access to the Menik Farm internment camp (set up late 2008 for the displaced from the fighting) was not forthcoming until February and then only to provide supplementary feeding – all other types of interventions were barred. But it was not that the organisation was inactive before this time. Public silence in external communications about the expulsion did not mean that there were no behind-the-scenes advocacy activities. In the November to December 2008 period a number of advocacy meetings were held in Colombo concerning access issues and other meetings were being planned for Geneva.

Thus, by December 2008 access looked dire. No agency wanted to speak out publicly. There was a lack of journalists and INGOs on the ground and so a decreasing amount of concrete information was available. For MSF, it was stated again that public communications had to be for a good reason and not to make the organisation feel better. But there was concern that silence would be equated to condoning the situation. What was being said by not saying anything? If no one spoke out would this be read to mean that the situation wasn't too bad?

In a retrospective MSF analysis it was admitted that tactical errors may have been made in the 2008/9 period, but it was stressed that, whatever the organisation had or had not done or could have done, humanitarian space had been in very short supply in Sri Lanka.[17] In MSF-H's view the GoSL had a plan for ending the war and it had been determined to follow through with it regardless of the criticism directed against it. Aid actors were allowed to participate in its implementation under strict conditions and had to forget about the principle of independent humanitarian action and unhindered access. The margin to negotiate was extremely thin.

This brings the discussion to the question of the confidentiality clause. What happens when the government completes the securitisation process and attempts to take away even the voices of organisations?

17 MSF-Holland Humanitarian Affairs Department report, 'Line in the sand: States' restrictions on humanitarian space' (2010).

The confidentiality clause[18]

In April and May 2009 MSF-H faced another dilemma, that of the demand by the GoSL that renewed, or new, Memoranda of Understanding (MoUs) would require the signing of confidentiality clauses that were meant to severely limit the ability of international NGOs to publicly communicate. This theme has already been reviewed from the government's perspective. This section analyses MSF-H's reaction to the requirement. Three aspects of the internal confidentiality clause debate will be discussed: the role of negotiation, internally and externally; the dilemma as an identity issue; and the implications concerning changes in organisational practice if such a clause were to be signed.

As with any government demand or request, MSF-H first had to decide whether it would comply or not. If yes, then the question would turn to how it would negotiate its compliance with the government. Interestingly, in this case the internal decision step was itself a difficult process of internal negotiation as the issue impacted directly on the organisation's witnessing role. As such the question was very sensitive and the debate became quite heated within the organisation. To some the confidentiality clause was not a banning of communications but simply a requirement of consultation before communications were made. The clause ended with the phrase: 'All information regarding the construction or service provision shall be provided to the MoH and no public comments shall be made by the partner, *without the concurrence of the Secretary, Ministry of Health* [italics added].' To others, however, it was clear that the intent was to gag organisations regardless of the logic of the wording. Irrespective of the reading of the clause, would the clause really be binding? Would it not, in fact, be possible to ignore it if the urge to speak out became overwhelming? Some felt that it was facile to state that the clause could be ignored if needed. Wouldn't breaking such a commitment undermine 'the organization's credibility as a reliable negotiation partner'? Some argued that 'such MoUs do not really change the reality on the ground, and that the clause does not make speaking out more risky than it already is', but such views were questioned by others in the organisation. And if signing was a 'voluntary act', and if there were in fact dire consequences, it would be hard then to complain about being gagged if the gag was put into one's mouth willingly.

In the end MSF-H decided to sign the MoU in May, as MSF-F had in April. In the final analysis it was considered that the price was not too high to pay to maintain a presence. The organisation would try to stay within the parameters as set down by the MoU. If a situation arose where the need to speak out was compelling then there would always be the possibility to ignore the MoU and risk being expelled. Interestingly, in a real sense there was no room for negotiation with the government on this question. On the part of the GoSL, in order for there to be a negotiation there had to be something to negotiate for, but in fact there

---

18 This section is based on HAD, 'Line in Sand' (2010), and interviews with MSF-Holland senior managers.

was nothing the GoSL wanted from INGOs which was worth backing down from its plan to devoice INGOs. They could potentially be useful if they stayed, but only if they kept quiet. At that point in time there were more pressing issues for the GoSL to be concerned about than the fall-out from organisations *choosing* not to stay by not agreeing to a clause in a MoU, a clause the government felt it could adequately explain and justify. Some within MSF, though, argued that there was something for the GoSL to negotiate, as they would not have asked for such a clause if they were not afraid of INGOs' voices. In this view, the government was in fact negotiating access rather than giving organisations a choice to leave. According to this analysis, MSF-H had more leverage than it realised and should have refused to sign. This viewpoint, though held by very senior managers, did not win out against the operational imperative to sign with the assurance that the organisation could then stay and hope to save lives.

Following from the above, for both sides the issue was framed as an identity question. For the GoSL it clearly was a justifiable requirement put into place by a sovereign state, as it had the right and, in its view, responsibility to control the activities of external agents as has been reviewed in detail. For MSF-H the question was how to deal with the identity aspects of the issue.

The confidentiality clause issue was considered in the end to be a 'fundamental' one for MSF and much more than just a 'piece of paper' as some had argued. Signing such a clause could be termed an 'explicit surrender of a large chunk of MSF's social mission', its social mission being both parts of its dual mandate of medical action and advocacy. Reminiscent of the 'building coffins for the dead' discussions from 2006, the fear was that MSF-H would become little more than a 'medical service provider' without its social mission remaining intact – that is, inclusive of the witnessing and speaking-out role. As with any organisation MSF-H was jealous of its self-identity and guarded against any actions that would endanger the sanctity of its identity as an emergency medical humanitarian organisation which spoke out about what it witnessed through its medical programming and proximity to the populations to which it provided aid.

It should be stressed here that in this bare life period there was little room for desecuritisation; the primary concern was survival, to at least remain present. The question about the confidentiality clause was less about arguing for the legitimacy of MSF and its work and more about whether accommodating to the government's demands was internally justifiable. The arguments were more internal rather than external. A comparison between the responses in the 2006/7 and the 2008/9 periods show graphically how changes in the context, internally and externally, link to the severity of the securitisation process, and thus limit the response options available to humanitarian organisations.

Summary

The Sri Lanka case study has been discussed extensively to provide a detailed example of how a humanitarian organisation responded to a context of securitisation. MSF-H took as the starting point the need to desecuritise – to proactively respond to the securitised discursive environment and the actions of the government. A careful reading of the securitisation discourse was attempted, and desecuritisation discourse was targeted at the political elites and the general population. The process of desecuritisation, however, was far from straightforward. The analysis of the securitisation discourse was patchy and less than systematic. There were disagreements about what sort of discourse was important to follow and which commentators MSF should listen to. The 'Asian way' discourse model was another topic of debate. Along with these questions about the process of discourse analysis were difficulties in determining the impact of MSF's attempt at desecuritisation. Impact is notoriously difficult to measure, whether concerning humanitarian interventions or advocacy activities. Access for the organisation was for the most part regained in early 2007; how much of this was a result of desecuritisation was questioned by the organisation. For the 2008/9 period, desecuritisation was not even on the table as a response.

Desecuritisation was, of course, not the only response – a modified form of accommodation was also utilised. The organisation tried to fulfil administrative requirements as much as possible, but as a tactic, rather than as a demonstration of agreement with the legitimacy of the securitisation process. Withdrawal was certainly an option, and as reported was considered if sufficient progress was not made in gaining access. Athough there is an instinct to counter-attack, this is a high-risk tactic, and one linked with the question of withdrawal, as attacking may leave no room for manoeuvre. Particularly in situations of insecurity, threatening the securitising agent may not be the best path to take. Finally, once prominently in the public sphere, it is almost impossible to conceal oneself.

In the Sri Lanka case, then, desecuritisation was mixed with accommodation, with desecuritisation tailing off as a response option as the situation concerning access became direr. Desecuritisation requires a certain amount of space to manoeuvre, and in an extreme context of securitisation, when expulsion has been resorted to by the government, accommodation may be the only response option left, barring withdrawal.

Thematic responses

Now let's turn to the response options as understood and used in the thematic case studies. Each theme will be briefly presented and their distinct features discussed. All of the case study findings will then be integrated into a summary at the end of the chapter.

Responses to the law

In Ethiopia, the law was used as securitisation discourse and organisations had to negotiate their space in the new legal environment. Response options were limited. Some organisations chose to withdraw from the country, as implementing their programmes was no longer feasible or their partnership model was too significantly disrupted. For the clear majority of those who stayed, accommodation was the primary response, as either the law was obeyed or the organisations faced (potential) sanctions and would be unable to stay. For those who chose this option there was a certain level of sympathy with the view of the government in expressing their sovereign rights.

There were serious limits to the ability of organisations to desecuritise, outside attempting to temper the negative consequences of the law on aid programming. Desecuritisation would not change the law, but could possibly help with presenting organisations as constructive contributors rather than as enemy agents. Desecuritisation activities included discussions with the government and encouraging other international actors, such as donors and the UN, to support the work of INGOs. However, in the absence of a free press or an audience outside the INGOs themselves, there were few channels of communication to utilise. Regardless of the potential for success, part of the desecuritisation process was to understand how the law was being used to securitise international organisations, and most organisations attempted this to a certain degree.

For some organisations, it was possible to try concealment – to fly under the radar and hope that the legal system would not notice non-compliance – but this was an unlikely scenario for a large and prominent international organisation. Having one's paperwork in order was also necessary to implement programmes, so concealment would prohibit action. It was not feasible to counter-attack against the use of the law, especially in an authoritarian regime, without the risk of being expelled.

Accommodation, therefore, was the most feasible and productive option for organisations in the Ethiopian context. In a context where the law is used aggressively to control organisations and where the law has teeth, accommodation is maybe the only option, barring a desecuritisation response that forces a fundamental change in the law, an unlikely scenario. Of interest is the use of desecuritisation as a way of at least moderating some of the negative effects of the law. One advantage to a situation where the law is discourse is that there is an easily identifiable reference point for counter-discourse, however effective that process is in practice.

Finally, the tension between international expectations of state behaviour and domestic legal considerations is to be further researched. What role do these differing perspectives play in how an organisation decides which responses to choose and which to reject? This tension may affect both the feasibility of accommodation and the desire to try to desecuritise.

Responses to fear

In a highly insecure context, where fear was used as securitisation discourse, INGOs also had limited options to respond. Given the nature of the securitisation discourse – the implicit threat of violence, backed by a history of security incidents against INGOs – any response was risky and INGOs feared missteps.

Next to withdrawal, accommodation was the safest response, since to keep from harm it was best to keep in line. However, it was sometimes difficult to know what the parameters of action were and if the rules were being followed. The risks of mistaking the rules of the game were very high. In order to accommodate one had to be sure about to what one was accommodating. In situations where the law was the primary channel of securitisation discourse, the rules were relatively clear. A situation of indistinction between law and violence was a much trickier space to manoeuvre through. As has been discussed, this was perhaps the point of using fear as discourse. In such a context, therefore, withdrawal was used by most organisations. The risks of playing the game were too high for most.

This is not to say that desecuritisation was not also a viable option. In fact, desecuritisation was a constant process for the organisations that chose to take the risk and stay. In such a dangerous context of securitisation it was vital that organisations try to decrease the level of threat that they posed to the government. There was always the hope of improving relations with the government. Direct access to political elites at the highest levels was difficult, though, and proxies had to be found through extensive networking. Regardless of the evaluation of the freedom of the press, media was available to be used to paint a positive picture of INGOs and their programming. The role of the public in the securitisation process was unclear, but it was important enough to be factored into any desecuritisation process. Press work was therefore essential. None of this was a straightforward process, however, and to a large extent organisations were operating blind – and certainly in a constant state of fear.

Counter-attacking is dangerous in any circumstance, but when dealing with security threats it may be foolhardy in the extreme. That said, some local Chechen staff working in humanitarian organisations considered it as the first option, in line with the perspective that the best defence is a good offence and *not* counter-attacking indicated weakness. This response was, understandably, too high-risk for organisations to take on board, and the tactic was mostly rejected.

Concealment is impossible in such a context. In such a well-controlled context of conflict it is obvious to the security services, federal and local, which organisations are present. Being present under the radar was an extremely dangerous strategy. A form of concealment, however, was used by most organisations in the sense that missions to Chechnya were implemented in a highly unpredictable manner and movements were kept as secret as possible. However, this referred more to actual physical movements of staff, especially expatriate staff, and did not necessarily assist with keeping the organisation itself free from danger.

Again, in this thematic review, responses centred around the three options of accommodation, desecuritisation and withdrawal. The balance changed, as withdrawal was the preferred option in such a dangerous context. But for those that remained, accommodation was a necessity, mixed with desecuritisation. But as with the past two cases, it was an open question how much desecuritisation activities actually accomplished.

Responses to expulsion

Humanitarian organisations have limited response options after an expulsion, the paucity of options a recurrent theme. Once out of the country there are limited paths for return or even communication. Once kicked out, organisations must take action if they wish to return, as it is unlikely that a government will search out such organisation and ask them to return. Exile is a useful way to characterise the effects of an expulsion on an INGO, although more work should be done to flesh out this concept.

Once expelled, accommodation took the form of sticking to the rules so that maybe the organisation could return to the country. Many organisations chose this option, but it involved some potentially serious compromises, and each organisation had to determine their own red line. How much were principles, and the organisation's identity, to be compromised for renewed access? Refusing to compromise was also an option, and withdrawal – in the sense of not trying to return – was a credible and understandable reaction.

Regarding desecuritisation, in such a situation it is difficult to conceive what the process would entail, as the ability to read the securitisation discourse ends once the expulsion has been implemented, as the organisation is no longer in the country, although governmental discourse continues after that. In this situation organisations would only be able to analyse what was produced for foreign consumption. Desecuritisation could include attempting to lessen the perceived threat from organisations, albeit from a distance; however, was the Government of Sudan receptive to such desecuritising discourse?

Counter-attacking, after leaving, was an option, but not in the hope of improving access: more for revenge, or to make a point that such action was unacceptable. This behaviour would form an interesting counter-point to the actions of the government. Concealment is obviously not possible if one is expelled, but may be possible for those who aren't.

An expulsion creates a unique situation in which an organisation becomes external in the external, trying to return to the internal. Normal response options are available, but must be viewed from a different spatial perspective. To return, accommodation may be the only viable option, although trying to desecuritise oneself, in the sense of decreasing one's threat level (to the government), could theoretically be possible, though the mechanisms for achieving this are unclear.

Summary

A few points in summary can be made from the case studies' findings. The securitisation response process needs further development, but some preliminary conclusions can be offered.

First, each situation has a different solution. This may appear obvious but is often not taken on board, with generic solutions too frequently attempted. What is important is to have a framework in mind and to be clear about one's options. How a specific context fits into the framework, and which options will be utilised, must be carefully considered. A careful reading of the context is the first step in any response.

Second, each response has its own pros and cons. Some seemingly have more cons than pros. It is hard to see how a counter-attack would be productive, for example, although it remains an intriguing option. It is the high-risk nature that makes it a dangerous response, but in some contexts it can be envisaged as a possibility, such as with a weak government with little power to enforce the threats inherent in the securitisation discourse. Concealment is also very difficult, especially in authoritarian regimes. Some organisations do try to fly under the radar and rely on remaining in that space. Once in full view, however, it is hard to go back into the shadows. Three options have more pros to recommend them. Withdrawal is always an option, but obvious compromises need to be made, balancing the needs of the populations against other organisational or principled reasons. This leaves desecuritisation and accommodation. Many organisations choose accommodation as the primary response, while some will try to desecuritise themselves, although in most cases the two options are paired. Differences will be found in the priority given to the options.

Third, the process must be taken seriously. Once an organisation has properly analysed how a securitisation process has been implemented and any relevant themes have been identified, the decision how to respond is critically important. Without a well-thought-through response the analysis is worthless. However, in many circumstances, responses to securitisation are not implemented systematically and decisions are made unconsciously or through instinct. A more logical, deliberative and well-grounded process is indicated.

And fourth, in the above discussion of response options, the absence of a deep discussion of the humanitarian principles may have been noticed. It is illuminating to locate where this discussion occurs. Certainly, principles are referenced in internal discussions. But this is often not done in a structured manner, or only superficially. In choosing response options, the absence of a clear framework grounded in principles is striking. The relationship between principles, politics and identities must therefore be reviewed. In the next chapter, this discussion of the response options will be added to the findings from the securitisation case studies and some overall conclusions will be made, all revolving around the central and unifying concepts of politics, principles and identity.

References

Gunaratna, H. (2006). Tell us are we welcome or not – MSF. *Island*, 10 October.
Labonte, M. T. and Edgerton, A. C. (2013). Towards a typology of humanitarian access denial. *Third World Quarterly*, 34(1), 39–57.

8

POLITICS, PRINCIPLES AND IDENTITY

> History consists, for the greater part, of the miseries brought upon the world by pride, ambition, avarice, revenge, lust, sedition, hypocrisy, ungoverned zeal, and all the train of disorderly appetites, which shake the public with the same…These vices are the causes of those storms. Religion, morals, laws, prerogatives, privileges, liberties, rights of men, are the pretexts.
>
> *Edmund Burke,* Reflections on the French Revolution[1]

Introduction

Edmund Burke had a deep suspicion of the utopian egalitarianism espoused by Robespierre and the French Revolutionaries and argued for practical political decision-making that considered the concrete socio-political situation rather than philosophical fancies. In this view, grandly stated ideology was but a pretext for policies derived from base human vices. In the opening quote, Burke makes this argument clearly, juxtaposing primal vices with normative pretexts. To some this is a cynical and pessimistic view, but to others a realistic portrayal of the political process. To a certain extent this basic dichotomy was also the starting point for this book. An argument can be made that the tensions between states and humanitarian INGOs are based on one actor espousing universal themes and the other managing practical political realities. But if so, which actor embodies which perspective?

The preceding chapters have shown that neither actor privileged one perspective over the other. The constructed relationship is more complex than a battle between pragmatic politicians and naïve do-gooders. The GoSL in securitising humanitarian INGOs used their ideals against them by holding them up to their own metric, finding them wanting. Although many in the international

---

1 Burke, 2010: 129.

community did not respect the stance of the GoSL in the war, the perspective of the government was based on universally held principles of sovereignty, statehood and national security. Humanitarian INGOs on their part acknowledged the rights and duties of the GoSL, but argued against its actions. INGOs themselves were often willing to set aside principles to remain relevant and present, and in the process dirtied their own hands on the political pitch.

In the thematic case studies, the law was used in ways that were, at face value, right and proper, or at least aligned with the rights and responsibilities of states and the political principles under which they operate. National security concerns also came into play, whether discussed transparently or falling under the rubric of fear. The consequences on humanitarian programming, however, were another matter, and the case studies have analysed these in detail. A sound interpretation of the meaning behind the states' actions was necessary for INGOs to properly respond, and they had various response options at their disposal.

The relationship is therefore more complicated than at first glance. A process of better mutual understanding à la Mill, is useful. As will be remembered, Mill argued that it was necessary to understand both sides before choosing a preferred view. The relationship, however, is more complex than two sides competing in a straightforward negotiation. It is not a matter of privileging one side over the other, but of understanding how the two sides are interconnected and how their relationship is constructed. What is important is to try to nuance the relationship, and to do so this chapter will tie together what has been learnt from the findings of the case studies. The goal is threefold. The first is to review the usefulness of the theoretical framework. The second is to compare and contrast the case studies, teasing out both common themes and unique features. This will be accomplished by reviewing state actions and INGO responses. And the third is to integrate these findings into the cross-cutting themes of indistinction and politics, principles and identity.

The theoretical framework

On one side of the metaphorical table sits a government and on the other side a humanitarian international non-governmental organisation. Each represents a normative framework – a government represents what has been referred to in this study as the norm of statehood and a humanitarian INGO represents the norm of humanitarianism. Norms in this sense are understood to be rules of behaviour and are socially constructed rather than dictates handed down by a superior power. The state system is fundamentally a constructed political entity. States are what they make themselves out to be and exist in dynamic tension with other states. A government, in the name of a state, must decide upon who is a friend and who is an enemy. This is an ever changing dynamic and one of the primary roles of a government is to make this calculation concerning both domestic and international actors. This prerogative, and in fact duty, to act and decide is one of the defining features of sovereignty. In extreme situations, such as during civil conflict, a state of exception can be conceptualised where customary rules are laid aside and a government uses its prerogative to decide to act boldly, determinedly and assertively, often outside the bounds of normal conduct. In a certain way, this behaviour is a standard, and essential, component of the norm of statehood. As has been seen, even a humanitarian organisation recognises a state's duty to take action of this sort in periods of national emergency. Rather than the fact of action, the debate is about the actual conduct of a response and how it relates to other norms in operation at the time, such as the humanitarian norm.

The humanitarian norm is essentially a moral norm – the humanitarian act is based on a moral commitment by humans to help other humans in need. Assisting others is considered right behaviour, a response to wrong behaviour that causes suffering. This moral act is in principle divorced from the political act. Humanitarianism NGOs do not make calculations about who is a friend and who is an enemy to defend their interests. Rather, humanitarian organisations decide on who needs assistance – on who is suffering because of political acts. Humanitarian organisations are, though, not sovereign entities and so cannot act without the consent of the political actors who control a population and a territory. Notwithstanding international legal frameworks that are meant to moderate the behaviour of governments, a specific government at a specific point in time will always, in practice, retain the prerogative to act.

There are three ways in which this normative dichotomy, and the theoretical framework built to analyse it, should be further nuanced. First, the state should be viewed as an internal agent, in contrast to an INGO that acts as an external entity. Second, the tensions between the nature of a humanitarian actor and the context of civil war must be factored into the analysis. And third, the methods by which principles are used by both states and INGOs should be considered.

Beyond the basic bi-polar relational construct between the actors, it should be understood that the state is the internal and the INGO is the external – it is not a relationship of two actors operating on the same plane, but of one actor representing the interests of a specific political space and one actor coming from the outside and, purportedly, representing a universal norm. States routinely interact with external agents – other states, inter-governmental institutions and international organisations – but under normal circumstances these interactions are on an international plane, that is, as one international agent interacting with another international agent. A state in this sense is an outward-facing political entity interacting with other international political institutions and representatives of international civil society organisations. The issue with humanitarian INGOs attempting to work in the midst of crisis is that the plane of interaction is at the domestic level – these external agents interact *in* the internal. It is an argument of this book that fact complicates the simplistic negotiation structure as is often presented by humanitarian INGOs.

To a large extent this explains many of the tense interactions as described in the case studies. One particularly vivid example is the role of expulsion. In Sri Lanka organisations were temporarily expelled from the area of conflict, but not the country. The same phenomenon occurred periodically in Ethiopia in relation to the presence of humanitarian organisations in the Ogaden region. The prime example was the whole-country expulsion of an entire set of INGOs from Sudan. The objective in all these cases was to eject the external from the internal. In can also be argued that the use of fear in the Chechnya case study had a similar effect, although expressed in a subtler way.

A second way in which the theoretical framework is made more complex is by the very nature of the work humanitarian INGOs seek to perform and the space within which INGOs attempt to operate. The context that has been examined in this study is that of civil war. This is an especially sensitive context for any state, particularly when external agents try to intercede. Obviously, the type of conflict and the nature of its sensitivity is context specific. In all these case studies, the conflicts were not countrywide affairs, although in the case of Sri Lanka in 2009 it neared this status given the profound effects on the entire country. Civil wars, then, also interact with a set of other national political and security concerns.

Aligning this to the first point, a distinction must be made between international agents that confront states on the international plane and INGOs that demand to interact with states on the domestic plane, where the ground on which this inter-action occurs is one of conflict or political instability. It should be emphasised that the space that is being considered here is not only a metaphorical or moral or even legal space, though it is also those; but at the most essential level it is a physical space. This physical space is the nexus of actual humanitarian interaction between aid providers and aid receivers. For regardless of the moral implications of the humanitarian act, humanitarian aid is essentially a materialistic endeavour. Without the ability to provide material aid to populations suffering from the effects of an emergency situation, where the material essentials of life are lacking and physical existence becomes precarious, the humanitarian act is null and void.[2] But as an INGO is an external agent, it is not a given that such access will be given to an internal, domestic, space, especially one as sensitive as a civil conflict.

Beyond the space of conflict itself, the case studies have pointed out clearly how other political and security concerns interact with the zone of conflict. For Chechnya, the conflict had to be tied to the evolving relationship between INGOs and Russia and to the developments of civil society in the country. The various levels of conflict and political insecurity in Ethiopia had to be tied to the country's development agenda. Obviously for Sudan, the involvement of the ICC intersected with the war in Darfur and the presence of INGOs. Finally, in Sri Lanka the deep cleavage between the Sinhalese political ideal and the Tamil fight for independence cut across the involvement of any international actor.

This brings forward the third feature that provides nuance to the theoretical framework, and that is the usage of principles by both parties to negotiate the

2 This is not to denigrate the importance of protection concerns in humanitarian pro-gramming, but even considering protection activities a certain physical access is most likely necessary.

provision of aid within this moral and physical space. Humanitarian INGOs present themselves as independent and neutral agents whose sole objective is to provide aid impartially. In this view, INGOs are independent of other external political actors and will not take sides in a military conflict. Additionally, aid will be provided to those in greatest need and not for any discriminatory purpose. As can be seen the three principles are tied together. A state locked into a civil conflict should be receptive to the implementation of these principles. A state will be assured that external agents will not support its enemies and that such agents will not be implementing the agenda of external political actors. And as one of a state's primary responsibilities is to see that its population is provided the essentials of life, then there should be no argument if those of its populations suffering the most should be provided aid, especially in cases where the government cannot do so. But again, these are indeed external, universalistic obligations which, from a state's perspective, may not sufficiently take into consideration the domestic context. This is again an issue of the interaction of the external in the internal. This also points to the conflict between the views of Mill and Burke. The role of principles will be revisited at the end of this chapter.

It should be stressed that the relationship between the actors is constructed. That is, the relationship is symbiotic and the negotiation is not mechanistic. The context within which the actors are negotiating informs the negotiations, and the mandate and behaviour of the actors also influences the way in which each actor reacts. Much of the tone of negotiations is dictated by perceptions. In fact, negotiations are conducted based more on perceptions than facts. Therefore, the analysis of discourse is vital, as the parties will often base their negotiation stances on what they understand to be the other's viewpoint and which they glean mostly from discourse. In this connection, it should be remembered that a way of understanding the concept of negotiation is as meaning constructed through discourse.

Connected to the process of negotiation should be added identity formation. As has been seen the internal formation of identity and identity politics both play important roles in how discourse is presented and how meaning is constructed. It should also be emphasised how identity can be constructed between actors on opposing sides of the metaphorical negotiation table. Concerning the norm of statehood two aspects should be highlighted: sovereignty and prerogative. In the Schmittian way, prerogative should be associated with decisionism – the importance of making decisions and acting rather than strictly following predetermined rules. In the case studies, the most effective methods of decision-making were the law and expulsion. The law returns repeatedly in the analysis as a useful tool for governments. The last-ditch tactic to expel the offending external actors is also always in the cards for governments.

The use of the Schmittian concepts of the political and the state of exception, and the related securitisation–desecuritisation process, has been productive in the process of better understanding how states and humanitarian INGOs interact. Previously reviewed explanations of the relationship between states and humanitarian INGOs have failed to provide a coherent framework with which to analyse and understand the relationship, or even in many ways to provide a framework at all, particularly given that the view of the states has been essentially missing in how INGOs have approached the state–INGO relationship. The analytical process proposed by this book has uncovered much about how states approach external actors and about how external actors react to the thoughts and actions of states. Based on this, the general findings from the four case studies will be reviewed, looking first at the state perspective and then at the INGO response.

The state perspective

These case studies have sought to understand the variables that go into a state's decision-making concerning the presence and actions of humanitarian INGOs. The presence of the external creates many problems for a state, represented by a government, to which it must respond. In situations where there is not a coincidence of objectives that would allow for a constructive relationship, and the presence of a humanitarian INGO is undesirable, one of the ways in which a government can respond is by securitising the external. Once an agent has been determined to be a threat discourse is used to paint a negative picture of the agent to justify acting to remove, or at least control, the threat. The end point of this process is to completely remove the threat – to outlaw the objectionable agent. Within a construct where a government believes it has the right and a duty – the prerogative – to make the political decision of who is a friend and who is an enemy, especially in a state of exception such as civil conflict, the securitisation process is a logical choice to manage the threat of external agents desiring to work on its territory. In this process, the necessity for a government to justify its actions should be noted, as there are limits to a government's prerogative (except in the case of a truly totalitarian regime), in that a government cannot act in complete isolation but must gain the support for its actions of its own population and, in certain circumstances, of external actors as well. Without this support the implementation of its securitisation policies will encounter unnecessary friction and may even fail if the active cooperation of the public or external actors is needed but not forthcoming. With this in mind, the next section will review the perspectives of the four states studied.

Securitisation in Sri Lanka 2006–2009

What shape did the theoretical framework take in the case of Sri Lanka? This book focused on the periods where the tensions between the Government of Sri Lanka and MSF-Holland were greatest. In examining the most problematic periods one can discover and analyse the most serious issues that interfered with a successful negotiation. What these periods had in common was the existence of an active conflict and a government under pressure – militarily and politically, internationally and domestically. These periods also saw the involvement of external actors, both in-country and engaged from abroad. Social and religious actors were active in influencing the government's handling of the Tamil question and the conflict. The context, civil war, was a state of exception where normal rules were to varying degrees sidestepped. The GoSL designated certain actors as enemies and others as friends. In both periods, NGOs – domestic and international – were labelled enemies and the GoSL used its prerogative to make decisions about how to manage these threats. The GoSL chose to securitise the unwanted NGO actors. As the analysis of the 2006/7 and 2008/9 periods has shown, the severity of the effects of this process changed over time, but the basics of the process remained the same and will be reviewed here. The structure of the securitisation process, as used in this book, should be remembered. A referent object is the entity that is being threatened, and the securitising actor is the agent which is acting against the threat and justifying those actions to the relevant audience. Other actors will also aid and abet the securitising process.

The referent object was the nation-state itself, or at least the nation-state as viewed by the government and the Sinhalese political and religious elites. What was being threatened was both the political order and the Sinhalese Buddhist identity of the nation. The existential threat to the nation-state came from the LTTE, and in the eyes of many by extension from the demands of the Tamil population as a whole. Many in Sri Lanka considered the very essence of the Sri Lankan nation-state to be at risk, and this justified taking strong action against any who were considered enemies to the normal social, religious, ethnic and political order. The challenge was to decide how best to respond to this threat. As part of this response it was necessary to decide which other actors were complicit and then decide on a plan of action to manage these additional threats. As has been examined in detail in chapters 2 and 3, NGOs were associated with the threat posed by the LTTE and the conflict. NGOs were therefore not a direct threat but were seen to be supporting, encouraging or in some way facilitating the LTTE. As has been seen, the category 'NGOs' was never very clearly defined. NGOs in general were reviled, not only international organisations, and the distinction between different types of NGOs was never well articulated. A complicating factor was the influence foreign agents had on local NGOs, blurring the line between external and internal agents. In the case study, the focus, however, was on humanitarian international NGOs that desired to work in the conflict zone.

What the above indicates is that the designation of a threat – the enemy designation – was far from clear and more nuanced than designating one actor as a foe. Humanitarian INGOs were, by extension and indirectly, seen to be threats, but only against the background of the LTTE threat. This is important for INGOs to understand, as it makes a difference whether they themselves were considered a threat or whether their connection to a problematic aspect of the context was at issue. Noteworthy is the confusion over the types of NGO involved, as this is also important for INGOs to be aware of – were NGOs as a group a threat? Or only those tainted by the external? What aspects in fact contributed to their negative perception?

The securitising actor was obviously the government, specifically the executive as well as the MoD authorities. In the two periods under study the presidential administration was led by the same set of political actors. The president himself retained the defence ministry portfolio, to which he assigned one of his brothers to the secretary position. Other assorted governmental agents communicated policy decisions, and the role of many of these has been examined. It is vital for INGOs to understand which political actor is the securitising agent – to identify who is actually making the decisions. The sovereign is the one who decides, and this is the actor with whom, ultimately, negotiations must take place.

Other actors involved with informing the relationship between the GoSL and INGOs were socio-political actors such as the JVP and JHU. These influenced the securitisation process through such political entities as the Parliamentary Select Committee (PSC) investigating the behaviour of NGOs. These other actors were more influential in 2006 than in the 2008/9 period as there was less divergence of opinion on how to prosecute the war in the latter period. This information is also very important to INGOs as the actors who influence the securitising agent may also be the ones it is most important to liaise with. At the least, the opinions of such actors should be monitored and the issues they consider important reflected upon in relation to the humanitarian project.

Finally, who precisely comprised the audience of the securitisation process was not always clear, but almost certainly it was partly the local Colombo political elites and partly the international community, which explains why there were so many stories in the English-language press. To be effective the audience must have been the politically important segment of the population. The audience could also have been the general population at times of election, but the Sinhalese press would have to be reviewed to confirm this. Actors such as the JVP and the JHU were also not likely to be readers of the English-language press, so for these actors a review of the Sinhalese press as well would have to be made to confirm the intensity of the securitisation discourse in Sinhala. There would of course be other media through which messages could be communicated – radio and television, meetings and other public fora, as well as ad hoc written artefacts such as posters, flyers and newsletters. It should be noted that in this case MSF discussed who the audience was and included the general population as part of the government's target audience, though the evidence does not support this view. Regardless, it is essential for an INGO wishing to engage in a process of desecuritisation to know who the securitisation audience is, as the same audience must be targeted to properly desecuritise oneself.

This securitisation process can also be looked at from a variety of perspectives, such as starting with the other actors involved, or even with the audience. This may assist in understanding the connections between the various actors, as it should in fact not be assumed that securitisation is a top-down process. The symbiotic relationship between the GoSL and the JVP and JHU is a good example of how the government was influenced by other actors. The process is dynamic and itself constructed over time, as again the changing relationship between the GoSL and other socio-political actors over the whole of the case study timeframe makes clear. It is more important, then, to look at the logic of the process that considers the views and desires of all the relevant actors than to focus exclusively on the perspective of the securitising agent itself. Understanding the underlying logic of the process, and the connections between the actors which informs this logic, will allow a securitised actor to know who to influence and what to monitor.

With this review of the Sri Lanka securitisation process in mind, it is time now to turn to the thematic discussions of securitisation discourse. In each discussion, the securitisation process will first be reviewed before the case's unique features will be described. The goal is to both gain more experience with using the theoretical framework while also expanding its usefulness.

Fear as discourse

Chechnya was a case of extreme violence for anyone involved in the crisis. Security was the overriding theme, whether one was an aid worker, a fighter or a civilian. The context was one of vagueness and fear. Each actor, each person, had a different engagement with violence and its associated fear. For an external agent attempting to work in an internal conflict characterised by such extreme violence, fear was at critical levels. The motto for humanitarian organisations was 'security trumps everything else'. For humanitarian organisations, the threat of kidnapping was the dominant fear.

Concerning the theoretical framework, in Russia the referent object was the state, as a personification of Russia – Russia as a political idea, a society, a political community. Any serious threat against core political institutions could be considered an existential threat against the state and, by extension, what it represented – the *idea* of Russia. The threats were myriad: civil society, political interference by the West, the work of human rights and 'democracy' groups, the Chechens fighting for independence, and anyone associated with this fight. Multiple layers were involved and interlinked. The Chechnya case could not be divorced from its Russian context and the political developments in the country. An external actor intersects with multiple layers concurrently. Concerning Chechnya itself, there was a conflation of the Chechens and NGOs; Chechnya and the West; and Chechnya and civil society interference in national political decision-making. Chechens, Chechnya and associated external actors involved with the conflict were securitised by the state through the media, in a similar way to the practice in Sri Lanka.

The general population in Russia had to be persuaded to accept the war in Chechnya and the associated brutality against fellow citizens of the country. A standard use of rhetoric of fear of the other was used to convince the population that the state response was justified. But parallel to this securitisation discourse, which concerned the conduct of the war, there was another track of discourse that directly targeted journalists and humanitarian NGOs working in and on Chechnya. This was a discourse of fear that had no audience outside the intended targets. Here, fear was less a rhetorical device and more a description of reality – Chechnya was dangerous and those who stepped out of line would be hurt. This is the realm of indistinction between law and violence. A curious comparison is the use of expulsion – rather than a threat of pain from being expelled, the threat was pain for remaining. In Sri Lanka, governmental statements, the media, editorials and actions were used. In Ethiopia, the law was used transparently. Fear is a more indeterminant discourse – invisible, and in a certain way silent – than the sort of textual discourse examined in the other case studies.

Identifying fear as the form of discourse begs the question, who was the agent behind the use of fear as securitisation discourse? Did a state agent create the insecurity or merely use the prevailing violent situation as a tool of control? More importantly, does the question of agency matter? Related to this, does 'truth' itself matter in such a securitised context? In a certain way, locating agency, and discovering the truth, may not matter if there is an established narrative set down which provides actors with rules to live by. For INGOs the question could only be: how do we stay safe? What should we do and not do?

It is worth pausing a moment and contemplating this question further. In the case of Chechnya and the use of fear as discourse, the question of agency stands out, and is in fact the crux of the matter – inherent in a context of fear is uncertainty, including its relationship to agency. But the other case studies also contain this question to varying degrees. Whereas in some cases it may be clearer who is making the decisions, it may still not be very clear to what extent decision-makers are purposely directing action or whether they are simply manipulating variables not of their own making. More fundamentally, the securitisation narrative itself may only be a useful theoretical construct; a narrative that is helpful to an organisation in negotiating with a state, but nevertheless not 'the truth'. But as asked above, if the narrative 'works', does it matter? More concerning for organisations is not being able to locate agency in the equation, for this makes it more difficult to identity the actor with whom to negotiate.

Stepping outside the case of Chechnya, it can be said that fear is always present as discourse and is an underlying component of the securitisation process. But in some cases, fear becomes the dominant theme and the friends and enemies distinction comes close to being literal. If there is general value to the concept of fear, it must be modified to fit the realities of each context, particularly around the roles of agency and the truth.

The law as discourse

In the Ethiopian case study, the form of securitisation was yet again different. The existential threat was the perceived political interference by foreign agents that challenged the ideological agenda of the regime. The EPRDF regime especially feared rights-based agendas. The disconnect between the government's development agenda and the emergency focus of humanitarian organisations was not to be tolerated. The civil conflict in the Ogaden was a particularly sensitive context. The external needed to be guided into the right direction, and the law was an available tool.

In the securitisation process the referent object was the Ethiopian people, but the government was also under threat. Yet, wasn't it the EPRDF regime that was the most threatened? Regime security was often the driving force in the government's actions. The concept of regime security brings an interesting wrinkle to the discussion. A black and white distinction between a government and a regime is not as important as the awareness of a difference. For the purposes of the theoretical framework, the point is that there may be an ideologically focused regime at the centre of a governmental apparatus that is protective of its own survival and where the set of people who constitute this ideological community conflate their survival with state survival. Such a distinction may assist in assigning agency and the locus of decision-making and, more importantly, in analysing motivation and threat identification. As with the case of Russia, which points to multiple layers of securitisation between the local and the national, there may also be multiple layers within the government, such as between the governmental apparatus and the central ideological regime.

The government was the securitising agent, but the indistinction between the regime and the government makes this judgement hard to make. Who was the sovereign? The audience of discourse were those actors who were the threat as well as the international community. Through the law a series of messages were communicated about how the socio-political order was to be constructed and how it must not be. The imposition of foreign norms would not be tolerated. The law was therefore a form of discourse, one that combined control with fear – stepping out of line would bring sanctions. It is noteworthy that, rather than relying on actions outside the law, the law itself was reinforced. The law needed to be interpreted by INGOs – there was meaning behind it and messages that were being given. The law was a political issue and in tension with the principles upon which agencies based their behaviour and thinking.

Compare this case with Sri Lanka, where the law was also used, such as with the Parliamentary Select Committee debates and the negotiations surrounding the signing of the MoU. In the Sudan case study, the expulsions were also in line with a legal code, although the event was precipitous and was explicitly political in intent. In Russia, the legal changes surrounding NGO registration was another example of the role of the law as a control mechanism, although they were not specifically targeted at operations in Chechnya. In Ethiopia the law was used more explicitly and transparently than in the other cases – was this because there were fewer discursive options to securitise threats, as there was not a free press? Or was it because of the way the Ethiopian governance system worked? Regime security must also have played a key role in encouraging the use of the protective power of the law.

Expulsion as discourse

What is being a good citizen? It is an intriguing question for INGOs to ask themselves – not because they want to be better citizens, but rather as a method to gauge governmental expectations. Regarding humanitarian INGOs working in Sudan in 2009, being a good citizen would consist of: being from and of Sudan;

not being beholden to foreign governments, donors, or intergovernmental organisations; not being representatives of international norms; being embedded with the Sudanese government; and being politically reliable. Most international organisations did not meet these expectations of good citizenship and were therefore ripe for being securitised.

The existential threat, or at least the impetus for the Sudanese government's reaction, was the ICC indictment: the head of state was being threatened with arrest. The referent object was therefore the sovereign and sovereignty. The ICC indictment was the state of exception and firm action was needed to respond to this direct attack on the sovereign.

The expulsions themselves were not outside the law, but did contravene normal expectations of how states engage with INGOs. This is a good example of a theme found in the other cases, where the layers can be articulated between domestic and international expectations of behaviour. Regardless of the legality of the expulsions order, the international community found the state's behaviour inappropriate. A similar reaction by the international community can be found in the 2009 period of the Sri Lankan case study.

The securitising agent was the government, the executive, which mobilised the bureaucratic apparatus. But as with Ethiopia, there was a convergence between the government and the regime. The audience of discourse was the international community – the West in particular. INGOs were interfering with the socio-political order. Their usefulness was questioned. And anyway, wasn't the humanitarian crisis overblown? But the main point was – the government would not be threatened. It is plausible that the choice of response was arbitrary, albeit convenient; it could have been another symbol of the West, and the symbolic punishment implemented in another fashion.

An important distinction can be made between within-country expulsions (single agency or corporate), such as described in the Ethiopia and Sri Lanka cases, and the corporate expulsions from the country, as witnessed in Sudan. The latter is much rarer and more extreme. Interestingly, the primary audience of the expulsion discourses was not as much the agencies themselves, but rather the Western political community in general. The expulsions were a brutal message.

The INGO perspective

Now that the state perspective has been reviewed, it is time to turn to INGOs. This section will not, however, describe a mirror image of the previous section, as, though the two sides are in tension, they are not as dissimilar as supposed. The interconnectedness of the two views will come out in the discussion.

MSF-Holland in Sri Lanka 2006–2009

In the Sri Lanka chapters, MSF-Holland was used as a sort of sounding board, not only to test how the GoSL reacted to the external attempting to work in the internal but also to understand how the external responded to the decisions made by the internal. As has been stressed, this relationship was constructed – the actions, perceptions and ideologies of the two actors influenced the behaviour of the other. But as the state is the sovereign agent, international organisations will always be in a reactive position (except, perhaps, where a state is very weak), and therefore the primary need is to interpret and theorise the behaviour of states. The task for INGOs is to understand, and then to try to influence through negotiation, the decisions which are made by states. These tasks are performed using the theoretical framework.

Obviously, the primary role of the government in granting access was acknowledged by MSF-H. The GoSL was the principle negotiation partner concerning access in the periods under study. At other periods, the LTTE was also an essential negotiation partner, but the negotiations were often implicit rather than explicit – if access were not blocked then access was assumed to have been approved by the LTTE. This was far from the case with the GoSL, as active cooperation by the government's bureaucracy was vital. MSF-H did not, however, understand very well the concept of the state of exception. It saw the state of exception more as arbitrary, at times illogical, behaviour, behaviour sometimes explained as an 'Asian way' of social interaction. The government's prerogative to decide was, nevertheless, explicitly understood. It was admitted, often begrudgingly, that the GoSL had a right and a duty to make decisions based on its national security concerns.[3] Acknowledging the GoSL's decisional prerogative was a first step, but the failure to understand the state of exception concept may have blinded the agency to an important governmental perspective. The state of exception perspective tells us that a government, in certain contexts, feels justified in laying aside normal rules and laws, for a higher purpose. Arguments can be had whether this is to destroy the old order in preparation for creating a new political and legal structure or whether it is a way to save the old order by temporarily ridding the political system of normal constitutional constraints. It can also be debated how conscious such a decision is on the part of a government. Regardless, it is important for external actors to understand the internally coherent prioritisation of national security over rules. A positivistic view of the juridical order becomes irrelevant as contextual changes drive decision-making. A deeper relationship with the key governmental actors would have assisted MSF-H with this understanding.

The role of other actors was in principle understood by MSF-H. In a standard context analysis model MSF-H would establish who the relevant actors were (relevant to the humanitarian context) and monitor their discourse and behaviour. The JVP and JHU were seen to be important and they appear in situation reports. But MSF-H did not have a full grasp of the various connections between the actors, such as the thread between the JVP and the Parliamentary Select Committee, and did not sufficiently grasp the meaning of the discourse such actors used that highly influenced the government. An in-depth discussion about the Parliamentary

---

3   Based on interviews with MSF-H senior managers.

Select Committee seems never to have happened. Gaining this knowledge would have entailed a deeper contextual understanding than MSF-H appeared to be either willing or capable to perform. The concept that other actors would influence the government's behaviour was understood, but how this actually occurred was not well grasped. The organisation's poor network did not assist it in such an analysis of the context.

Related to this last point, the referent object was also not clear to MSF-H. There was only a superficial understanding of the Sinhalese Buddhist nationalist perspective and its impact on political decision-making. An understanding of this perspective was vital to understanding much of the behaviour of the government. In fact, without this understanding the government's urge to think of the context as a state of exception was less comprehensible. These approaches should also have guided the agency's search for who the audience of the government's discourse was. There was much debate about this within MSF but little consensus. Was it the elites? The average Sri Lankan? Also, intriguingly, the question of audience was considered to be more about security concerns than the status of the organisation. The idea appeared to be that the government's discourse may have instigated a violent reaction to the agency's personnel. What was missed was the concept that organisations were being securitised and the discourse was an integral part of this process, rather than only an indication of what the government was thinking.

In general, the discursive context was poorly grasped by MSF-H and the source of discourse was not always identified. This was again the case with reflecting on the influence of such actors as the JVP and Parliamentary Select Committee. Newspapers were monitored and analysed, but the impact of discourse *on* the government was not well understood. The discourse monitored was more about the discourse the government used against INGOs. MSF-H's own discourse was also not well reflected upon by the organisation. One way in which this was particularly true was in the use of principles. Principles, regardless of whether they are universal or not, are often not well understand by governmental actors. Principles, though potentially as useful to states as INGOs in creating a less politically and militarily risky, and more mutually beneficial, space for humanitarian aid to be delivered, had to be correctly explained and understood by government authorities. The potential for misinterpretation was great. For example, independence could be considered to be shorthand for government avoidance, neutrality as actively not supporting military action, and impartiality as desiring to only work with Tamils. It is not clear that MSF-H properly explained these principles to the government. And in many ways principles were even side-lined by MSF in the negotiation process in both periods, as the organisation's medical identity was often in tension with its identity as a principled humanitarian INGO.

Nonetheless, MSF-H did attempt to desecuritise itself. Discursive responses were made to discursive indicators that were being tracked, such as the accusations of illegality of INGOs and INGO partisanship towards the LTTE. But, in a way, MSF took the negative discourse by the government mostly upon itself and exaggerated its role and influence. Some senior managers believe that in the 2006 period the organisation overreacted in its response, especially in considering with-drawal. Patience turned out to be a better tactic. What was also confused in the equation was the difference between MSF-H and other international actors. Was it understood in 2008/9 that all international actors were being conflated into a threat? MSF tended to be self-centred in this way. The Asian way desecuritisation approach recommended by MSF-H in a certain way coincided with the government's attitude, though it was more about MSF-H's ability to know what was going on rather than an appreciation of the government's anti-Western feelings. In 2006 the attempt was valid and may have done some good, but in the last period little could have been done to ameliorate the situation. The international will always lag behind the domestic and be forced to react.

It is interesting to note that much of the above critique was shared by post facto internal evaluations of MSF-H operations during the periods considered. But though some of the weaknesses correlate, such as poor networking and superficial context analysis, what is missing in the MSF-H view are the reasons why these tactics were essential. It may be that a better understanding of why a government acts in the way it does, based on the proposed theoretical framework, will help an agency to approach access negotiations better prepared. This is not to say that MSF-H failed in the 2006/7 period to gain access – perseverance paid off and some aspects of it desecuritisation approach may have worked. Principles were commu-nicated, albeit not to best effect and not always when they should have been. Given that the relationship is constructed, a better mutual understanding can assist an INGO in more constructively negotiating access under normal circumstances, though as has been graphically demonstrated in some circumstances, such as the end of the conflict, no manner of negotiation would have gained MSF-H access.

Reviewing the response using the response choices will form a baseline for the subsequent cases. Desecuritisation was the preferred option, and to a certain extent was accomplished by MSF-H through negotiation and perseverance, although there was a fair bit of accommodation in the organisation's actions. Withdrawal was contemplated but not carried out. What of the other tactics? Counter-attacking was not attempted, and concealment was not possible.

Responding to fear

How to live in the indistinct space between the law and violence, in a constant environment of fear? INGOs had various reactions. Withdrawal was the most common and was by far the safest option. Even for those that stayed, strict security protocols were put into place that relied on lack of expat presence – a remote management style of programme implementation. Self-censorship was also common – watch what you do, watch what you say, watch even what you think. The second-guessing of decisions, analysis and speech was rife.

Is desecuritisation possible in such a context? Desecuritisation may in most cases be the best response, but how to desecuritise yourself against a securitising agent that operates in the shadows? Or is the best policy to accommodate the dictates of the agreed-upon narrative? The essential point was to have a narrative and stick to it. Yet, as the narrative was in many ways built on guesswork, it was important to accept a high-level of ambiguity and not be too precious about discovering 'the truth'. Needless to say, this is an extremely uncomfortable space – physically and intellectually – for INGOs to inhabit.

The damage fear does to principles can also be severe. How does an organisation remain true to its principles when the overriding goal is to not get kidnapped? Security management becomes the primary lens through which all action, or non-action, is evaluated. Is there room for principles in these calculations? Impartiality necessitates helping those most in need, but this is difficult if one is afraid to reach them. Fear also affects making an independent assessment of needs, as one has to fit into the tight restrictions laid down by the state, as well as the dominant narrative that guides behaviour. Neutrality becomes especially important, as even being perceived to be involved in political controversies is extremely dangerous. Witnessing, and communicating what one sees, is a risky endeavour. Flipping this around, however, brings out the question of how this reticence to speak out and advocate is seen and perceived by the populations one is working with; not communicating also sends a strong message. In such a context, it is important to be seen to be independent from foreign political influence, but in a highly politicised environment where political identities are at the basis of securitisation, it is hard to completely depoliticise oneself. And after all, as an INGO, an external actor, one is, at some level, a representative of a foreign viewpoint and potentially a different political ideal.

Counter-attacking would have been suicidal, although there was periodic advice by the Chechens to do just that. In such a context of insecurity it was considered to be an extremely high-risk tactic. Interestingly, concealment was in certain ways attempted, particularly related to remote management. But it was naïve to think that the presence of international humanitarian organisations could go undetected.

All of this has a perverse effect on the primary goal of humans helping humans in need. Living, and working, in fear, in a context of vagueness, with every decision tortured, is not conducive to the negotiation of access, let alone the implementation of effective humanitarian programming.

Responding to the law

The law, as a set of written rules and regulations, penalties and sanctions, dos and don'ts, is out in the open to be studied and used as guidance for behaviour. What is behind the law, however, needs careful analysis. The response to a new law is not only in reference to what is out in the open, but on what motivated the law in the first place. Politics and identity, as has been seen, are often at the basis of the law.

There are various ways to manage the legal, administrative and, most importantly, political fall-out regarding programmes: try to save what you can and bin the rest; withdrawal; or accommodation. Accommodation involves compromise on programming but also on principles. As with Chechnya, accommodating to the political demands of a state may have adverse effects on reaching the populations most in need, and certainly making an independent assessment will be difficult. The perception of neutrality is also compromised, as being seen to be aligned with one political agenda may not assist one in accessing the populations one wishes to reach. Concerning development programming, it may be possible to take a long-term view and adapt, particularly if there is an alignment between agendas. But for emergency organisations it is a trickier calculation. This is where the mandate of the organisation becomes important, as each organisation will have a different tolerance for accommodation and will make the choice whether to withdraw based on different calculations.

The balancing act is, then, to differentiate between what is possible and what is inconsistent with both the dictates of the law and one's principles. Is this, in effect, the limit to desecuritisation in such a context – to justify, outwardly and inwardly, what one will and will not do? For, in such a situation the law will not be changed, particularly given the meaning behind the law and the fact of an ideologically strident regime responsible for those changes.

Counter-attacking was not contemplated by any of the organisations researched. Concealment, as was found in the Russian case, was not a viable option.

Expulsion as discourse

When INGOs are no longer good citizens, they can be expelled and sent into exile. As with the other cases, even if the options are clear they are not easy to choose between. Serious compromises must be made if return is contemplated, compromises that entail at least a certain level of accommodation. To top it all, as exiles INGOs are starting from a very weak position. As exiles, withdrawal is not really the correct perspective, as the INGOs have been forced out of the country. The choice is whether to fight to get back in or not, depending on the attitude of the organisation. As with the other cases, principles are at stake.

At this point in the discussion the principles at stake are familiar. The road back to a space where an organisation can freely assess needs and access vulnerable populations, unhindered by political interference, was long, and the levels of accommodation demanded too much for some. A price to pay was remaining quiescent and strictly neutral, keeping far away from any political controversies. It was an open question how far along the path to accommodation one had to go before one's humanitarian identity was endangered. Was the goal to assist the vulnerable populations in Darfur or satisfy the political demands of the state? As in the Ethiopian situation, there was also an indistinction between the state, as represented by a government, and the regime. It could be asked whether compromising on principles was the price to pay for regime security and, based on this, an opening back into the country.

As with the other cases, counter-attacking was not an option, and neither was concealment. Desecuritisation as a method of returning had it merits, and some organisations did pursue this, in a way, by changing their names in order to no longer be in the same category as those expelled. This was something of a bookkeeping trick, but access negotiations sometimes have odd rules in play. Desecuritisation in this sense was less through discourse, however, and did not substantially improve the organisation's reputation. This may, therefore, be better considered as accommodation.

Summary reflections

The case studies found that it was valuable to examine the relationship between states and international humanitarian non-governmental organisations in terms of the Schmittian concepts of the political and the state of exception, both intimately tied to notions of state prerogative and sovereignty. In addition, the securitisation approach was found to be a useful method for understanding the way states interact with INGOs, while the response categories assisted in understanding the choices INGOs had for reacting to state policies and discourse. Though 'the sovereignty card' – the idea that states use sovereignty as a pretext for poor behaviour – is often used as a shorthand by INGOs to describe the rationale behind the actions by governments, a more nuanced explanation was needed. This study found that sovereignty per se was not the dominant explanatory concept. Rather, how a government views its decision-making prerogative, when and how it conceptualises a state of exception, how it designates who is a friend and who is an enemy, and how enemies are subsequently securitised are the most pertinent concepts to consider. The role of discourse in these processes has been emphasised in this book. Taken together these concepts form the proposed theoretical framework, the basis for understanding how states and humanitarian INGOs negotiate and construct their relationship. A major finding in this book is that the relationship is more complex than being a purely two-sided negotiation structure. The theoretical framework has tried to introduce the most pertinent variables, but these are only indications of the complexity.

Humanitarian INGOs would benefit from referencing the theoretical framework in their approach to negotiating access, although such shifts in worldviews are not easy for large organisations to make. Understanding the securitisation process would be particularly useful for such INGOs. Paired with this is understanding better the options for responding to a securitised context. A firmer grounding in how discourse is used to create such a securitised environment is also essential to enable INGOs to decide how best to react to the policies and actions of states. In this negotiation process, it would also behove governments to more fully recognise the benefits of humanitarian principles in addressing some of their own concerns. But as noted in regard to the use of principles in negotiations, the onus is on the humanitarian INGOs themselves to properly communicate the usefulness of principles.

The previous sections covered a lot of ground, a few points of which should be extracted for further discussion. The goal of this book is not to elaborate a theory for the sake of it, but rather to produce a useful framework and a method of analysis for understanding the relationship between states and humanitarian INGOs. As one becomes more practised in using the framework it should recede further into the background, leaving a certain interpretive mindset in place, a way of thinking that helps INGOs better implement their humanitarian programming. A parallel process is to polish the rough theoretical edges and to align better theory with practice.

Indistinction

Indistinction came out in the case studies as a key concept. Indistinction affects both sides in a negotiation. Clearly, in a situation of securitisation the motivations and intent of a state are not transparent to an INGO. No matter how hard a humanitarian organisation tries to interpret and understand the actions and discourse of a state, there will remain unknowns. But a state also works in a context of indistinction regarding the thoughts and actions of INGOs. This section will present some preliminary reflections on the concept of indistinction in the securitisation process.

One question of interest is the role of the law. The theoretical starting point is that, in a state of exception, a state would act outside the law. The law would not be obliterated but (at least) temporarily overridden to respond to the dictates of the emergency. In the context of a humanitarian crisis, however, this concept must be modified, for in fact much of the securitisation process appears not to be extra-legal, at least domestically. In replying to the presence of the external, a state may easily use the law to enforce conformity, punish troublemakers and keep out the riff-raff. In Ethiopia the law was reinforced, in Sudan the expulsions were almost certainly not illegal. In Chechnya, although fear did not rely on a specific interpretation of the law, the law was used heavily by the state as a control mechanism. And in the case of Sri Lanka, notwithstanding the harsh anti-NGO rhetoric and aggressive stance of the Parliamentary Select Committee, it is hard to pinpoint a case of the law being grossly overridden. Even in the case of NGOs being barred from working in the conflict-affected areas in 2009, this was easily justified within the normal bounds of the law. In fact, many in the international community commented on how careful the government of Sri Lanka was to keep within the law.

Domestically, then, the law should be viewed as a useful tool, one pliable enough to help a state meet the dictates of an emergency situation. INGOs may still have many questions about the motivations behind a law and the application of the law may not be clear, but nevertheless the concept of domestic law applying to civil society is understood, if not appreciated. In some cases the law may be overridden, but in most this is not necessary. International norms are another matter, however, as are expectations about state behaviour in the minds of international actors. It can be argued that this is a realm of indistinction and confusion. There are many ways in which the relationship between INGOs and states can be evaluated, and against international norms is one important reference point. There are expectations about the conduct of states, based partly on international legal frameworks, partly on humanitarian principles, partly on the moral outlook of humanitarians and partly on history. The set of these expectations have been reviewed above. The point here is that often what is thought of as being 'outside' normal behaviour is not domestic action but action that contradicts expectations based on international norms. This is an indistinction between norms.

Another space of indistinction is between the law and violence, a space where fear plays a leading role. Like a vacuum, this space must be filled. Managed insecurity, as graphically demonstrated in the Chechnya case, can serve as effective filler. This can be looked at as discourse, a discourse of fear. Thinking of it as discourse makes it easier to analyse and fit into a framework. Fear is indistinct, but still analysable. But, in the narrative constructed from this analysis, what of agency and truth? This is yet another layer of indistinction. It is, after all, the usefulness of the narrative that is most important, on both sides, rather than ontological and epistemological questions. From the state perspective, for example, an existential threat can be characterised as political interference and the need to keep the state at the centre, regardless of whether INGOs intend harm or not. The fear of interference is what is important. From the perspective of an INGO, a narrative may be built to guide how to remain safe and retain access while not contradicting one's principles. As long as the narrative works, how important is it that the INGO understands precisely who is behind the insecurity? These are open questions and cannot yet be answered definitively.

On the side of INGOs, in a situation dominated by fear and indistinction, where the power of the law, punishment, incapacitation, deterrence and retribution all play a major role, how to react? How is the space of indistinction, and what fills it, engaged with? The case studies have described various tactics. Accommodation entails compromises, and principles must be considered. Withdrawal also has its cost, as then vulnerable populations do not receive assistance. Desecuritisation has real limits and must be based on a firm analysis. It may not always be possible to decrease the level of perceived threat your organisation displays to a state. INGO action must be based on an interpretation of the motivations and concerns of states. INGOs cannot 'black box' states – they are not monolithic entities, not all alike, and political agendas change over time. In addition, on the INGO side, principles are also not monolithic and must be continuously re-evaluated and reassessed. Identities on both sides change over time. Indistinction must be met head on.

Politics, principles and identity

The above reflections can be distilled down into a discussion of politics, principles and identity, the key themes that tie everything together.

For many organisations, the first hurdle when considering how best to engage with states is to attend to the question of the role of politics in humanitarian action. The findings from this book's case studies clearly support the view that the environment within which INGOs work is political. States are political actors, as are the governments that represent them, and even more so the ideological regimes which often dominate the political process. This is clear. Also readily apparent is the fact that humanitarian crises are, fundamentally, political crises. This is the case whether the crisis is a famine, a civil conflict, involves a mass movement of people – within or across borders – or is, as is often the case, a combination of them all. Even natural disasters are not really 'natural', but human-made and, ultimately, the result of political decisions. Such humanitarian crises are, in fact, some of the most politically sensitive contexts imaginable.

Any actor, especially an external actor, trying to intervene in such circumstances must engage with a highly politicised context and form a relationship with all relevant political actors. This seemingly obvious point is stressed because of the resistance – sometimes fierce – to the idea of political engagement within the sector. As detailed earlier, there is a view that humanitarian principles necessitate an apolitical stance by humanitarian organisations, a misreading of the principles. Humanitarian organisations should not engage *as* political actors and need to remain neutral in their political engagement, but their actions and presence will have sometimes profound political consequences and will be perceived as political action by the political actors cohabitating the political pitch. This is an essential point for humanitarian INGOs to accept and internalise.

It is, therefore, necessary for INGOs to understand the political motivations of states and the political context, and as well understand their own political roles. A political analysis defines the ground. The friend and enemy distinction, the establishment of a state of exception, and the securitisation process all form a part of the political process. Any theoretical framework must begin from this starting point. This is equally the case regarding the desecuritisation process. Whichever option an INGO uses to react to being securitised – accommodation, withdrawal, desecuritisation, counter-attacking or concealment – depends not only on a political analysis but also on proactive political engagement. This can be an ugly affair, and a role for which INGOs are often ill prepared. This must change within the sector.

As has been discussed above, INGOs base much of what they do on humanitarian principles and sometimes misread their intention, narrowing the parameters of engagement. Just as INGOs believe that politics is for states and they themselves are apolitical, it is also believed that only INGOs have principles. The case study findings have shown, however, that states also rely on principles, whether formal or informal constructs. Political principles are, of course, those related to statehood and sovereignty and their use has been covered extensively in the case studies. Interestingly, whereas states often think principles are an excuse for not respecting the rights and responsibilities of states, INGOs may think that political principles are an excuse for cynical and self-serving action. Political principles may be derisively labelled ideology by INGOs, particularly when voiced by 'authoritarian' regimes.

These assumptions and labels should be dispensed with to allow for a more level-headed discussion. Commonly, principles carry a moral weight, and thus, when attributed to an actor, a certain credibility is given to their actions. As the above discussion indicates, this is the crux of the matter. To be reconciled is the concept of the moral in the humanitarian project with the political dictates of the crisis. This is for *all* actors to balance. This book argues for a clash of the moral with the political, the humanitarian project grounded in the moral principle of humans helping humans, and states representing hard political choices. This basic tension remains, but as the case studies have shown, the actually existing world is a messy place. It cannot be that humanitarians have a lock on principles, or moral action, and state action is by definition immoral. Yet, at the level of negotiation, the moral principles at the heart of humanitarian action isn't a bad place to start, and there is no shame on the part of a state to explain the difficult political decisions it faces.

In the end, there are going to be tensions between the two distinct identities – states and INGOs are fundamentally different. It is no accident that *non*-governmental organisations establish their identity in opposition to governments. Civil society, also, in a fundamental sense stands in opposition to state coercion. In this discussion this is the ending point, but it is also an analytical starting point. Notwithstanding the differences in identity, the field of action is shared, while the population requiring assistance is owned by neither. With a better understanding is this clash of identities surmountable, for the good of the vulnerable populations deserving assistance? It may be asked, though, why INGOs do not often take up these ways of looking at things. And why do states seem not to want to deal with these issues?

On the part of states, it is a real struggle to have direct discussions on these issues. The reasons are far from clear and may link to fear and indistinction. On the surface it would appear that it is to the benefit of states to talk openly about their relationship with humanitarian INGOs. Maybe the outcomes are unclear, are too messy or cannot be properly managed? It may also be a failure to admit the usefulness of the humanitarian project itself. As the review of the history of state–aid agency interactions revealed, much of the aid rhetoric can be perceived as being anti-state. In the developing relationship, from the period where states were at the centre to a period where sovereignty was being questioned and the role of states was becoming less clear, states would of course react. This is the very starting point for this research project. The 're-emergence of states', the 'strong state perspective', is indicative of the issue. Discussing directly the role humanitarian organisations, particularly international organisations – the external – may be a step too far for states and might be seen to be giving credibility to actors that may be useful but must be controlled and managed. This question of identity is a crucial issue for states.

On the part of humanitarian INGOs, the issue revolves around the nature of the political and its relationship with principles. As stated above, this issue must be dealt with in the minds of humanitarian organisations. States are not wrong when they accuse INGOs of using principles to justify non-engagement with political actors. INGOs are often fearful, it seems, that political engagement will dilute their moral authority. This is an identity question that must be taken seriously. It is also wondered whether a lack of capacity plays a role – would a better-prepared and educated organisation do a better job in engaging politically? This book argues that this is the case and so presents a way for INGOs to work through an analysis and build a narrative that works.

At the end of the day, humanitarian INGOs must do a better job at communicating their specific nature and the norms upon which they operate. States must do a better job in differentiating between the various types of international actors, their specific mandates and their limitations. Each side has much to learn about the other, as Mill suggested in the introduction's opening quote. But Burke's concerns also need to be attended to, as there are limits to how well the relationship can be built. Politics, principles and identities are powerful forces that will inform how the negotiation process progresses and the relationship is constructed.

References

Burke, E. (2010). *Reflection on the Revolution in France*. New York: Barnes & Noble.

Mill, J. S. (2002). *The Basic Writings of John Stuart Mill: On Liberty, the Subjection of Women and Utilitarianism*. New York: The Modern Library.

Schmitt, C. (2005). *Political Theology: Four Chapters on the Concept of Sovereignty* (2nd edition). Chicago: Chicago University Press.

Schmitt, C. (2007). *The Concept of the Political* (expanded edition). Chicago: Chicago University Press.

CONCLUSION

The future

The preceding chapters have made the case for the utility of the theoretical framework. There are inherent tensions between states and international humanitarian NGOs. On the side of the state, the concepts of prerogative and decisionism, the friend and enemy distinction and the state of exception, the norms of sovereignty and statehood and, most importantly, securitisation have all been covered in depth. And on the side of humanitarian INGOs, humanitarian principles, the moral norms underpinning humanitarianism and the response options of desecuritisation, accommodation, withdrawal, counter-attacking and concealment have been all been reviewed. The case studies have contributed to fine-tuning the theoretical framework, hopefully helping to turn it from being merely a theoretical whimsy into a practical tool.

The last chapter concluded the analysis with a discussion of the themes of politics, principles and identity, attempting to tie together what has been learned. But this is only the starting point for research, reflection and practical engagement with this issue. This concluding chapter therefore looks towards the future. The normal expectation of the future is that things will be better. This is the case for our own lives, and in the aid sector the focus is on making the lives of those assisted better. It is a never-ending quest to improve our ability to do so. The remainder of this chapter will propose concrete steps to assist, in whatever small way, in reaching this goal

To start with, a thought experiment could be proposed that would ask an INGO to explore how better decisions could have been made in a concrete case. What decisions and actions would have avoided the development of difficult relations with the state under consideration? But this is only half the story, as the states themselves also make decisions and INGOs must react to these decisions. As has been discussed extensively, one key in this process is for INGOs to gain a better understanding of the political context. No one who has worked in the aid industry for any length of time would ever be so naïve to believe that there could be a fundamental change in how the political system works. The key is to better understand how the system works. All that can be hoped for is to find a better method for reconciling the clash of interests, and maybe even moderating the worst excesses, on both sides of the negotiating table. States also have a responsibility to engage with the humanitarian norm in a more constructive manner.

There is a middle ground between the deep cynicism of Burke and the progressive attitude of Mill. The goal of this chapter is to better establish that space by outlining how the relationship between states and INGOs can be more constructively approached. These reflections will be centred on a proposed research agenda and will include practical suggestions for fostering a better understanding.

A research proposal

One worry expressed by many contacted for this research concerns the academic–practitioner divide. The relationship remains bi-polar, with only cursory interactions between the two 'sides'. It is strongly argued that this divide must be broken down and the space in the middle reinforced. Theoretical frameworks have the potential to assist practitioners in developing their thinking, and of course practitioners must be forthcoming in sharing their experiences with academics so that the theories they develop are useful. The state–INGO relationship is a good example of a theme that would benefit from a more constructive engagement between academics and practitioners. This book's research has tried to take this perspective, but to be successful as a research project this approach must be continued. In this research, a theoretical framework was proposed, tested and tweaked. Now it is to be used, as without take-up the theory is a mere curiosity. The recommendations as described below should be understood to be within this general approach. These reflections speak to a wide variety of research questions, methodological issues and practice-oriented recommendations.

First, the objects of research must be clarified. To start with, this research deals with aid agencies that implement humanitarian programming during humanitarian crises. Purely developmental organisations may or may not benefit from using the theoretical framework, but this book and its research agenda have not considered that question. Given that caveat, much more work needs to be done on examining the differences between multi-mandate and humanitarian organisations, as this book does not explore these differences very deeply. The bulk of this research implicated humanitarian organisations, and when multi-mandate organisations were examined they were treated as another type of humanitarian organisation. In other words, not as separate entities, but part of the same set. The case studies were opened up to be inclusive, but there remain other pertinent variables attached to each perspective and some of these are discussed below. One practical recommendation would be to conduct a case study around the operations of a single multi-mandate organisation, preferably named, such as in the MSF-H in Sri Lanka case study. This would entail dividing the two types of organisation into different sets.

In addition, within the two sets – humanitarian and multi-mandate – not all organisations are of the same type, approach and mandate. The humanitarian set, however, may, by nature, have less variance. It can be argued that humanitarian organisations focused solely on humanitarian crises implement a smaller set of programme types, set shorter-term objectives, and their programmes should always be informed by the humanitarian principles. The elements that go into this set have grown over time: a good example is emergency education activities. Multi-mandate organisations have a wider range of activities that they implement outside humanitarian crises, and what the linkages are between those and the ones implemented in humanitarian crises is an interesting question. The inclusion logic may be pertinent to how an organisation approaches its relationship with the state. For example, if a programme normally implemented in a development context is chosen for a humanitarian context, such as education, but involves close collaboration with the government, how does that affect the organisation's engagement with the government? Beyond types of programme, the mandate and worldview of the organisation may inform the relationship with the state. Multi-mandate organisations, even those with a strong and well-resourced humanitarian branch, may have a different set of conceptual tools that they bring to negotiating access and envisaging the role of the state.

Within both sets, examples of mandates are many and differing mandates may also inform an organisation's relationship with states. Considering multi-mandate organisations, for example, do faith-based organisations have a different viewpoint? What about campaigning actors that also implement aid programming, both developmental and humanitarian? What of those organisations that put a special focus on capacity-building activities? Issues revolving around the building of relationships with grassroots actors, or the links to religious actors, or the necessity of capacity building, are important aspects to consider more closely. In addition, what about the different types of developmental programming which organisations focus on outside their humanitarian programming, such as education, health, agriculture? How do these perspectives affect the political worldview of the organisation? The question here relates to how much multi-mandate organisations need to maintain good links with governmental actors or specific community representatives to fulfil their dual mandates. Some of these distinctions are of course also relevant to humanitarian organisations.

One final distinction relates to funding. Many organisations rely for a large proportion of their funding on institutional donors, mostly governmental or inter-governmental in nature. This is the case for humanitarian as well as multi-mandate organisations. The intriguing question is how much do donor links change the political calculations made by organisations? Do the political leanings of the donor countries affect how funded organisations conceptualise their relationships with states?

For all types of organisations, there may also be a difference in political and cultural perspectives based on where an organisation comes from. This book's research focused on the experiences of Western international NGOs. INGOs from other backgrounds may have a different perspective on many of these issues. Humani-tarianism, and aid in general, has often been approached as a universal norm, but this is a contested question that must be further engaged with. As a larger set of non-Western organisations are appearing in humanitarian crises, this is an urgent task.

This research has also focused solely on international NGOs and not considered the United Nations or the Red Cross movement. These other types of institution will have their own specific challenges given their differing status and mandates. The operational agencies of the United Nations, such as the World Food Programme (WFP) and UNICEF, represent an inter-governmental organisation, and some agencies, such as the UNHCR – the refugee agency – are treaty organisations. In other words, they have legal identities and are guardians over certain international treaties – in the case of UNHCR, for example, over International Refugee Law. The International Committee of the Red Cross (ICRC) has a formal role as guardian of International Humanitarian Law, and national Red Cross societies also have legal identities in their own countries. How far these types of agency fit into the theoretical framework is an open question, although the ICRC has appeared from time to time as a fellow humanitarian traveller in this book's research.

National NGOs are also in a unique category. They do not represent the external in the internal, with the possible exception of cases where they come from a distinctly different part of the country. Yet even here they cannot be comparable to international organisations, as national NGOs are, by definition, of the country in which they are established. They will, therefore, have a special relationship with the state and may not fit into the theoretical framework. An added complication is the situation, as seen graphically in the Ethiopia case study, where there is an inti-mate relationship between international and national NGOs. We saw how the Ethiopian government handled this relationship. So, in this way, national NGOs may be linked to the external in the view of governments, to the detriment of the ability of national NGOs to obtain funding and implement their programmes.

Each one of the above-mentioned organisations also has a different relationship with the humanitarian principles. Even within the set of humanitarian organisations attitudes to the principles differ. Some reject neutrality as a principle as it limits other types of action, such as advocacy and communication activities. Other principles are added based on a development mindset, such as accountability or solidarity. It is for each organisation to integrate their varying takes on principles into how their relationship with states plays out.

There are, therefore, many aspects of the object of study to be nuanced. All of these themes and distinctions must be integrated into the research since they introduce a large number of additional variables into the equation. The theoretical framework must be flexible enough to encompass maybe different views and perspectives.

Regardless of which type of NGO is considered, one very important issue that affects everyone is the growth in NGO laws. As this research has indicated, NGO laws must be viewed as a form of discourse and the motivations behind them analysed; therefore, there is a danger in addressing them too superficially or simply as a convenient administrative response to a perceived challenge to sovereignty. But this is not to say that the theme itself should not be tackled head on, as it is a crucially important development. This theme is a stand-alone topic that urgently needs further research and attention.

From the domestic situation to the international, there are many other changes in how states view aid globally and their responsibilities connected to the provision of aid. Variations in the impact of the Responsibility to Protect framework and human rights norms need to be better integrated into the theoretical framework. Other themes to be integrated are localisation and building the capacity of first responders. There seems to be a movement towards increasing the capacity of local responses, with the clear implication that the role of international agencies should be limited. How does this trend affect the relationship between states and humanitarian INGOs, whether multi-mandate or purely humanitarian?

The most glaring gap in the study is, quite obviously, the absence of primary research from the state's viewpoint. Any future research must fully integrate state representatives. It can be argued that states have as much stake in understanding the relationship as INGOs, however the incentive is less. It has certainly been the case for the research discussed in this book that constructive contact with states has been nil. As discussed in the preface, this is not through want of trying. A productive way to reach states has not yet been found, and this question, probably more than any other in this chapter, is one that needs further attention.

One specific issue that arose from the Sri Lanka research that should be researched more is the role of Asian values and Asian concepts of sovereignty in informing such a state–INGO relationship. In the Sri Lanka case both MSF-H and the GoSL referred to the Eastern-Western differences in world-view and ways of communicating, but this study only superficially examined this vital issue. This of course applies to the Asian region as a whole, though it is suspected that, though there are commonalities, each context has its own unique voice and view. Other areas of the world may also have a similar regional dynamic pertinent to the theoretical framework.

These regional variations bring the discussion to the limited number of contexts that have thus far been studied. Whole areas of the world, such as Latin America and the Middle East and North Africa (MENA) region, have been left unstudied. But it should be stressed that this is not a developing world phenomenon. State–INGO relations are difficult in Europe as well, as the European 'migration crisis' has shown. An indicative list of potential future case studies would include: Colombia, focusing on the complicated web of NGO laws in place; Hungary, in the context of a democratic state in Europe putting into place barriers to civil society actors working with migrants; Syria, as a case of extremely violent civil war with a punitive government and a completely divided country; Australia, in connection to barriers to access for NGOs working with refugees; and Canada, as a reference point of a context with no conflict and no troublesome NGO laws.

Finally, it should be noted that securitisation is not the only end point for the state–INGO interaction. Although it is proposed that the generic negotiation structure will remain valid in any humanitarian crisis where humanitarian INGOs and states interact, securitisation as a process may not be the only way in which this relationship develops. The clash between the two norms sets does not necessarily imply a situation of securitisation. There may be other ways in which states react to the external in the internal that does not involve the characterisation of such actors as threats that need to be managed outside normal legal bounds. For example, a situation can be envisaged where a state, while still maintaining the right of pre-rogative, interacts in a less extreme way towards international actors and strictly respects normal rules, laws and regulations related to humanitarian activities. In such a context, there may still be severe tensions between the state as a political actor and a humanitarian INGO as a moral actor, but without the state villainising the external and in fact allowing it to work in the internal. These types of contexts should be searched for and researched in depth as counterpoints to the contexts reviewed above.

A few methodological recommendations should also be mentioned. A more comprehensive discourse analysis methodology is indicated which is theoretically sound and comparable but also sensitive to the particulars of any given context. Local languages should not be ignored, as for example this study limited itself to analysing only English language discourse. Regardless of the language, it may be useful also to quantify the use of specific terms, that is, to track the frequency of how different terms and concepts are used. It is of primary importance to develop a methodology for INGOs to analyse discourse better. More work is also needed on the process-tracing procedure to better align it with the needs of this type of research, including more reflection on what other types of empirical evidence may be available to provide increased depth and variety to such research.

Changes in practice

The above has outlined a proposed research agenda which aims at strengthening the usefulness of the theoretical framework and increasing INGO's understanding of states and how the political works. More difficult is the change in mindset within the sector that a better understanding promises. This book has focused on the securitisation process, but a better situation would be cooperation rather than tensions.

Outside of research, more discussion is needed between the actors. Research helps guide the discussion, but the discussion itself is important to have. Best would be a series of interactions between states and INGOs of various sorts in a structured set of discussions. The reticence to discuss openly and directly these issues must be broken down. Much work is being done at the lower, local and community levels, such as localisation and first responders support. And at the highest policy levels discussions are held in the abstract. The missing middle is the engagement between national governments and INGOs, and engagement on the particulars of their cases – not in the abstract, but about the concrete issues at hand. Quite honestly, although both sides of the equation have to make efforts, on this point the onus is on the states.

For INGOs it is recommended that there is a structured development of the theoretical framework. It should be coupled with a context analysis and networking agenda. As mentioned above, a thought experiment would be for the organisation to look at what could have been done better, on their part and also on the part of the state. This is not to suggest yet another onerous system being put into place. It is, rather, a mindset issue, a development of a way of thinking that allows for a realistic analysis of the political factors at play. This change in mindset and practice takes time and perseverance.

It is hoped that some of these recommendations may be taken up by practitioners, academics and states in a joint effort, with a view to improving the relationship between states and humanitarian INGOs, of any type, not for their own benefit, but to improve the assistance available for vulnerable populations.

INDEX

Note: Page numbers in **bold** type refer to **tables**
Page numbers in *italic* type refer to *figures*
Page numbers followed by 'n' refer to notes

academic–practitioner divide 195
access 4n21; changing 48; constraining 24, 82, 88; controlling 134; delayed 153, 154; denying 4, 61; difficult 136; emergency 120, 148; facilitating 75, 152, 153, 157; impossible 147, 148; losing 120, 161; negotiating 165, 188; physical 174; possible 149; price of 62; prioritising 149; unhindered 158, 163, 187
accommodation 148, 150, 185, 186–188
accountability 52, 116, 119
accounting 118, 119
accusations 147, 152
action 8, 41; capacity for 104; drastic 140; exceptional 60–64; moral 9, 173; political 173; prohibited 93; quick 52; unjustified 88
Action Contre la Faim 48; killings 48, 58
actors: armed 82, 83; moral 5; political 18, 47
adaptation 120
administration 115, 116, 117, 118, 120
administrative barriers 93, 152, 154
administrative requirements 148, 150
adulation 98
advocacy 44, 73, 117; behind-the-scenes 163; humanitarian 73; political 135; safe space 100; silent 148
agency 103, 104–105, 122, 132, 180

agenda: foreign 114; hidden 26–27, 57; human rights 46, 81, 180; ideological 123; military 162; national security 80, 81; political 18, 135; research 11, 194; security 101; state 26; Western 97
agents: external 173, 174, 175; international 173, 174; revolutionary 124; securitising 33, 67, 106, 124, 140, 177–178, 181–182
aid 19, 174; coordinating 27; development 2; distribution 50, 51, 53, 74; instrumentalising 24; needs-based 20; as political tool 19–20, 22; rhetoric 192; structure 101; workers 58, 59, 103
allegations 148, 151
allegiance 102
ambiguity 82, 86, 94, 102
Amnesty International 114
anti-globalisation 46
armed actors 82, 83
arrest warrant 134, 137, 139
Asian values 15, 135, 198
Asian way 55–56, 55n4, 88, 147, 152, 155, 183; desecuritisation 160
assistance 173
attacks 157
audience: general public 160; identifying 34, 184; international community 124, 140, 181, 182; international NGOs 105, 107,

124, 179, 181; politically important 67, 178; receptive 33–34; relevant 177
auditing 50, 115, 119
autarky 121
authoritarian regimes 28, 29, 30, 81, 98, 135
authoritarianism 116
authority: coercive 17; moral 192; non-state 26; political 17; threatening 26, 28; top-down 158
autonomy 17

bare life status 71, 79, 88, 130, 168
barriers, administrative/bureaucratic 93, 152, 154
Bashir, O. H. A 133, 134
behaviour: appropriate 14, 15; illogical 183; inappropriate 182; interpreting 183; modifying 125; normative standard 123; right 173
Belgium 134
beliefs 68; cultural 110
bias 73
borders 112, 158
Bradley, M. 85, 86
bureaucracy 23, 61, 63–64, 146
bureaucratic barriers 93, 152, 154
bureaucratic complexity 98
Burke, E. 171

camps 137
Canada 130
capacity-building 117, 198
care, duty of 84
case studies 5, 7–8; future 198; methodology 35; multi-mandate organisation 195
categories 113
ceasefire agreement 58, 71, 74, 86
censorship, self- 29, 116, 185
centre 112, 120, 122
charges 147, 152
charities 113
Charities and Societies Agency (Ethiopia) 113
Charities and Societies Proclamation (Ethiopia, 2009) 112, 113–121
Chechnya 10, 92, 100–107, 174, 179–180
children 117
China 98
citizenship 130, 132, 139, 181–182
civil society 21, 22, 99, 112, 151; growth 53, 113; oppositional 192; role of 116; threatened 119
civil war 10, 31, 174; Darfur (Sudan) 133–141, see also Sri Lankan civil war
civilian population 80, 83

clandestine dealings 65
clues 93
coercion 17, 94, 110, 111, 120, 125
coherence 23
Cold War 19–20
collaboration 120
colour revolutions 97
communication 136; absent 186; channels 8; indirect 155; objectives 163; public 99, 153; restricted 164; verbal 154
compassion 58, 59
competition 52
compliance 120
complicity 29, 149, 163
Comprehensive Peace Agreement (Sudan, 2005) 136
compromise 120, 138, 187
concealment 143, 169
condemnation 59
conditionality 20
confidentiality clauses 78, 79, 89, 164–169
conflict: border 112; framing 162; long-term 149; zone 79, 119, 120, 139, 145, see also civil war; war
conflictual relationship 30
confusion 64, 66, 67, 177
consent, state 27, 158
conspiracy 152
constructive engagement 116
consultation 164
contexts 36; ambiguous 86; domestic 175; of fear 94; local 78, 83; political 8, 18, 23, 100, 149, 181; reading 83, 149; security 105; sensitive 174; violent 94
control 112, 116; asserting 137; by fear 134, 180; information 28, 97; strategy 102; tactics 100; tool of 180; top-down 110
cooperation 84, 120, 162
coordination 64, 115; poor 52
counter-attacking 143, 169, 186
counter-terrorism 100, 106, 156, 158
credibility 29, 162, 191
crimes, international 133
criminal law 130
crisis 1–2, 19, 147; ambiguous 86; capacity to cope 26; Darfur 128, 132–138; defining 23, 27; humanitarian 18; legitimacy 46; perceived 149; political 190
critique 98
cultural identity 44
culture: organisational 120; understanding 148

Darfur (Sudan) 128, 132–138
death: civil 131; murders/killings 48, 58, 59, 102, 103

debates 2, 88, 147–150, 164
decision-making 17, 175; explaining 75;
   important factors 44; locus 181; political
   19, 44; state 173
decisionism 172
defence 88, 93
delays 153, 154
democracy, revolutionary 119
democratisation 20, 22
deniability, plausible 155
denial 4, 142n1
deportation 65–67, 129, 129n2, 130,
   131, 139
desecuritisation 34, 143–169, 184, 185;
   Asian way 160; limits 187
development: aid 2; goals 118, 180;
   organisations 2n4, 18–19; programming
   19, 187; strategic 22
dharmista samajaya 42
dichotomies 54, 83, 161
differentiation 41, 48
dignity 60
diplomatic support 154
diplomats 79, 153, 161
disaster 49, 191; zone 138, 139
disciplinary process 130
discourse 6, 7; conceptualising 3, 37;
   expulsion as 11, 129–141, 181–182,
   187–188; fear as 10, 92–107, 179–180,
   190; indicators 155–160, 184; invisible
   180; law as 10–11, 109–125, 180–181;
   monitoring 183, 184; political 86, 87;
   securitisation 179; security 94; state 25;
   threat 33
discourse analysis 36–37, 175; methodology
   199; tools 155
discursive environments 8, 36–37
discursive process 68
discussion 199
dishonesty 137
displaced people 133, 137, 159
domestic context 5, 6
donor coordination 122
donors 21, 196; influencing 24
Dunant, J. H. 17
Dunantist organisations 17, 18

education, emergency 194
efficiency 116
elites 67, 68, 139, 155, 177
embassies 153
emergency 23; education 194; health 120;
   intervention 119; national 173;
   programming 119, 184; state of 31,
   32, 94

enemy 5, 7, 175; designation 177; and
   friend distinction 6, 30, 45–68, 99, 107,
   124, 131
equality 17
Eritrea 123
ethics, medical 44
Ethiopia 10, 109–125, 138, 174, 181–182;
   Charities and Societies Agency 113;
   Charities and Societies Proclamation
   (2009) 112, 113–121; People's
   Revolutionary Democratic Front 112
ethnic cleansing 133
ethnic identity 129
ethnicity 42
euphemism 94
Europe 198
evil, lesser 84
exception, state of 6, 31, 60–64, 101, 110,
   124, 173, 183
exceptionalism 32n6
exile 79, 129, 131, 132, 138, 187;
   internal 138
existential threat 33, 101, 106, 123,
   124, 177
expatriates 117, 120, 153, 154
expulsion 65, 73–75, 79, 89, 101, 125, 173;
   aborted 145; corporate 129, 131, 132,
   182; denouncing 161; as discourse 11,
   129–141, 181–182, 187–188; fear of 93;
   justifying 137; mass 131, 161
external 9; in internal 14–37, 130, 173
external agents 173, 174, 175

facts 132
famine 120
fear 28, 129, 139; control by 134, 180; as
   discourse 10, 92–107, 179–180, 190; of
   expulsion 93; impact on principles 186;
   responding to 185–186; rhetoric of 179
food, convoys 74
foreign funding 113, 114, 118
foreign interference 52, 59, 76, 118, 123,
   137, 180
foreign policy 19–20, 23
foreigners 58
framing 79
France 144, 145
friend and enemy distinction 6, 30, 45–68,
   99, 107, 124, 131
funding 21, 26; cap 118; foreign 113, 114,
   118; misused 52–53, 54; sources 196
future 11, 194

gag order 79
gagging 164

good 18
government: agencies 61, 64;
  conceptualising 17; obstructive 24;
  pressured 176; and regime 181;
  representatives 97; tools of 95;
  uncoordinated 146; view of 188;
  weak 169
government prerogative 172, 174, 176, 183;
  defining 31; state of exception 34
Greece, ancient 130
greed 55
groupings 102
Guatemala 95
guessing 103, 186

harassment 129
Hassan, A. 134
health emergencies 120
hidden agenda 26–27, 57
historical review 19–23
Holland, Médecins Sans Frontières 27,
  41–69, 43n2, 71–90, 144–145, 160–169,
  183–185
Holmes, J. 85
homeland 131, 132
hostage 102
housing 52
Huguenots 129
human rights 72–73, 80; abuses 73; agenda
  46, 81, 180; law 162; onslaught 72;
  organisations 101, 106, 114
humanitarian circus 52
humanitarian intervention 22, 73, 158
humanitarian organisations 115, 196;
  international non-governmental 1–2,
  19–25, 182–188, 197; laws 97, 99,
  112, 113–121, 146, 197–198;
  national 1n2
humanitarian project 2
humanitarian space 71, 82, 83, 89, 136, 138;
  creating 150; decreasing 98, 146;
  restricted 163; unique 162
humanitarianism 192; conceptualising
  17–19
humanity 18

ideals 171
identity 5, 11, 29, 33, 190–193; beliefs 68;
  clash 125; corporate 130; cultural 44;
  discussions 67; ethnic 129; formation 175;
  international 77; issues 168; labelling 42;
  mistaken 65; opposing 192; organisational
  44–45; political 186; politics 81, 175;
  religious 129; self- 48, 68, 96; Tamil 42;
  Western 57

ideology 33, 171, 191; Ethiopia 114, 122;
  Sri Lankan 42; Western 3, 46
immigrant 139
immigration policy 130
impartiality 175; in authoritarian states 28;
  definition 18
impunity 103, 136
inaction 103
incoherence 64, 66, 67
independence 23; definition 17
indeterminacy 103
indistinction 93–100, 105, 137, 139, 189
individuals 131
influence 102, 161, 179; political 20;
  Western 15, 21, 22, 97, 106
information control 28, 97
insecurity 10, 61, 67, 92, 134
institutional isomorphism 111, 115
instrumentalisation 24, 84, 138
intelligentsia 159
intentionality 104
inter-governmental organisations 21
interaction, plane of 173
interference 3, 23, 123; external 106;
  foreign 52, 59, 76, 118, 123, 137,
  177; international 80; political
  114, 116
internal 9; external in 14–37, 130, 173
internally displaced persons 133,
  137, 159
international agents 173, 174
International Committee of the Red Cross
  74, 75, 78, 197; murders 103
international community 59–60, 72n1, 83;
  defining 85; tension with 137
International Criminal Court (ICC) 133,
  134, 135, 137
International Humanitarian Law (IHL) 74,
  75, 120, 162
international law 17n2
international norms 15, 22, 83–84, 99, 124,
  162, 182, 189
international organisations 21
international pressure 99
International Rescue Committee (IRC) 135
interpretation 125
intervention 73; coordinated 23;
  humanitarian 22, 73, 158; right of 158
invisibility 103–104

Janatha Vimukthi Peramuna (People's
  Liberation Front) 45, 46, 48, 50, 82,
  156, 183
Juche 122
just society 42

justice, social 42
justification 155, 176

Keen, D. 84
kidnapping 102, 102n4, 103, 104, 134, 179
killings 48, 58, 59, 102, 103
knowledge: historical 36; transfer 117

language 175; political 93, 94; symbolic 110
law: criminal 130; defining 109; deportation 130; as discourse 10–11, 109–125, 180–181; exceptions to 31; fear of 93; human rights 162; humanitarian organisations 97, 99, 112, 113–121, 146, 196–198; international 17n2; International Humanitarian Law 74, 75, 109, 120, 162; interpreting 125; NGO 97, 99, 112, 113–121, 146, 197–198; response to 186–187; socially constructed 110; as tool 175, 189; violating 33; and violence 94, 95, 105, 110–111, 125, 129, 190; weaponised 110
lawfare 125
layers 179
legal code 32
legal obligations 83–84
legitimacy 15, 29, 60, 73n2; crisis 46
legitimisation 87
letters 150, 151, 152, 154
leverage 161, 168
Liberation Tigers of Tamil Eelam 42–43, 45, 46; defeating 80; supporting 56–57, 64–68, 76, 82, 145, 177
lifting bags 65, 66
literature review 3–4
lives, saving 19, 23, 59
lobbying 148
local organisations 53

mandates 157, 186
manipulation 26, 28, 29; discursive 138
material assistance 19, 174
matrix 102, 105, 142
meaning 41; constructed 175
Médecins Sans Frontières 43–44, 144n2; accusations against 64, 65, 76–77, 87; Belgium 134; Cold War era 20n3; France 144, 145; Holland 27, 41–69, 43n2, 71–90, 144–145, 160–169, 183–185; Spain 144, 145; Sri Lankan civil war 10, 41–69, 71–90, 144–169; and strong states 27–30
media 8, 36, 37, 68, 71, 145, 146; intellectual 159; international 148;

interpreting 156, 178; national 178; negative 156
mediation, social 123
medical ethics 44
medical organisation 161
medical service provider 168
medical supplies 74, 75
Medicos Del Mundo 64, 65, 145
memories of violence 95
messages, indirect 155
military agenda 162
Mill, J. S. 1, 172
mindset change 199
minorities 130
misinformation campaign 146
misinterpretation 184
mistrust 115
misunderstanding 73, 77, 78, 80, 83, 150
monitoring 64, 76
mood change 147
moral action 9, 173
moral actors 5
moral authority 192
moral hazard 20
moral principles 191, 192
moral project 5, 19
moral universe 2
morality 25, 191, 192
motivation 181
multi-mandate organisations 18, 115, 117, 195
murders 48, 58, 59, 102, 103
Muslim people 158
myths 111

name-clearing 147
narrative 2, 3, 85, 86, 103, 104, 125; explanation 36; identifying 190
nation-building 112
national emergency 173
national NGOs 197
National Peace Council (Sri Lanka) 78
national security threat 22, 88, 89
nationalism 100; Sinhalese Buddhist 46, 83, 177, 184
nationalist parties 45, 50
needs 20, 24, 115, 118, 119, 152, 186
negotiation 5, 164; context of 175; preparation 185; purpose 7; structure 34, 35
neo-colonialism 52, 55
neutrality 135, 175, 186; compromised 162; definition 17; and information control 28
Niland, N. 85

Non-Aligned Movement summit (2006) 156, 157
non-governmental organisations 50n3; growth 21
non-interference 46
normality 88
normative framework 172
norms: defining 14–15; expression 81; foreign 124, 181; humanitarian 26, 173; indistinction between 191; influence 30; international 15, 22, 83–84, 99, 124, 162, 182, 189; legal 32, 83, 181; local 15; moral 173; political 84; sets of 9, 14, 26; social 110; in tension 14
North Korea 122, 123
North Western Provincial Council 62, 63

opinion, public 99, 106, 156, 160, 176, 178, 179
opportunity cost 135
opposition 112
order: social 130; threat to 123
organisation 41; types 113, 196
Orwell, G. 93
ostracism 130
outlawing 79, 89, 176
overreaction 185
Oxfam 136

paperwork 97
Parliamentary Select Committee (Sri Lanka) 50, 65, 75–78
paternalism 153
peace 80, 86
perceptions 175
periphery 112, 120, 122
perseverance 185
perspectives: government 37, 188; humanitarian international NGOs 23–25; practitioner 85; state 25, 26–27, 176–182
police 152
political act 173
political actors 18, 47
political agenda 18, 135
political community 140
political contexts 8, 18, 23, 100, 149, 191, 194
political discourse 86, 87
political elites 67, 68, 139, 155, 177
political engagement 192
political environment 156
political footballs 137
political identity 186
political influence 20

political issues 134
political reality 132, 171
political roles 191
political space 3
political speech 93
political system 195; international 3
politicisation 157
politics 5, 8, 11, 42, 122, 190–193; defining 30, 99; fear 94, 100–107; identity 81, 175
popularity 106
possibility 99
Post-Tsunami Operations Management Scheme 49–50
power: arbiter of 95; central 130, 139; centralised 122
practice 41; changing 199–200; wasteful 54–55
practitioners 85, 196
pragmatism 120, 121
precedent 136
president 134, 139, 158, 178
press conference 151
pressure 52, 148
pretexts 171
principles 5, 11, 44, 125, 190–193; absent 161, 170; compromising 187; and fear 187; humanitarian 17–18, 24, 120, 157; and law 11; misinterpreting 184; moral 181, 192; political 191; prioritising 197; respecting 25, 157; state 9; using 174–175
private sphere 17
process 105; tracing 35, 36, 144
profit 55
programming restrictions 117–118
promises 53
protection 117, 130, 171n2
protector 106
public campaign 153, 155
public opinion 99, 106, 156, 160, 176, 178, 179
public sector 21
public statement 147
public voice 29, 78, 99
publicity: negative 28, 145, 146, 151; positive 148
punishment 98, 131, 138
puppet master 105

ransom 102
reactive position 183
reality, political 132, 171
rebel groups 47
rebel movement 122

rebellion 129
Red Cross 74, 75, 78, 103, 197
red lines 85, 149
referent object 33, 67, 106, 123, 177, 179, 180; identifying 184
regime 109, 181; authoritarian 28, 29, 30, 81, 98, 135; ideological 119; security 122, 124, 181; threatened 124
registration 97; requirements 97
relationships: constructed 175; triangular 81–86
relevance 162
religious identity 129
remaining 180
reports 75–78
representation 17, 120
repression 28, 98, 121
reputation 99, 120, 149
research: agenda 11, 194; proposal 195–199
response, first 198
responsibility 57–58, 75, 159
Responsibility to Protect (R2P) 22–23
retaliation 135, 137
retribution 103, 111, 130
return 138, 187
revolutionary agent 124
revolutionary democracy 119
revolutions 97
rights: discourse 115, 116, see also human rights
rights-based programming 117, 118, 119
rules 93, 159, 180, 183
Russia 96–100, 129, 174, 179
Rwanda 122

safety 75
sanctions 20
sans frontieriste perspective 20
Schmitt, C. 30, 175
secessionist movement 100
second-guessing 185
secrecy 112
securitisation 6, 10, 25, 31–34, 176; analysis 41; bare life 10; Chechnya 106–107; complete 71; and discourse 8; discourse 101, 179; expulsion as 139–140; fear as 104–107; justifying 25, 87; messages 54; response options 6–7, 11, 142–170, **143**, 191; Sri Lanka 67–68, 89, 176–179
securitisation process 107, 109; and law 123–125
securitising agent 33, 67, 106, 124, 140, 177–178, 181–182

securitising move 33
security 179; agenda 101; conceptualising 33; concerns 62; context 105; incidents 103; national 22, 81, 88, 89, 146; regime 122, 124, 181; risk 145; services 105; threat 48, 62–63; threatening 77
self-censorship 29, 116, 185
self-help organisations 113
self-identity 48, 68, 96
self-interest 26, 87
sensationalism 159
service provision 101
shadow puppets 86
shelter 52
signals 147, 152, 155, 156
silence 20, 75, 78, 84, 104, 106, 186; justified 102; public 163
Sinhalese Buddhist nationalism 46, 83, 177, 184
Sinhalese people 56–57
slander 149
social construction 111
social justice 42
social mediation 123
social mission 168
social order 130
social problems 101
societies 113
society 17; just 42, see also civil society
sources 36–37
South Africa 122
sovereign 178, 181, 182
sovereignty 2; absolute 60; card 188; conceptualising 16–17, 21, 22; conditional 20; defining 6, 172; interference 26; internal 46; protecting 131, 139, 182; re-asserting 132; Sri Lankan 59–60; tools of 94; weaponising 25
space: physical 174; political 3; uncomfortable 183, see also humanitarian space
Spain 144, 145
speaking out 29, 79, 99–100, 103, 106, 163–164
speech, political 93
speeches 156, 158
speed 52, 53
spying 119
Sri Lanka 143–169, 174; as case study 35; Freedom Party 45; Government 10, 45–68, 71–90, 160, 162, 168, 178; ideology 42; National Peace Council 78; Parliamentary Select Committee 50, 65, 75–78; securitisation 67–68, 89, 176–179;

sovereignty 59–60; tsunami 49, 50–53,
62, 65–66
Sri Lankan civil war 42–43, 72–75, 79–80,
82, 84, 86, 177; Médecins Sans Frontières
10, 41–69, 71–90, 144–169
stability 42, 94
standards, double 89
state: agenda 26; assertive 23; cynical 25;
decision-making 177; defining 16; enemy
of 130; expected behaviour 189;
humanitarian responsibilities 27; idea of
179; and international non-governmental
organisations 19–23; international
recognition 16, 17; motivation 189;
motivations 191; obstructive 24; as
people's representative 115; prerogative
31, 34; representatives 198; repressive
121; responsibilities 21; responsibility to
protect 22; system 15, 172; threatened
106, 131, 139, 140, 174, 182; totalitarian
122; unified 80; view of 26–27, 176–182;
and violence 94, *see also* strong states
state of emergency 31, 32, 94
statehood 172, 173, 175; conceptualising
15–17
strong states 2, 20, 27, 96, 109, 192; and
Médecins Sans Frontières 27–30
structures 81
Sudan 11, 109, 129–141, 174, 181–182;
Comprehensive Peace Agreement (2005)
136; Darfur 128, 132–138
suffering 173
surveillance 113
survival 168
suspicion 155
symbol, Western 140, 192

Tamil identity 42
Tamil Relief Organisation 57
Tamil Tigers *see* Liberation Tigers of Tamil
Eelam
targets, vulnerable 137
tension 137, 173
Terror, Global War on 22, 162
terrorism 156; counter- 100, 106, 156, 158
theoretical framework 7–9, 30–37, 41;
developing 200; in practice 195;
reviewing 171–176
third party involvement 31
threat 7; credible 125; defining 25, 131;
designating 177; ethnic 129; existential
33, 101, 106, 123, 124, 177; external
177; grave 139; identifying 181;
international 185; national security 22,
88, 89; perceived 28; removing 177;

response to 94; security 48, 62–63;
sensing 30; state 106, 131, 139, 140, 177;
to order 123, 130; underlying 94;
Western 97
Tokyo Donors' Conference 159
totalitarian state 122
tourist visas 63
transparency 150
trauma 94, 95, 102
travel restrictions 134
triangular relationships 81–86
trigger event 145
trustworthiness 130
truth 104, 105, 125, 180, 190
tsunami (Sri Lanka) 49, 50; response 50–53,
62, 65–66

uncertainty 86, 92, 104, 180
understanding 36, 148; contextual 86;
mutual 172, 185
unfairness 140
United Nations (UN) 137, 197; General
Assembly 158; integrated missions 23;
World Food Program 74, 197
United States of America (USA) 130
unity 112, 121
unknowns 102, 104

vagueness 94
values 110; Asian 15, 135, 198; social 111
verstehen 36
vices 171
victims 23
views, public 8, 36
violence 92; extreme 179; and law 94–95,
105, 110–111, 125, 129, 190; memories
of 95
violent contexts 94
visas 134, 146, 153; delayed 155; procedure
64; revoking 65, 66, 67; tourist 63
visions, contested 81
voice, public 29, 78, 99
voicelessness 104
voices: devoicing 164, 168; international 83;
muted 79; outlawing 89

war 95, 179; accepting 106; border 112;
Chechnya 100–101, 179–180; Cold
War 19–20; on terror 22, 162;
traditional 100, *see also* civil war;
Sri Lankan civil war
warning 157
wastefulness 54, 119
weaponised law 110
weaponising sovereignty 25

weapons 110; culture 103
Weber, M. 17
Western agenda 97
Western cooperation 136
Western identity 57
Western ideology 3, 46
Western influence 15, 21, 22, 97, 106
Western models 56
Western symbol 140

Western worldview 23
withdrawal 149, 150, 185
witnesses 81, 137
witnessing 29, 44, 106, 162, 183
work permits 58, 61, 120, 146
workers, aid 58, 59, 103

Zambia 122
Zimbabwe 114

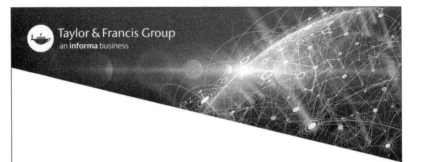